# DARLING OF MISFORTUNE

# EDWIN BOOTH: 1833-1893

# BY RICHARD LOCKRIDGE

> No, oh no! There's but one Hamlet to my
> mind—that's my brother, Edwin. You see,
> between ourselves, he is Hamlet—melan-
> choly and all.—JOHN WILKES BOOTH,
> *on hearing his own Hamlet praised.*

THE CENTURY CO.
*New York* · *London*

FOR *Frances*

# ACKNOWLEDGMENTS

A LONG LIST MIGHT BE MADE OF SOURCES FROM WHICH THE author has drawn the material upon which this biography is based. It is with no thought of ingratitude that he omits that list here, where it would form a bibliography, and refers the reader to the specific citations contained in footnotes. Previously published material which has been utilized was consulted, for the most part, in the reference and newspaper rooms of the New York Public Library and was made available through the efficient efforts of the staff of that institution.

Unpublished material, much of it priceless, was made available to the author through the courtesy of The Players, a club for actors founded by Edwin Booth and, increasingly, an invaluable museum of the theater. The author's deepest thanks are due the club, its secretary, its librarian, and the librarian's most energetic and able assistant.

The author alone is responsible for errors of name, place, fact, and inference. Where such errors are absent the sole responsibility belongs to Mr. Howard Devree, who, with a kindness which leaves the author permanently in his debt, took the manuscript sheets as they were written and scrubbed them as clean as was humanly possible of the encrustation of error which overlaid them.

*New York, 1932*

# CONTENTS

..ix..

# ILLUSTRATIONS

# DARLING OF MISFORTUNE

# I

## PROLOGUE

TO RAISE THE CURTAIN ON THE LIFE OF EDWIN BOOTH, tragedian, is to reveal a melodrama of abashing theatricalism. We shall find it preposterously extravagant, and then we must remember that it is a melodrama written by Fate. No lesser playwright could have escaped catcalls while offering such a tale; the superior smiles which come to the faces of those who are asked to believe too much would have been the inevitable return for his abundant generosity. Only Fate could have brought it off; only Fate could have crowded into one life such heaped-up misfortune, or made so obvious and immediate the compensation allowed for that misfortune. As the play proceeds, we shall more than once suspect that it is all quite too impossible and that Fate's indifference to the limits of our credulity is equaled only by her bland refusal to have anything to do with subtlety.

To find any merely human dramatist who would dare a tenth as much, we must return to Shakspere and his imitators, and even then we shall discover that one major calamity was usually considered quite enough. If in yesterday's extravagant melodrama we discover a romantic and beautiful youth marrying the girl of his heart we are not at all surprised to find the girl dying, poetically, in the next act. But, if we are not observing some "Perils of Pauline," we expect it will be allowed to go with that—unless, to be sure, the romantic and beautiful youth chooses to kill himself on her tomb.

What we do not look for, and what we will as a cultivated audience by no means allow, is that the hero shall thereafter go on from catastrophe to catastrophe, leading a life fraught with insanity, sudden death, participation in national cataclysms, and endurance of unmerited financial disaster. When we find such luxuriance, we suspect, quite rightly, that the playwright has no idea where to stop, no realization of the effectiveness of understatement. And if we discover, further, that the unlikely tale has been tricked out in even more unlikely furbelows—rescues from drunkenness, unmerited disgrace, hairbreadth escapes from assassination, and so on—and that the whole goes forward to the off-stage thunders and flashings of prodigious natural phenomena, the chances are we relegate the whole matter to the Bowery. Or to the cinema.

But not even the cinema will have such melodrama, nowadays. No longer does its grinding camera reel out the serial of old, with each instalment ending in a plunge of the hero and heroine over a cliff. Nowadays, even in the cinema, we are lucky if anything happens at all, and if the playwright does not assure us that the only catastrophe is that there is no catastrophe and that the romantic youth and the girl of his heart really grow old and bored together.

We have, in short, learned where to stop. If, in doing that, we have forgotten how to start, at least no one can accuse us of extravagance. Only Fate ignores our newer rules; only Fate feels under no compulsion to remain credible. Possibly she does not really care whether the audience believes or not, being entirely satisfied that she leaves no room for the slightest doubt in the minds of her actors.

If she had felt herself constrained within the limits of the plausible, she would hardly have begun the life of Edwin Booth in a shower of meteors and ended it amid the flashes of lightning. That sort of thing is entirely too obvious. Nor would she have brought in the old caul trick, equipping her future tragedian with that magical symbol of yesterday. She would have realized that we cannot take cauls seriously; that they belong in the superstitious past, with witches' brews and powdered toads. We reject all this. And Fate grins. She continues with her melodrama.

A few tricks, to be sure, she missed. Edwin Booth was not actually bound to the platform of a buzz-saw, although some of the critical denunciations he endured, some of the disappointments he survived, must have seemed to him quite as sharp. He was not lashed to the tracks in front of an approaching express-train, though he did, to be sure, once rescue Robert Lincoln, the son of the man Wilkes Booth killed, from a not utterly dissimilar predicament. Nor did any single villain pursue him always, although he found villains enough, and called them that. But all the rest can be promised in the play: irregular birth, clouded boyhood, the tragedy of the beloved's death, the horror of a brother's crime, financial disaster, the dark cloud of insanity—all these. For Edwin Booth was a man ill fated.

In that rôle the public had every opportunity to observe him, while he lived. The public watched, in understandable bewilderment, the piling up of misfortune upon this one man. The prominence of his profession, and his prominence in it, together with the accident of circumstance, saw to it that disaster should never visit him secretly, at dead of night. The thunderbolts always struck Edwin Booth at high noon. The lightning played about him then. The sun of his natural art, the flashes of his fate, combined to make him, for his generation, a hero doubly in the spotlight. He was given a double prominence, a double visibility. It remained only for him to bear himself well and appropriately, on the stage and off. He bore himself so. There was nothing for the public to do but applaud.

The applause was partly for his art, partly for the man. The proportions of this mixture have long been the subject of debate. There have been some to insist that only the peculiar prominence given him by the assassination of 1865, by the spectacular failure of his theater, and by the rest of his misfortunes, accounted for his prominence on the stage. And others have insisted that he would still have been famous and great as a player if he had lived a very ordinary life, being never the subject of great national sympathy and the beneficiary of notoriety. The truth lies somewhere between.

It is certainly true that he had greatness as an actor. And it is also true that he was, in a manner of speaking, kicked upstairs. So many prodigious things happened to him, in such quick succession, that the public began to believe him mythological. And as he was a victim, the public felt for him a peculiar sympathy, which finally mounted almost to adoration, that mixture of emotions with which it generally greets those who try gallantly and fail through no fault of their own. So Napoleon lost an empire at Waterloo and gained sentimental immortality.

Booth was exactly the man for the part. Reserved and shy, he baffled understanding, and so the general public was spared the necessity of thinking of him as a man very like the common run of men. The rôle of misfortune's darling requires a Hamlet-like exterior; and that exterior, if it is to be really convincing, should be backed by a Hamlet-like maladjustment to routine life. This exterior, and this character, Fate gave Booth, as compensations. He became the Hamlet of his generation, on the stage and off. "He is Hamlet," his brother said. He was letter-perfect and face-perfect and gesture-perfect in the rôle; if he was not also thought-perfect, few but his close friends, who were not many, suspected it. And he was enough of an actor, in life as well as in art, to emphasize his fitness for the part given him. When he found out fully what the audience expected, he was showman enough to supply by art such slight cementing as nature required to make its façade perfect.

It was to glimpse that façade, one of the most perfectly consistent the century produced, that thousands all over the country flocked to see Booth play. Thousands more, of course, went also to see the player, and would not have gone if there had not been in the playing, also, a measure of perfection. Only, one may doubt whether the playing alone would have brought farmers and their wives trudging down dirt roads to the rail lines, that they might watch and wave as the special train carrying the actor on tour flashed by. Not merely to see Shakspere's Hamlet would so many have thronged the small towns in which he played one-night stands, paid the high prices demanded, crowded and overcrowded the hotels and slept in them on corridor cots.

Those trudged, and slept fitfully, to see the darling of misfortune. Every new catastrophe increased his fascination; from each new knock-down blow he arose, like the combatant of legend, strengthened by his contact with the earth. But the private man suffered; and finally, after this buffeting of Fate had continued for a reasonable number of years, the man did not get up again. But even in his death he was in a way fortunate. He did not long outlive the setting of his star. The art to which he had devoted his life and life itself came simultaneously to an end. The final curtain fell on drama satisfactorily rounded off. Everything had been appropriate to everything else.

Most particularly, perhaps, is that appropriateness revealed as one considers the similarity of the parts he played in life to those he played upon the stage. On the stage he acted always, or almost always, the hero of poetic tragedy. Always he was the tragedian. He was, indeed, the last of the tragedians; and as that began to be suspected it was one thing more to enhance his prominence. "He left no disciples, no successor to take up his mantle when he discarded it. When he made his final bow, the curtain—so far as the

American stage was concerned—fell also upon the legitimate drama." [1]

"The legitimate drama": we must, at the risk of didacticism, be clear on that before the curtain rises. Mr. Towse, who wrote the sentences above clasped by inverted commas, did not have in mind what the present-day producer means when he speaks of the "legitimate." Mr. Earl Carroll can now claim a new and spectacular theater, destined for spectacular and aphrodisiac revues, as a "home of the legitimate." But the word, as limited by Mr. Towse, and as employed in the past century, would have had to be stretched woefully to cover the plays of Mr. Eugene O'Neill. The tragedians ruled the "legitimate" of yesterday. They were a race of monarchs. Monarchs and kingdom have vanished together, for all practical purposes. The kingdom, the "legitimate," was that body of poetic tragedy and romance which is Shaksperian in tone. Shakspere's plays were the backbone of the "legitimate." Playwrights who contributed the other dramas of the tragedian's repertory followed as they might.

Always the plays swung around a central character which was far beyond life-size. All emotions, all misfortunes, were grand and final. Violence, insanity, black guilt, and death were the materials; the gods and the abstractions were called upon in speeches of the utmost magnificence. It was the day of the grand manner. Like them, Booth's life was a poetic tragedy in the grand manner, with none of the ingredients missing. It should be written in blank verse.

[1] J. Ranken Towse: "Sixty Years of the Theater." Funk & Wagnalls Company, New York, 1916.

# II

## A TRAGEDIAN IS BORN

EDWIN BOOTH WAS THE FOURTH SON OF JUNIUS BRUTUS BOOTH, tragedian, and Mary Ann Holmes, of whom little is known. He was a brother of the Booth who killed Lincoln and who had, it can hardly be doubted, inherited a tinge of insanity from his father. Edwin was born on November 13, 1833, in the deep country outside Baltimore, in a house shaded somberly by towering trees. Near by was a spring in which generations of bullfrogs have croaked unhappily but unmolested. They croaked when he was born, and that night there was a shower of meteors which amazed the servants in their shanty behind the tragedian's house. He was born with a caul, and that set the servants to nodding. They said young Edwin was born lucky, and mumbled to the young mother that the caul must be kept. For many years Mary Ann Booth, who had come to America bravely with an erratic husband, saved that object which promised high fortune to her son, and it was passed on to him, an indistinguishable thing but perhaps a symbol of destiny. The meteors, which were even more spectacular, could not be saved. But they were remembered.

Junius and Mary had come to the United States twelve

years before, bringing with them a piebald pony named Peacock and, one assumes, a bundle of press cuttings. Edwin's father was then twenty-five years old and had already made a name for himself. He had also been previously married, in the confused days of his early youth, and had solved that problem for the time being by leaving it abruptly. The problem followed him, but at a respectable distance. The fame which he had acquired during a brief but exciting tilt with Edmund Kean had, however, preceded him.

Junius was born on May 1, 1796, in the parish of St. Pancras, London, to a father who had no apparent interest in the theater. The father, Richard, was a solicitor, whose only deviation from the pattern of respectability had occurred during the American Revolutionary War, when he had run away from home and reached Paris, whence he indited a letter to John Wilkes, the reformer and agitator, expressing his "ardent desire to serve in the Glorious Cause of Freedom." Richard's father, who was John, a silversmith, captured and returned him, apologizing to the famous Wilkes, who was a distant relative, for the youth's presumption. After that, Richard studied law quietly and practised it without notable adventures.

In after years Edwin made some effort to trace his ancestry beyond his great-grandfather, who made a spoon upon which the young Booths in America cut their teeth. He was unsuccessful. A genealogist burrowed, at his direction, through the records, but reported from the British Museum that he could learn nothing of John Booth's father. He sent along a copy of John Booth's will, for what it might be worth. Edwin, who had hoped to trace his ancestry to the Barton Booth who acted in Colley Cibber's day, and who was a member of a Booth family which had married into the peerage, was disappointed. He was forced to find what satisfaction he could in the prevailing theory that all the Booths of England are descended from the first of something like that name—Adam de Boothes.

The De Boothes are assumed to have gone to England from Normandy either with or shortly after William. Adam, the first of whom record exists, lived early in the thirteenth century. In all the studies made of the family he is the starting-point. The De Boothes became good Englishmen, shortened the name, and by the time John Booth made silver spoons for his great-grandchildren had spread until the country was thick with Booths, of all degrees but all good Englishmen. From this stock, it may be assumed, Edwin came. There have, however, been other assumptions. At one time the patriotic Anglo-Saxons of the United States were very anxious to disavow any blood relationship with a handsome young man referred to by the most conservative as a "monster." It was felt that something might be gained if the Booths were relegated to a racial minority, and much was made of the swarthy skin, dark eyes, and heavy noses which were family characteristics.

It was then announced, on the evidence of a hearty wish, that the Booths were really of Spanish-Jewish blood and that the name had once been Beth. Others, equally ingenious, said that they were Jews from Portugal and that they had been Boothbys before they were Booths. It was recalled that Junius once assured a Unitarian minister that he, too, was a monotheist, being a Jew, and a devout reader of the Talmud. Junius was, however, inclined to be mischievous, particularly with clergymen, and he was also a devout reader of the Koran. (He once considered, indeed, the advisability of naming a daughter Ayesha, after one of Mohammed's wives, and changed his mind only when he thought of naming her Asia "in remembrance of that country where God first walked with man.")

All this is speculation. No one really knows who preceded John Booth. Two sons, Wilkes and Richard, came after him. The first followed his father's trade, inheriting his tools and shop and being lost to fame among them. There was always a suggestion of the hand-craftsman in the Booth family. Richard, having paid his abortive tribute to the cause of freedom, married and begot Junius, who grew into a sturdy, handsome youth, with a head as classical as his name.

Junius was given a sound education and destined for the law. But the law bored him and he turned from it to the arts—at first, with easy catholicity, to all the arts. He hovered over them like a young eagle over woolly lambs, swooping first toward one, then toward another. He thought of writing, and thought better of it. Painting intrigued his fancy, but he shied away. He contemplated sculpture. Then he espied the stage, and no longer hesitated. Ignoring whatever mild protests may have come from his legal father, who must have had a soft spot for the vagaries of youth, young Junius found himself a place in a stock company at Deptford. There, on December 13, 1813—thirteen seems to have been the Booth number—he made his début.

He played at Deptford off and on for four years,

rising to stock-company stardom. That rise brought him to the rôles of the tragedian, and once he played in the stead of the great Edmund Kean, who was ill at Brighton. Kean was then the brightest Roman candle of all in England. It was being noted, in that unforgotten phrase, that to see him play was like reading Shakspere by flashes of lightning. It was an honor for young Booth to play in his place, as Sir Giles Overreach in "A New Way to Pay Old Debts." That was one of the parts sacred to tragedians.

Junius played in the Kean tradition, which was the only tradition. He was, in other words, as much like a lightning storm as possible. He raved and ranted, doubtless, as he strode through his parts. His Richard III shook the scenery; as Sir Edward Mortimer in "The Iron Chest" he made even his fellow-actors tremble; as Pescara he was sinister until the audience gasped. He traveled in the provinces with the company and ventured across the channel, appearing several times in Brussels and elsewhere.

On one of these trips he met Mary (or Marie) Christine Adelaide Delanoy and took her back to England. They were married, on May 8, 1815, in London. Two children were born, a daughter who died in infancy and a son who lived to accompany his mother to the United States years later. This was to be referred to afterward in the Booth family annals as a "youthful misalliance," but for the moment it had all the aspects of permanence. The young people seemed contented enough together as Booth continued in the provinces and began to write letters to the directors of the London theaters of tragedy, Covent Garden and Drury Lane, advancing his claims to preferment. They were still contented enough, so far as any one knows, when Booth got his chance and was invited to appear at Covent Garden. His salary remained at its provincial level, one pound a week.

The elder Booth's first appearance in London was as Richard. With that appearance he came, automatically, into rivalry with Kean, who was electrifying Drury Lane. Comparisons were inevitable and instant. They were strictly comparisons, not contrasts. Most of the reviewers found him very like Kean, in appearance, in voice, in method. "Surely one of nature's duplicates," observed Bell's "Weekly Messenger." Kean shook his head indignantly at this encroachment, but Booth was not displeased. He was like Kean, and Kean was great, ergo . . . ergo, he asked a rise in salary. He suggested five pounds a week. The management regarded this as rather sudden and suggested patience. Patience, Junius singularly lacked. Almost before he knew it he was party to a violent quarrel; before he entirely realized what it was all about he had risen to great heights as a public curiosity, been talked about and abused from one end of London to another, revealed that in temperament at any rate he was second to none.

The story of his struggle with Kean and the London managers has been often told, but it is too amusing to be passed over entirely. It played its part, moreover, in sending him to the United States with his pony and a new wife. Perhaps without that struggle Edwin Booth would have starred in the English heavens, not in ours. Certainly the struggle cut short Junius's career in England and made him so famous that a career in America was inevitable.

It is the story of an absurd and touchy man—perhaps of two men absurd and touchy. It began with Kean and his annoyed observation of this new rival. The management of His Majesty's Theater in Drury Lane also observed, with like annoyance. Kean and his directors put their heads together. Then they moved, en masse, on a cab and drove hurriedly to Covent Garden. They snatched up a bewildered, fuming Booth and bore him away. They set him down at a table, and placed before him a contract and pen and ink. They flattered him, and showed him the dotted line.

Booth already had a contract with the Covent Garden management, of course. But, with one thing and another—wine was no doubt flowing freely—he forgot that. He signed with a flourish and became an actor of the Drury Lane Theater. He did not read his contract very carefully, after finding it provided the salary increase he wanted and that it offered a way to show the Covent Garden directors a thing or two. He was to play with Kean, and straightway did, appearing as Iago to Kean's Othello.

The public had in those days an eager, personal interest in things of the stage which has in the ensuing hundred-odd years noticeably abated. It heard of this new development and flocked to the opening. When Booth appeared he was greeted vociferously by the pit. "I know my price," he remarked, within his rôle, but with meaningful emphasis. The pit shouted in glee. The directors of Covent Garden glowered in the distance, the villains of the piece. Then the tumult died and Booth thought to read his contract. He discovered, to his consternation, that he had pledged himself not to appear in any of the parts then being played by Mr. Edmund Kean. That was by no means so jolly. There were only certain parts suitable to the tragedian, and Kean played them all. Booth was in a fair way not to be a tragedian at all.

This thought put him into a lather and then into a fever. He reported himself ill and unable to play. Then he recovered and dashed back, headlong, to Covent Garden. He was welcomed. There on February 25—he had still been only two weeks in London, it will be noticed—he made another début. The pit, happy at this disturbance, flocked to Covent Garden. But this time it did not cheer. Possibly it thought Booth a bad sport; possibly it considered him a noisy child. In any case it had a new opportunity to express its emotions, audibly. This time it jeered, it hissed, it made unmannerly sounds. Neither Booth nor those in his cast could be heard beyond the footlights. Placards were prepared for this emergency.

"Mr. Booth Wishes to Apologize!" one of them announced. The crowd booed enthusiastically. "Can English Gentlemen Condemn Unheard?" inquired another, plaintively flattering. English gentlemen could, and did. Finally the performace had to be abandoned altogether. The next few days were exciting. With open glee the newspapers noticed the imbroglio. It got into the courts, Drury Lane instituting, and at once withdrawing, a suit. Furious charges were hurled back and forth. The directors of Drury Lane had wantonly stirred up the pit at Covent Garden. They had done nothing of the kind.

Gradually it simmered down. On March 1, Booth was

allowed to appear again and make his apology. The play
proceeded. But all this did Booth no immediate good. A
few weeks later he was back in the provinces, touring once
again, and Kean was still undisputed monarch of the London stage. The pretender never thereafter managed to dis-
turb that reign, although he lingered three years longer in
England.

The girl from Brussels was still with him. But the first
fine frenzy was over. Late in 1820, Booth deserted his young
wife, whether in any sense justifiably does not now appear,
and on January 18, 1821, he married, in the home of a lady
of quality, one Mary Ann Holmes. Of Miss Holmes her
daughter Asia says nothing in her discreet biography.[1] Who
she was and whence she came—these are mysteries. Later
gossip described her as a Drury Lane flower-girl. It is only
evident that she married Junius Brutus Booth, who was
already married, a fact of which it is quite possible she was
ignorant. Booth could hardly have shared that innocence,
one imagines.

Some three months after their marriage Junius and
his second Mary sailed for America on the schooner
*Two Brothers.* They landed at Norfolk on June 30 and the
newspapers announced the arrival of "the Booth." Six days
later Junius made his American début in "Richard III" at
Richmond. A few days after that he somewhat astonished
his new associates by walking the twenty-five miles or so
from Richmond to Petersburg, having an engagement to fill

[1] Asia Booth Clarke: "Junius Brutus Booth (the Elder)." Later
reissued in a limited edition as "The Elder and the Younger Booth."
J. R. Osgood & Co., Boston.

and having missed the bus. He arrived, perspiring and weary, only a few minutes before curtain time. A contemporary reports that he looked "like a well-developed boy of about sixteen." It was difficult for any one to believe that this was "the Booth"; his acting during the early scenes seems to have done little to reassure the house-manager. But finally, shaking off his weariness, he began to play the part for all it and he were worth; and both, make no mistake, were worth much in the theater.

This trudge, so characteristic of the elder Booth's haphazard progress through the external world, forms the basis for one of the first of a hundred anecdotes told of Junius Brutus Booth in the United States. Many of them are amusing and some of them very likely true. It is hardly to the purpose to repeat them in these pages, however much they may cry out for repetition to an audience which conceivably has not heard them.

Perhaps once in a drunken frenzy he stood over the captain of a lumber schooner, on which he had inexplicably taken passage from New York to Annapolis, and forced that unfortunate mariner to drink bowl after bowl of Epsom salt, pointing pistols at him meanwhile and assuring him boisterously that he must be physicked else he die.

Possibly, on another occasion, he refused to perish on Richmond's sword in a performance of "Richard III" and instead first battled with unaccustomed fury against the surprised Richmond and then chased him from the theater, down an alley, and to the refuge of a passing horse-car. Edwin, in after years, specifically denied that story, adding that it had been told about almost every tragedian since

Shakspere wrote. Probably he was quite right. But certainly
Junius's nose was broken when he was at the height of his
fame, and it is more than likely that Thomas Flynn, the
comedian, broke it with a pewter mug during a social occasion which could not have been quite sober. If Flynn did
this, Booth bore him no grudge. When Edwin was born
and named for Edwin Forrest, his father christened him
also Thomas, for Flynn. This name Edwin Booth never
used; still, he had it.

Nor is there any doubt that after Junius's first success
in New York (he began, as Richard, at the Park Theater
on October 2, 1821) it suddenly occurred to him that he
might better keep a lighthouse. He was touring the South
at the time and may have seen a lighthouse which took his
fancy. He decided that he would, in a phrase later made
ridiculous, "get away from it all." Early in 1822 he discussed the matter with a customs collector, one Blount,
and made application for the Hatteras Light. He learned
that it offered its keeper three hundred dollars a year, a
house, oil for the light, and twenty not very inspiring acres
to farm. He was seriously considering this retreat when a
theatrical manager found out about it and intervened, thus
performing a service to the American merchant marine
which can hardly be reckoned. Diverted, Booth decided to
become a farmer instead.

That summer yellow fever was rife in Baltimore, where
he had more or less established himself. From it Junius
retreated, taking his wife, their first child—Junius—and
Peacock the pony into the heavily wooded country to the
north. He bought a farm of a hundred and fifty acres about

twenty-five miles from Baltimore and near Bel Air. It was connected with town only by two ruts through the forest. It was densely wooded. "The forest scenery was romantic and beautiful," writes Asia. "There were huge rocks with tiny cascades; streams and springs of delightful water gushing out in the most remote places."

There was no house on the land, but Booth found one on the adjacent farm. Its owners had built it, solidly, of logs as a temporary residence until their farm-house was vacated by another family which had leased it. When Booth came on the scene the lease had just expired and the log house was therefore vacant. Booth purchased it. He put rollers under it and, while the neighbors looked on in amazement, moved it across several fields and finally set it down in a clearing near a spring. A great sycamore arched over it. He had the cabin plastered and whitewashed, and added to it as his family grew.

The house had four rooms and a loft by the time Asia was old enough to remember anything, and later she was to describe it as a "picturesque and comfortable abode." In the general room Junius kept his library. It included the works of Shelley, Coleridge, Keats, Racine, and Dante; English and French dictionaries, Burton's "Anatomy of Melancholy," Plutarch, the Koran, Locke's "Essay on the Human Understanding" and one or two others, including, of course, a complete Shakspere.

In this house, nine of Booth's ten children were born. It lasted well; indeed, it was torn down only in comparatively recent times, although a few years before his death Junius, prosperous, built another house which he called

Tudor Hall. This second dwelling was occupied by the family until the time of the Civil War, when it was rented. It was purchased in 1878 from Mary Booth, the widow, by Samuel A. S. Kyle and on his death in 1893 became the property of his widow, who still occupies it. She is now Mrs. Ella V. Mahoney, and has written pleasantly of the house and of the family which once occupied it.

The log house was for years the center of "the farm," so always referred to by the Booths. Not long after the land was purchased, Junius found himself too much occupied with the stage to till the soil, and his father came to the United States to act in the capacity of farmer. Richard Booth remained there until his death, tending to such farming as was done. The increasing family led a curious life which Junius, whether at home or abroad, directed.

Junius Booth was, for one thing, a strict vegetarian—on humanitarian grounds. He forbade his family to eat meat, although the servants might buy it elsewhere if they insisted. No living thing on the farm was killed with Junius's sanction. The black snakes were immune from punishment; and even their cousins, the poisonous copperheads, must not be harmed. The frog in the spring, and his descendants, lived sacrosanct lives; in a country of opossum-hunting the Booth opossums dwelt content and unmolested. For several years Junius even refused to allow the sheep to be branded, but he compromised on this point while he still had a few sheep to brand.

In all respects his domination of his family seems to have been moderately kindly but complete. He frowned upon discussion of the theater, in his home, hoping that none of his children would be tempted to follow in his footsteps. He urged the strenuous life, even upon his father. "Rise early," he once wrote to the elderly solicitor. "Walk or use some exercise in the open air and, when going to bed, drink a *warm* liquid—either weak grog, gruel or even water; drink nearly or quite a pint at one draught." Then one waited and was soon asleep; particularly, no doubt, if grog was handy. A little lettuce, eaten beforehand, would be found helpful, since "much opium, but in a harmless quantity, is contained in that vegetable." Junius himself found grog helpful in avoiding insomnia. He was rather famous for it. The "comfortable lethargy" his father sought was often enough attained by the son, in the back rooms of saloons.

When he was at home Junius himself would rise early and dig in his garden, whistling as he dug. But as he grew older and his fame increased he had less and less time for digging. For upward of twenty years he played in the American theaters, appearing often in the seaboard cities and frequently venturing inland. In 1825 he returned to England and played with success there, although the theater in which he appeared, the Royalty, burned as he concluded his engagement and his losses were considerable. He played also on the Continent, and returned in 1827, studying Italian as he came. He also found occasion on this voyage to cow a maniac with "the unflinching gaze of self-possession." And in 1828 he played in New Orleans, Racine's "Adromaque," presumably in French. He and Edwin Forrest were great friends and sometimes played together.

As time went on he became increasingly erratic, his

natural excitability frequently being heightened by his natural inclination toward hearty drinking. While Edwin was still a boy Junius began to disappear periodically and anxious searches were made for him through all the saloons available. He was usually found in one of them, and thence supported to the stage, where, if legend is to be believed, he gave those superior performances always credited to drunken actors and drunken newspaper men. Once—Otis Skinner repeats this story—he was being led across the stage toward his dressing-room on such an occasion when he heard through the curtain the impatient murmuring of the audience out front. Wrenching free, he rushed forward, parted the curtains, and, clinging to them for support, appeared before the waiting crowd.

"Shut up!" he shouted, at the top of his powerful voice. "Shut up! Keep still and in ten minutes I'll give you the goddamnedest Lear you ever saw in your lives." He did, of course. Are we to be denied romance?

And there was another time when he tried to commit suicide, leaping into the sea. Then he was rescued, considerably calmer, by Flynn, and it is reported that he anxiously begged Flynn, as the comedian pulled him into a small boat, to be careful, lest he upset it and drown them all. And there was another time when he invited all his neighbors around Bel Air to the funeral of a horse, and still another when he summoned a clergyman to preach a eulogy over the bodies of some dozens of pigeons. And once he wandered for days in the fields.

But these things were not mentioned, although they were well enough understood, while the children were

# Edwin Booth

growing up. Of them Junius Brutus was the first, born before the family moved to the farm. After him came as rapidly as nature permitted Rosalie Ann, Henry Byron, Mary Ann, Frederick, Elizabeth, Edwin Thomas, Asia, Joseph Adrian, and John Wilkes. Henry, Mary Ann, Frederick, and Elizabeth died in childhood. The others grew healthily enough, playing in the woods. Contrary to their father's wishes, the theater was early in their blood. The boys climbed to the crotch of a low cherry tree and spouted Shakspere to the frogs. The servants watched with excited glee while Wilkes, on the piebald pony or on Captain, a much larger animal, galloped through the woods, waving a Mexican war saber and declaiming as he rode. And, remembering the heavenly fireworks and the caul, they were polite to young Edwin, who was less spectacular than his youngest brother and not so much his father's favorite, except when there was something to be done.

The favorite was always Wilkes—so fiery, so reckless, so debonair. He was his mother's particular love. Mary Ann Holmes must have loved erratic boys and men. She gloried in him and feared for him. He was "good-hearted, harmless, wild, harebrained," as Edwin remembered him. Once in mid-July he harnessed the oddly assorted horses to a sleigh and drove in triumph through the woods to Bel Air, scraping all the iron from the runners. His father smiled.

None of the flock was very carefully educated. Edwin's education, and probably the education of the others, began under the care of Miss Susan Hyde at a school for boys and girls where, as Asia says, "the rudiments were well inculcated and the gentle instructress presided as the Minerva of

25...

her little circle." One may trust Asia always for the euphonious. They attended a country school conducted by a maiden lady. Later, Edwin was placed under an elderly Frenchman, Louis Dugas, who had been a West Indian naval officer and had retired to give his attention to the young. He wrote his own school-books, encouraged dramatic readings, and taught fencing.

Still later, Edwin went to school irregularly in Baltimore, where more dramatic readings were indulged in, and where at odd moments a Signor Picioli taught him a little of the violin. He learned also to strum on the banjo and to sing negro songs. He was a gangling boy, sallow, slight, but with a beautifully formed head and sad brown eyes. His father thought he might become a cabinet-maker. A good trade, that. Edwin could hang up his shingle in Bel Air.

# III

## A TRAGEDIAN BEGINS

IT IS THE HABIT OF MEN WHO LIVE BY THE STRAINING OF THEIR nerves and their emotions, while assuring themselves that intellect supports them, to urge the simpler life upon their children. Writers gravely assure their young sons that true happiness lies in digging ditches, and refer feelingly to the honest sweat they have never shed; actors speak harshly of the stage as a profession, citing its manifold disadvantages, and push their offspring toward cabinet-making. They may even believe themselves to be quite sincere. Junius Booth convinced one of his sons he was quite sincere. Edwin always believed that his father wished for him "some more healthful work, anything that was *true*, rather than that he should be of that unreal world where nothing is but what is not."

"If I had it all to do over again," Junius doubtless assured his son, in the familiar words. If he had it all to do over again he would fell trees or plane lumber or devote himself to farming. "Never think of the stage," the father urged, while dragging his son steadily toward it. "Shun this life!" exhorted Junius, hurling Edwin into it. "Make furniture," he ordered, and thrust a prompt-book into the willing hands of the youth. Edwin respected his father far too much ever to see entirely through all this. But, as he followed his begetter from dressing-room to dressing-room, he must have had occasional doubts. Even to a boy in his early teens, it must have seemed rather curious preparation for a life of honest toil.

Junius urged carpentering, inspired acting, and fitted Edwin for neither. He did not apprentice him; he did not send him to school. Edwin himself said later, with some truth, that "chance, not predilection for the stage," determined his way of life. The same chance was a determining factor in his way of meeting life. With no straining for interpretation, we may see in Edwin's youth the seed of what he became, both as man and as actor.

Booth often said, in his later years, that he had suffered "from the lack of what my father could easily have given me in youth, and which he himself possessed." He was referring to formal education, to the Latin and Greek which he, like Shakspere, got on well enough without. Junius was well educated. He was, moreover, a natural linguist, who could learn Italian on a voyage home—no small accomplishment, if he really learned it, even when one considers the length of voyages in 1825. Very possibly he had the educated man's light opinion of education, never prizing what he had never lacked. His son, naturally enough, came to overprize what he had never had. When Edwin had a child of his own, his chief urging was that she study . . . study.

Increasingly, as he grew older and went up higher in the scheme of things, he lamented his lack. He came to move among educated men and women, knowing poets and writers and artists who had come down from Harvard and Yale and whose manners innocently reflected their learning. It was a day when Latin and French and Italian tag lines were prevalent in speech and the written word. A more utilitarian civilization puts small value on such ornaments, and it is even a little difficult to understand the unhappiness it was to Edwin Booth that he was ready with no tags.

There is one letter, to his daughter, which reveals this unhappiness rather touchingly. He began it in high good humor, playfully tossing together such few Latin words as he knew and giving what he hoped were Latin endings to English words. Half-way through it struck him suddenly that this was all pretense, that he was aping his betters. The letter tails off in a mood as near one of bitterness against his father as Edwin ever knew.

Always he was to find his "idiocy and vanity too weak to support him against a full charged scholar." He dreaded to meet "professors." He said once that his friends called him a "natural." Fitzhugh Ludlow said he was a "splendid savage." "I'm stupidly awkward, I know, and get scared at trifles and hesitate to meet professors. I can't get over my schoolboy awkwardness." So he described his own state of mind. At the time he wrote he was crowned king of the tragedians; he knew almost every one of importance; he was a brilliant and envied figure, notable for self-possession which verged on polite hauteur.

There was, of course, no plot on his father's part to keep Edwin from education. The elder actor's belief in the simple life did not go so far as that. Junius Booth probably thought very little about it, one way or another. When Edwin went to school in Baltimore it was his mother's doing. She would have kept him at his books if it had not proved inconvenient. Even when it proved much more convenient to have him elsewhere, she insisted that he take his books along. He did. He did not open them very often, but he had them. He carried them into the dressing-rooms of half the theaters in the United States. No doubt they were sometimes under his arm when he sought his wandering father in saloons. Edwin was kept in contact with the world of letters.

The problem which confronted the Booth family during Edwin's teens was Mr. Booth. At his best he could do what he wished with his audiences. But he could never do very much with himself. When he ventured away from the farm, often starting in a carriage to which Peacock and Captain, one about twice the size of the other, were hitched, his family hoped for the best and feared the worst. They never knew when a message would come back to them from the manager of a theater somewhere, anxiously inquiring whether they had seen his star of the evening.

When such messages came, one of two things had happened. Either, as was more often the case, Booth had had a drop too much and was sleeping it off in the alcove of some bar-room or his excited mind had gone momentarily astray. If it was the first, then the problem was merely to find him, rouse him, and set him on the stage, where he might be trusted to act. Such incidents were unfortunate, but more or less to be expected by the families of actors in the early and middle years of the last century. The recurrent spells of mild insanity were, however, a special problem of the Booths.

It was discovered that, in moments of strain, Edwin had a quieting effect upon his father which others lacked. "My presence seemed necessary to him when at his work," Edwin says, "although at other times he almost ignored me, perhaps because his other children were more vivacious and amused him more." It was when he was at work that Junius needed care. When he was at home, playing at the simple life to which he was academically drawn, he was for the most part calm enough. The strain of performances, of traveling, of bad hotels, undid him. Then he needed a guardian. Edwin very early became that guardian. He could not travel with his father and go to school. Therefore he went no more to school.

He might start to school in the autumn. For a few days or even weeks he would study. Then a message would come from his mother. Edwin must join his father—at Washington, perhaps, or Richmond; perhaps in Boston or New York. "Take your school-books," his mother commanded. Edwin was off, to join his father and spend the winter touring. "Did you bring your books?" his father would demand sternly, when he arrived. Edwin would show them. Junius would nod gravely, his duty done. Then he would take his son to the dressing-room. "Stay there," he would admonish. "Stay there and study." Then, in glamorous costume, Junius strode forth.

Edwin would try to study, his mind elsewhere. Words from the stage would float to his ears. Then he would give it up. Then "the idle boy, ignoring Lindley Murray and such small deer, seldom seeing the actors, listened at the keyhole to the garbled text of the mighty dramatists as given in the acting versions of the plays." Who could study problems of interest, or learn hard grammar, when into his ears poured resounding words, delivered with the fire and fury which made a great tragedian? Perhaps he should have been learning Latin declensions. Instead, "at an early age my memory became stored with the words of *all* the parts of every play in which my father performed." He had some trouble forgetting mannerisms and inflections when he began to act for himself.

Those hours in the dressing-room, with the school-books laid aside and ears open to Shakspere, must have been the happiest, as well as the most profitable, of Edwin's boyhood. But that was only part of it. Junius was by no means always on the stage. When he was not, his son was his secretary, his buffer, his guardian. When Thomas R. Gould the sculptor arrived, full of his vast admiration for Junius and untold quantities of dull conversation, it was Edwin's task to entertain him while Edwin's father hid under the bed. And when Junius, mistaking a pause in the conversation for its termination, yelled from his cover, "Is that damned bore gone yet?" it was for Edwin to be as tactful as circumstances permitted. It was Edwin's task to see that his father was protected from the outside world, and from himself. When Junius sawed the air, up and down with his right arm, it was Edwin's task to be on the alert. That peculiar motion meant that Junius was getting thirsty and would have drink. It was a signal to get him to bed, if possible.

From city to city the two went, the boy slight and pale, with sad brown eyes; the man growing stockier, his classic beauty somewhat marred by a broken nose, his eyes filled with Roman severity. From city to city they went, from bad hotel to worse, from theater to theater. They played in New York near Five Points, where the Bowery begins and where the gangs were already fighting in the streets. They played in Boston, where they stopped one night at the Pemberton House, an aging hotel built around a court and with stables occupying one wing. They were given a room on the ground floor, from which opened a dark, unventilated closet, rank with the smells of the stables which were beyond its farther wall. They could hear the stamping of tired horses.

They were staying there one night when, after the performance, Junius began to saw the air. It was midnight, and the streets were deserted. Edwin led his father home, steering him past inviting doorways. He got him safe in the room and shut the door, heaving a sigh of relief. But Junius looked around the room with disfavor and announced that he was going for a walk. Young Edwin, weary and anxious for bed, braced himself to meet this new emergency. He promised that, if his father would stay at home, he would entertain him. He would talk of any subject on earth which appealed to the tragedian. He would sing coon songs and strum his banjo, whatever the other guests might think.

Junius shook his head severely. He was going for a walk. He needed the night air. Edwin should go to bed. Junius would not think of keeping his son up longer. Was he an unnatural father, with no thought for the strengthening of young bones? Let sleep knit up the raveled sleave of care. As for himself, he was going for a walk. He got up, fixing his commanding eye upon his bothersome offspring, and started for the door. Magnificently he glared at his son. He was going for a walk! His proud eye met his son's disbelief and challenged back, "What of it?"

But between him and the door stood Edwin, slight and boyish but also glaring. Booth met Booth, and Edwin had an eye of his own. "You shall not go," announced the stripling, no doubt trembling inwardly at his own audacity. Junius stared at him in shocked amazement. This was mutiny. But he hesitated in his movement toward the door. Suddenly he turned and, speaking never a word, stalked into the closet! He slammed and locked the door. Edwin, startled, stared at the door. Then he called, tentatively, "Father?" There was no answer. "The Booth" was sulking.

Edwin's young imagination began to paint horrors. His father, on stepping into that airless room, had been instantly overcome by some noxious gas. He was lying now in the darkness, unable to move, unable to speak. With his last strength he was trying to lift himself to unlock the door, and failing! It was midnight and Edwin was alone. Behind a locked door his father was dying—dying because of a youth's impertinent challenge. Edwin began to shout. "Father! Father!" There was no answer. Edwin pounded on the door. No response. The boy began to cry hysterically, pounding with all his strength. He begged for an answer from the closet. There was no answer. Finally he desisted. He grew cold and calm. His father was dead. He must go for help.

The silence lasted only for a moment. Then Junius, listening within, began to wonder what was going on. Just as Edwin was about to depart by one door, the tragedian threw open the other and stalked back into the room. With great dignity, and no word, he strode to the bedside. He undressed, still with such dignity as that activity allows, and clambered in. He did not speak. Edwin did not speak. After a time the boy was quieter and slept.

Edwin told his sister another experience, somewhat similar, and she reports it, also. Again it was in Boston, which seems to have affected Booth curiously. This night it was Junius's fancy not to go home at all after playing, but to take another of those nocturnal walks to which he was addicted. But he insisted that Edwin go home, again pointing out the necessity of ample sleep for a growing boy. Edwin said that he would like to take a little walk, also. Junius glared, but started off at a tragedian's pace. Edwin hurried after him. The father increased his speed, and the son his. They raced through the dark streets, under the wooden awnings, Edwin hanging on for grim duty. Then Junius laughed, perhaps admiringly, and slackened. Edwin came up with him and they walked on. Breath regained, Junius was off again and again Edwin trotted to keep up.

The tragedian swung in under the shed of a long market building and began to pace from end to end of it. Neither spoke. Sometimes Junius chuckled; sometimes he glared. Edwin matched his mood and his stride as well as he was able. Back and forth they went, back and forth. Finally the darkness turned gray and they were still walking. Then the first shafts of sunlight crept in under the shed. Junius, torn between anger and amusement, gave it up. He led the way back to the hotel and they went to bed.

Such nights were, of course, unusual, or Edwin would never have told of them. But for years the boy maintained a hardly broken vigil over the man. Often he lost in these combats and then he searched for his father in the saloons, usually finding him. He met the other actors of the time. Hearty Forrest patted him on the head and predicted a great future, while Edwin nodded with weariness. And Edwin looked, with curious envy, at other boys whose fathers led circumspect lives, seldom visiting theaters, almost never getting publicly drunk. Other boys were the protected, not the protectors. Other boys went to school.

And the other boys looked curiously at him, admiring and wondering. He was of another world. He traveled and talked with actors, the vagabonds of society. The most respectable proud ladies of Boston looked at Junius and his son, when they looked, as at curiosities. Edwin was not of the stuff which glories in that regard. His whole life proves it. Enforced unconventionality has its own rebound. Ministers' sons are not alone in their revolt.

Edwin was a proud boy. He was proud of his father, immensely proud. But he was at the same time torn by a desire for social acceptance. Boys cannot be outcasts without pain. Edwin, hypersensitive, felt himself more of an outcast than he ever was. He overestimated the already

*From the Collection of the Ehrich Galleries, New York*

JUNIUS BRUTUS BOOTH AS SIR EDWARD MORTIMER
*Painted by John Neagle*

crumbling barrier between people of the stage and those they entertain. He tremendously overstressed the gulf between the formally and the partly educated. Although one cf many children, he spent most of his time with adults. "When I was a little boy," he explained afterward to a little girl, "I had no opportunity to learn the different games and sports of childhood, for I was traveling most of the time."

He was at it when he was thirteen, and when he was fourteen and fifteen. By that time he knew most of his father's parts. They were the parts of all tragedians. The backbone of every repertory was Shakspere; and of Shakspere, Richard III, one of Junius Booth's favorite parts, Hamlet, Shylock, Macbeth, and Othello or Iago (depending upon the physical characteristics of the actor). "Lear" also was played and frequently "Julius Cæsar," in which the tragedian might be either Brutus or Antony, now and then Cassius.

To these were added the rôles of Sir Edward Mortimer in "The Iron Chest," Colman's melodrama (which was usually given without music), and Sir Giles Overreach in "A New Way to Pay Old Debts." Sir Edward Bulwer-Lytton's "Richelieu" was to come a little later into its full popularity, although William Charles Macready played it first in 1839. The rôle of Pescara in "The Apostate" also was a favorite of the elder school and, in later days, Tom Taylor was to add to the repertory a Hugo adaptation which he called "The Fool's Revenge."

Each tragedian had his favorites among these, and most had their own specialties in addition. Thus Forrest, although he was an accepted tragedian, succumbed to an epidemic of Indian plays when he was in his prime, and appeared as various noble savages. Jack Cade also was a favorite part of his. And Edwin Booth, some years later, appeared as Raphael in a rather dreadful little romance called "The Marble Heart"—which had a far longer life than it deserved, but is now mercifully forgotten.

Shakspere was always the inner citadel. The other plays were, by all modern standards, extremely bad. But they had one thing in common: each of them had a central character of satisfactory importance and the proper purple patches of which the actors could make "points." One of the best of these, as an example, is found in "Richelieu":

> "Mark, where she stands!—around her form I draw
> The awful circle of our solemn church!
> Set but a foot within that holy ground,
> And on thy head—yea, though it wore a crown—
> I launch the curse of Rome!"

It was for such moments that the older tragedians played. For those fine outbursts they husbanded their strength, walking softly, even listlessly, through the routine of the play, drawing themselves up when they saw a "point" approaching. Most of them were not at all averse to striding down stage at such moments, facing the audience, and letting the pit and gallery have it full force. Forrest used to do that.

Do not laugh too easily, or utter "ham" too confidently under the breath. It was ham, to be sure; it was noisy and obvious and it led to unbecoming raising of the voice. But it was great fun for everybody, and probably would be to-day. The heroic speeches kept the tragedians on top for many years. They rode the candences of blank verse, and those cadences are as irresistible as the measures of a brass band. They strutted and made believe, most of them off the stage as well as on. Much fustian entered into it; many black capes were swept across the shoulders of many stalwarts. Still, for all their obvious absurdity, they ruled the roost by human right.

In the early days they usually wandered freely, unburdened by supporting companies. The companies, trained in all the parts favored by the stars, awaited them. Towns so small that they have not had even road companies for years were then smaller still, but they had stock companies. These companies waited to surround such stars as Junius Booth with the appropriate gestures, content to serve as background to magnificence. It mattered very little to the stars what was the skill of their support. They appeared rather in cued monologues than in plays. No one thought of balanced performances; no one pretended that the drama reflected life. The drama reflected elocution, and all knew it and liked it. If they did not like it, they could go to the comedians. Only a few of the larger cities had standing companies which could take the foreground on necessity, although most of the companies had leading men who could play Iago to the star's Othello, Horatio to the tragedian's Hamlet, or Cassius to his Brutus.

Edwin's father was one of these stars and he shone widely, ranging the country. Edwin trailed after him, taking the part only of confidential aid, until September 10,

1849. He was then some two months less than sixteen years old. His début was at the Boston Museum, and it was not, as has been sometimes reported, the result of a last-minute decision. It is true that an overburdened stage-manager, called upon to play several small parts in addition to his other duties, may have rebelled and called for help. It may have been his happy thought to draft for one of these rôles the younger Booth. But Edwin was not rushed into his costume at a moment's notice. There was time enough for the astute manager of the theater to take full advantage of the situation and to advertise, in the billings, thus:

Last Night But Three of Mr. J. B. Booth, who will appear as

### THE DUKE OF GLOSTER

Tressel .........................Edwin Booth

His First Appearance on Any Stage on Monday evening, September 10, 1849, in Shakespeare's Tragedy of Richard III, or the Battle of Bosworth Field.

Duke of Gloster ..................Mr. Booth
Tressel .........................Edwin Booth

Typographically this is but a suggestion, of course. The printing of ancient playbills was a strange and fearsome thing. Capital letters reared themselves in the most curious places; Old English was always within reach. And every program-printer in those days seems to have had handy individual fonts peculiar to himself—and very peculiar to the page, with violent ornamentation depending everywhere.

*Edwin Booth*

Edwin went on, after borrowing his father's spurs and answering to that gentleman's satisfaction a short catechism: "Who was Tressel? What did he do?" and the like. Edwin spoke his few lines. "It is a great pity that eminent men should have such mediocre children," observed Rufus Choate from his seat in the audience, to the companion next him. "Did you do well?" inquired Junius. "I think so," replied Edwin, doubtfully. "Give me my spurs," said Junius and the momentous occasion had passed.

Edwin was then, by his own later report, "a sight." "I wore my hair down to my shoulders like a woman," he remarked. "I had a sallow complexion and a thin face and went around looking like a crushed tragedian." He must have looked, also, like a sleepy boy. But Joseph Jefferson, who first saw him at sixteen, thought of him afterward as "the handsomest boy I remember ever to have seen. With his dark hair and deep eyes he was like one of Murillo's Italian peasant boys." Jefferson also thought him "more attractive, more interesting, more beautiful" than his father, who, after all, had a broken nose. A few years later a newspaper reviewer was to report him, excitedly, as "Apollo-like in beauty, grace and manly perfection of form," to term his eyes "large and lustrous"—although, in the phraseology of an earlier day, he wrote as if Booth had only one eye—his forehead "high and noble" and his nose and mouth "of the pure Grecian type."

At the time of Booth's first appearance trouble was brewing about slavery and the Fugitive Slave Law was engrossing the attention of the press. News came from abroad by steamship and appeared on the front page of the "Herald," conveniently summed up in a head-line which read, "Five Days Later." Daniel Webster was making speeches. Forrest and Booth shared the tragic field, with Forrest ascendant. But even then there were stirrings against the native American star. Walt Whitman, who for two years was violently the dramatic critic of the "Brooklyn Eagle," was inveighing against Forrest's "loud mouthed ranting" and deploring that so many young actors took him for a model. Whitman was far ahead of his beloved democracy on this point, however. The general public loved ranting and could hardly be given too much of it. The louder the voice the greater the art. That was the general belief.

It remained to be seen whether Edwin Booth would qualify as a tragedian. His first appearance had been none too promising; his voice faded out before it reached the gallery, which was fatal. But he was only a boy of sixteen, with much to learn besides the words of the parts he might play. He was born to the purple, but he had to prove his ability to wear it. If he were too slight, or insufficiently magnificent, it might be his lot to appear as one of those leading men supporting the real stars, male and female. He might then be called upon to play many rôles far afield from the tradition, including even the melodramas of the rising Dion Boucicault. He might make money in other fields, but not the highest fame.

Fame and fortune both awaited if the purple fitted. He might expect, in that event, to be treated with the utmost consideration by critics and to be accepted as a defender of the "legitimate." He might also expect to be compared, line by line, gesture by gesture, with all preceding and contemporary tragedians. He would find the most cultured audiences waiting to hear him, and ears and minds throughout the country trained to the cadences of English blank verse. He might look forward to the day when he could ask, first fifty, then sixty, per cent of the gross intake on the nights he played. He might look ahead, also, to being always a lone eagle, supported on the stage invariably by inferiors who would expect little more than kindness and to be told where to stand.

He would play in the robes of kings and princes, of cardinals and all the mighty of the earth. He would be by turns heroic and sinister; he would always have resounding lines to speak. He would never, conceivably, find himself cast as a character faintly resembling any one he would meet in everyday life. He would have very little everyday life, when it came to that. He had examples of such stars in his father and Edwin Forrest. It must have seemed to him, as a beginner, that the pinnacle toward which he aimed was very solidly occupied.

Edwin was, after his début, apprenticed to the stage. There was no more talk of cabinet-making. He played on occasion thereafter with his father. Junius—

made no great objection to my acting with him, although he never gave me instruction, professional advice or encouragement in any form; he had, doubtless, resolved to make me work my way unaided; and although his seeming indifference was painful then, it compelled me to exercise my callow wits. It made me *think*.

Perhaps Junius' sympathies were so freely given to the animal world that he had few left for his young son.

In addition to playing with his father, Edwin served in a Baltimore stock company managed by Theodore Barton. There he was under contract to play any part assigned and to receive six dollars a week. He appeared in many minor characters, changes of bill being frequent. He was not generally considered particularly promising and had the distinction of being roundly berated for incompetence by one Madame Ciocca, a passing star. He must have been bad indeed to earn such notice.

During the autumn of 1850, on September 27, Edwin was with his father again, making his first appearance in New York at the National Theater as Wilford in "The Iron Chest." (Wilford is, it may be noted, a considerable step up from Tressel.) During that autumn and winter he played elsewhere, part of the time with his father, and in the summer he and his friend John Sleeper Clarke, who was two months and ten days his senior, gave dramatic readings in the court-house at Bel Air.

The two boys rigged up a stage and benches—a little training as a carpenter might have come in well, after all —and had bills printed in Baltimore, riding there for them. A negro boy entrusted with posting their sheets pasted most of them upside down to convenient walls. A considerable audience gathered, despite this, possibly because of it, and they divided at the door, male and female to side and side. The boys delivered Shaksperian set-pieces with enthusiasm and vigor, sang coon songs, and played the banjo. No report on the box-office receipts has come down to us.

In 1851, Edwin played for the first time in a tragedian's rôle, appearing as Richard in place of his father, who

EDWIN BOOTH AT THE AGE OF SIXTEEN

announced himself ill and unable to leave his room. The Booths always believed that the illness was feigned so that Edwin might have his chance. "But what will they do?" Edwin inquired anxiously, as the elder actor announced his decision not to go to the theater. The carriage, with Richard's costume, was waiting below in the street. No warning had been given the theater. "Go play it yourself," Junius commanded, and fell to contemplating his physical derangement. From this view Edwin could not move him, and so he himself went as commanded. He reported the difficulty, apologetically, to John R. Scott, the house-manager. "You play it," said Scott.

Perhaps it was a conspiracy, after all. Edwin was dressed in the robes, which were several sizes too large. He went on the stage and it is reported that the audience, although amazed, was kindly. Edwin always felt that his performance had been excruciatingly bad. When he returned to the hotel he found his father as he had left him, apparently lost in thought. Edwin afterward believed that Junius had been in the theater, and perhaps he had. And perhaps, given three hours without a guardian, he had been elsewhere.

So Edwin's apprenticeship went on. "I had seven years of it," he wrote later to a young actor who was leaving his company for one where more varied training was promised. "Most of my labor was in the field of comedy—walking gentleman, burlesque and low comedy parts—the while my soul was yearning for high tragedy." He adds, Polonius-wise, that he did his best in all he was cast for and that the unpleasant experience did him a world of good. So he paid the elderly man's tribute to the hallowed school of hard knocks; the human tribute to the theory that anything sufficiently unpleasant must be salutary.

At about this time family affairs for the moment overshadowed those of the theater. Suddenly the past of Junius rose up to plague him. Mary Christine Adelaide Booth, left so long ago in London, appeared in Baltimore and with her a son, Richard. Perhaps after preliminary discussions, perhaps suddenly, Mary Christine filed suit for absolute divorce from Junius on March 26, 1851.[1] She petitioned the judges of the Baltimore County Court. In the petition, which has long grown yellow in a box in the cellar of the Superior Court building, she came "humbly complaining" that she had been married to Junius Brutus Booth, then "a citizen and subject of said Kingdom of Great Britain" but now a resident of Baltimore, on the eighth day of May, 1815, in the city of London. She filed a certificate showing that the ceremony was performed by

[1] Copies of the papers filed in the case have been certified at the request of the author by the clerk of the Superior Court of Baltimore City, which has assumed jurisdiction, and are in possession of the author. The whole question of J. B. B.'s first marriage and its legal termination has been in rather pointless dispute for many years, although while Edwin Booth was still living the Baltimore "Sun" investigated and printed the facts substantially as given here. This did not, however, dissipate the confusion. As late as 1929, Lloyd Lewis in his "Myths After Lincoln" (Harcourt, Brace and Company, New York) treated Junius Booth's first marriage, his children by that marriage, and the divorce in 1851 as if they were among the myths of which he wrote. As a matter of record, it may be noted, also, that at the time of Mary Christine Booth's death, Edwin Booth flatly denied, in letters to newspapers, that his father had been married more than once. Filial devotion, evidently, gained the upper hand.

Nathaniel Fork, B.A., curate of St. George, Bloomsbury, County of London.

She set forth that she had thereafter lived with the said Junius, as his lawful wife, and that she had borne to him a daughter who died in infancy and a son still living. "In or about the month of January, 1821," however, "the said Junius Brutus Booth, without any intimation whatever or any justifiable cause whatsoever, abandoned your oratrix and came to the United States." He had continued since in that abandonment. And, further, he had left England "in company with a woman with whom he has been in the habit of adulterous intercourse from that time to the present; and that he has lived for many years in the city of Baltimore with said woman and does now treat and recognize said woman as his wife and that he has by her a large family of children." Mary Adelaide paused for breath, and the judgment of the court.

It was not long in coming. Junius did not deny the charges. His solicitors answered for him on March 28, simply: "This respondent admits the facts stated in said bill to be true and assents to a decree as prayed." On April 18, Judge John C. Hand, presiding, signed a decree granting the divorce and assessing the costs against the defendant. On May 10, 1851, the marriage—or remarriage—of Junius Brutus Booth and Mary Ann Holmes was recorded in the same court. Mary Christine died in Baltimore seven years later, at the age of sixty-eight, and was buried in a Catholic cemetery.

It was this incident, magnified and distorted by an embittered press, which was revived fifteen years later. It was then reported, among other things, that the first Mrs. Booth had died of a broken heart, induced by the cruelty of the treatment she had undergone. Hearts must have broken slowly in those days.

At the time very little attention was paid to the matter by the press. Critics of modern newspapers doubtless will credit this to delicacy and lament that a similar attitude is not now prevalent. They will be mistaken, of course. When Forrest and his wife ended their married life at about this time, in a long court wrangle, the newspapers were full of it. To print the details they even cut short some of their most circumstantial accounts of trials for rape.

Junius tarried in the East for a year after his matrimonial affairs were straightened out. Then he listened receptively to the suggestion of his eldest son that he visit California, which lay knee-deep in gold. Son Junius had come on from the far West, where for some years he had been an actor and theater-manager. He promised his father honor and money. Junius started with him, leaving Edwin behind. But he became ill in New York and missed the boat. So says the gentle Asia. A little later he returned to New York, this time with Edwin—who could be trusted to see him safe on any boat. They sailed that summer to the new country, where Edwin's apprenticeship was to be continued.

# IV

## THE YOUNG MAN GOES WEST

CALIFORNIA WAS STILL A FABULOUS LAND IN 1852. ONLY THE day before it had called fabulously to the East, offering gold in great nuggets for the taking, and the East had fabulously answered. The hardiest of those east of the Mississippi had streamed overland with pick and shovel and had sent back tales of miraculous wealth. Their entertainers had followed to establish saloons and dance-halls. The publicans and the prostitutes had gone, and those who offered less rhapsodic commodities—the storekeepers and the restaurant men.

And the actors went, also. Separated from her husband, Mrs. Catherine Sinclair Forrest was one of the first to seek fortune in this new land of promise. She had set up shop in San Francisco. Junius Brutus Booth the younger had been there for several years. He had not attained riches, but he had been where riches were. What California needed, he promised, was a star of his father's caliber. "Come West, old man," he begged. The gold-hunters were eager for the drama. They would pay for it with little bags of precious dust.

Junius and his sons set forth. They did not attempt the

long overland crossing, nor yet the tedious, risky sail around South America. They split the difference, crossing by the Isthmus. They sailed from New York to Aspinwall, without incident. They were poled up the Chagres River on flatboats, with their trunks piled in the center. The natives observed them from the bush. When the river was no longer navigable, the travelers took to mules, edging slowly toward the Pacific. They slept at night curled on top of wine-casks. They heard the natives sharpening machetes in the underbrush, and shivered. But they reached the Pacific and sailed up to San Francisco.

It was a rude city, hastily expanded. Beards were untrimmed in San Francisco and trousers were crammed into boots. But there were waistcoats of flamboyance and nuggets as big as men's fists, and the dust of gold was weighed in scales. Junius noted that there was no lack of saloons and promised himself some pleasant evenings. But first he must act for a time, and this he did, opening at the Jenny Lind Theater under the management of his elder son. He tore into "Richard III" and "The Iron Chest" with zest and the miners greeted his efforts with applause and gold. This for a time. Then business began to fall off. The first flush was gone and not every one was a millionaire. Not every one even believed that he would be a millionaire to-morrow —a state of mind which had been quite as good as the fact for the entertainers. And possibly the dance-halls had joys the legitimate could not offer.

The Booths, after a rather short stay at the Jenny Lind, moved over to Sacramento, where all took benefits, with only moderate success. "You should play Hamlet," commented Junius to Edwin, on seeing the slim youth in the sable garb he had donned for the rôle of Jaffier. "If I have another benefit I will," said Edwin.

They returned to San Francisco, but the flow of gold which had been anticipated was dammed somewhere. Junius shook his head and lamented the culture of the East. He spent more and more time in saloons, whence his sons more and more frequently fetched him. Now and then, no doubt, all three Booths grew tipsy together—no great task for Junius and Edwin, who were always uncommonly susceptible. It has been reported, in explanation of the elder Booth's intemperate habits, that he was intoxicated with only a drink or two, where others might consume a dozen and stay above table. Edwin seems to have inherited that limitation of capacity.

But, despite everything, Junius was growing homesick. He did not like this wild West, particularly since it did not promise quicker fortune than more civilized regions. He was all for starting back at once. He insisted that his elder son, who had profited nothing from the experiment, nevertheless pay him the minimum fee agreed upon. This the junior Junius did, although it left him nearly impoverished. Junius Senior beckoned to Edwin and started off. But Edwin did not budge. His brother nodded approvingly. The great Junius looked his surprise and alarm. Edwin was staying on.

He felt that he had been long enough a guardian. If he was going to succeed as an actor, it was high time that he came from under his father's wing, where he could hope to be no more than an adjunct, and struck out for himself. Edwin had reached that point, which is reached by even the most conscientious youth, when living for somebody else begins to seem unfair to oneself. He had decided that he must see what he could make of standing on his own legs. Here, where the Booth name was still a vague sound, notwithstanding the younger Junius's efforts to advertise it, was a place to start. Here, while enjoying the aid of his elder brother, he could nevertheless sail under his own colors. And, anyway, he liked California. It was new and young, it was romantic. It excited him and called him. He would stay on.

They argued it out, the Booths, and Father Junius sailed alone. Edwin, feeling that he had burned his bridges, and also, a little, that he was derelict to duty, watched his father go. Probably, once the die was cast, old Junius joyed in his liberty. When his father's ship was out of sight Edwin turned back to face San Francisco and his own future.

He had hardly begun this Western apprenticeship when he heard of his father's death. The news came while Edwin, as a member of a company headed by D. W. Waller, was snow-bound in Grass Valley, in the heart of the gold district. The company had played at various towns inland, including Nevada City, and had reached the straggling camp which called itself Grass Valley—because most of the grass had been torn up or trampled down—in time for a big snow-storm. But despite almost impassable roads, the mail got through, and in it was a black-bordered envelop for Edwin. His father had died on a Mississippi steamboat, which chugged up-stream from New Orleans. He had left the Louisiana city ill and his illness had developed rapidly.

He died in his cabin, with a steward and a stranger by his bed. The body was sent to Baltimore and buried there.

Edwin and some others plodded through the snow from Grass Valley—according to some reports, for fifty miles—before they could find means of transportation back to San Francisco. There he found more details of his father's death and burial, together with the advice to remain where he was, since he could do nothing in the East. He reproached himself and was reassured and reproached himself again, as will sensitive persons who feel that somehow they might have prevented catastrophe. But Junius was nearing sixty when he died; he had had a full and busy life and attained fame; he could rest in peace.

Edwin continued his apprenticeship. For a time he played in a company of which his brother was co-manager, and for a time it prospered. Then he met D. C. Anderson, a character actor, some years his senior, and they struck up a friendship. They found hotels bad and prices high and decided they could do better by themselves. They rented a two-room house on a plot two hundred by seventy-five feet and, looking out upon this domain, dubbed it "the ranch." They did their own cooking and housekeeping, in slap-dash fashion, and Booth drifted easily into the bohemian life he was afterward to deprecate so earnestly.

Our picture of those days is marred by the discretion of friends and relatives. All of them, Asia prominently, wrote to combat a legend. That legend had it that Edwin Booth was a hard-drinking man all his life, that he was as often drunk as sober, that he indulged—this was darkly hinted—in all manner of secret dissipations. That legend was entirely false. The picture it painted never had any real counterpart in life. And of course his friends wrote of him with that picture in mind and with the determination to eradicate it. The result is that they have sometimes given to their hero the repellent aspect of a plaster saint. Only now and then does his real character creep out, particularly during his earlier years. It is not until, some years later, the habit of saving his letters grew among his friends that we can see Booth as a man, not as an idol.

And until he began to speak thus for himself in letters from which not even a faithful daughter could edit all vitality, although she certainly managed to edit most of the biographical material from them, we must rely on such fragments as were let slip. Now and then some one, like Mrs. Thomas Bailey Aldrich, blurted indiscreetly, and added to the man a warmth and vitality others scarce allow him. For inwardly Booth was no brooding giant. He was a friendly, gentle man, upon whom a mask was thrust. He wore the mask, after he had adopted it, with a half-humorous realization. It was convenient. But he never wore the mask of a saint.

Asia slips a little in her task of dehumanizing when she tells how once some one who had long owed him twenty dollars repaid the sum in gold. Edwin, with Anderson at his side, no doubt, turned in at the next gambling-place. He staked his sudden wealth. He lost. So. He and Anderson journeyed on.

Those were not the days, nor was San Francisco the place, for prigs. Anderson and Booth must have lived with casual zest on their "ranch," drinking when it pleased them, so long as they were sober to play in the evening; risking what money they had where it might be doubled. Anderson, whom Booth never forgot, must have kept a paternal eye on the handsome youngster and a hand on his arm after a glass too much. But he gave him his fling, none the less. In those days there was no solemn talk of Booth's "devil," his inability to keep his thirst within convenient limits. It was not a devil in those days. Those were Booth's *Wanderjahre*. They must have been, in many respects, the happiest he ever knew. No moralists anxious—and anxious with cause, mind—to protect Edwin's reputation can quite put the snuffer down over their gaiety.

It was not the gaiety of riotous living, of course. There was plenty of work in it, the adventurous work of a young man finding himself. After his brother's company faded away, Booth played with Mrs. Sinclair. He appeared with Laura Keene, who had left New York some years before and wandered West and who was soon to return to New York for new successes and failures as one of the first women managers in the American theater. Miss Keene blamed Booth's bad acting for her lack of success. And Booth, following in his father's footsteps, played again in "Richard III" and this time made something of a stir. In April, 1853, he played for the first time in the rôle which he was to make preëminently his—Hamlet. That occasion is noted by the "Daily Alta California" of San Francisco thus:

For the benefit of Mr. Booth, the favorite play of "Hamlet" was produced at this establishment last night, Mr. Booth supporting the principal part and making his first appearance in that difficult character. As a first appearance it may be considered highly creditable and we can even predict a high degree of success for the promising young artist when he shall have overcome a few disagreeable faults of intonation and reached a profounder conception of the part.

Even though the "Daily Alta California" had its reservations, Booth's audience was delighted. It found in the young actor what later and more sophisticated audiences were to find, the perfect physical embodiment of the accepted Hamlet. "He was Hamlet, melancholy and all," as Wilkes Booth said later. He was slight and dark and his eyes were mournful; his face and voice were beautiful but sad. The pale cast of thought seemed to lie over him. It caught in his long dark hair; was implicit in his slight grace. He was a tragic poet in the flesh. Even his elder brother was impressed, although he warned the youth that there were many hard knocks ahead. A young journalist, Ferdinand C. Ewer, wrote in tempered praise in a magazine he was then editing, and to his intelligent understanding Edwin reacted quickly. He and Ewer became friends and remained so until Ewer's death many years later.

Mrs. Sinclair's theater having captured such business as there was, and Booth's appearances with her having ended, the rising actor looked around for new activities. Then a wandering tragedian named James Stark returned from Australia. There, not in California, lay fame and fortune, he declared. Stark had acquired neither, but Booth, who saw something new to do and was young enough to try anything—he was barely twenty, this fortunate youth—did not press too hard upon that point. He infected Anderson and Laura Keene with his enthusiasm and they set sail for Australia early in 1854. It took them seventy-two days to get there. They reached Sydney and Edwin appeared as Shylock, no slight undertaking for a twenty-year-old. They had some success in Sydney, but failed in Melbourne, and Miss Keene hurried back, as fast as slow boats would take her, to civilization. We shall meet her next on the other side of the world.

It was not long before Booth, Anderson, and the rest followed her, for there was neither fame nor fortune in Australia, after all. The venture was brief, inglorious, but rather good fun. Edwin and Anderson almost were hit on the head by a falling cocoanut, Asia reports, but Edwin had a premonition and moved and the nut fell harmlessly between them. Success missed them, too. They started back, pausing at Honolulu with several others who had joined in their exodus from Australia.

Although Booth was still a boy, he is reported to have been their leader. Certainly he was their star. He raised fifty dollars in the group and rented the Royal Hawaiian Theater for a month. They raised enough more to have bills printed and were penniless in the middle of the Pacific. The native boys to whom they turned over their bills for posting revealed a curious appetite for the paste which went with the bills. They ate the paste, smacked their lips, and threw the bills away. Then Booth and the rest, who were a little less hungry, posted the bills themselves.

His Majesty King Kamehameha IV was a patron of one of the first performances, but, since his predecessor had just died, he could not appear publicly in the auditorium.

A chair was rigged up for him in the wings and there he sat in state, magnificently guarded on each side, but forced to relinquish his chair when it had to be used as a throne by a king whose crown was pasteboard. Kamehameha is reported to have enjoyed the performance. And on March 10, 1855, Edwin played Sir Edward, as a yellowed playbill is still extant to prove, and after it Master Dobbs in "the laughable farce of *The Omnibus*."

They made enough, after a few weeks, to book passage for California and they sailed away, richer in experience and with the spectacle of the large, dark king engraved in their memories. They reached San Francisco early in the summer and Booth again joined Mrs. Sinclair, who still was prospering. He played various parts and the company was at one time billed as the San Francisco Minstrels, in which, it was promised, "the highly popular artists, Mr. Wheatleigh, Mr. Edwin Booth, Mrs. Henry Sedley, Mrs. C. N. Sinclair, Mrs. Wheatleigh, together with other ladies and gentlemen of the profession, will appear." Edwin played the Duke de Chartres in "the elegant comedy, *Follies of a Night*," opposite Mrs. Sinclair.

Dates do not always jibe in the scattered records of this Western period, but it was probably after that that Booth went to Sacramento, either with or without Benjamin Baker, a generous and ingratiating soul, expansive as over-yeasted bread, who was already known as "Uncle Ben" to all the actors on the coast. He later extended that sentimental relationship eastward, becoming uncle to every one. He was given to tall claims and he made them concerning Edwin Booth, probably with very little warrant in fact.

"Did I know Ted?" he was accustomed to exclaim in tones of mock amazement, even when no one had put the question. "Did I know Ted? Why, everybody knows I was his first manager. If it hadn't been for me, that boy . . ." And so on.

That boy would never have amounted to anything if it had not been for Uncle Ben. Or if it had not been, a little later, for William Stuart. There were always plenty to point to Booth and cry out, "See what I have done!" Booth seldom answered; never publicly.

Uncle Ben Baker was, he says, Booth's manager in 1855. He led him to Sacramento, where the young man acted for some weeks at least, first without and later with Mrs. Sinclair. They put on together, at about this time, "The Marble Heart," which had not previously been produced on the American continent. There was no crying need for it, even then. It failed, deservedly. And Booth, says Baker, played in support of a young woman who had just escaped from the Mormons in Salt Lake and was capitalizing the fact for all it was worth.

"We worked the sympathy racket and packed the house every night," Baker assured a reporter for the New York "Star" ten years later. Nineteen thirty-two would not have phrased it differently. And Baker said also, in that interview, that Booth played the ghost to the Hamlet of a stage-struck dancing master named Clapp, and with him dodged a rain of vegetables. Booth was then a "long-legged stripling, awkward as a young duck," said Baker. Booth could hardly have been noticeably long-legged at any time.

But whatever his appearance, and however Baker may have labored in his behalf, the Sacramento engagement was another failure. Booth joined a road company, led by an actor named Moulton. It was excellent fun, and all came under the head of apprenticeship. Edwin was having a good and early start; he could afford to try what was new. This was new enough. They were strolling players, riding horseback. Their luggage followed in a single wagon, which carried also a band (three horns) and such properties as were essential. They wandered through the camps, playing where they could, taking what came. All went well enough for a time; the camps were roughly gay at night, the actors were stormily greeted, but with friendliness.

Then camps began to catch fire just as the players quitted them. It was vexing and inexplicable. Perhaps there was among them some one who liked to see the sparks fly upward. Five camps flew upward in quick succession and the miners began to speak of Booth grimly as the "fiery star." The horns played and as brave a face was put upon it as might be, but the camps grew less friendly. The players saw frowns instead of smiles, and little knots of men gathered to talk under their breath and to stare at the actors.

Then the undercurrent of hostility broke out. The actors were chased from one town, Booth fleeing on horseback. They circled and convened again and went on. At the next town a sheriff met them. They had been none too prosperous and certain accounts were unsettled. All their possessions were seized. Booth's horse went into the common pool. The band lost its horns.

Edwin Booth

The sheriff suggested that Sacramento was a good place for actors. Safe, he said, significantly. The actors started trudging home. They had no money, no horses, no band to keep their spirits up. The roads were dusty and the way was long. As Booth plodded wearily toward the city he considered his situation. For six years, now, he had been on and off the stage. For four years he had been acting in California, in a great variety of parts. He had played Hamlet and Shylock and Richard III and Master Dobbs. He had made no money out of it, but he had kept alive. He had been part of a rough, unfettered life, and he was already growing tired of it. He thought longingly of "the farm" back in Maryland and of the cities of the East. Things, as Ben Baker had assured him before he left Sacramento, were "getting dusty" in the West. He swished a stick abstractedly against weeds. It was a long way from California . . . to anywhere.

He wondered whether, after all, he was to be a great tragedian. Perhaps it would be better, he told himself, to get back East as best he could and find himself a permanent place in some stock company. In New York would be best. Miss Keene was already there. Before she left she had mentioned something about his being her leading man. There would be a steady salary in that, anyway. It might reach a hundred dollars a week—big pay. There would be no more plodding through snow-drifts, no more slogging over dusty roads. He could live well in the East on that salary, and enjoy comforts. He could sit idle, if he wished, and smoke a pipe. He could reflect. He would not dine sketchily on meals that he and Anderson scrambled together on the ranch. He could eat now and then in the best hotels.

And he had, after all, made some sort of reputation in California. Friends in the East had sent him back clippings which had been reprinted there, telling of his appearance as Hamlet and predicting his greater success. That reputation would help, even if Miss Keene's promise came to nothing. He would hardly fail of some sort of engagement. And he was homesick. The East beckoned. He was in Sacramento and penniless and his thoughts turned toward New York. But how was he to get there?

He made a new friend, M. B. Butler, an architect, to whom the world of the theater owes not a little. Booth told Butler of his desire to go home. Butler agreed that that would be best. They considered ways and means. Butler was a friend in need. He arranged a benefit in Sacramento; and when that produced only enough to pay Booth's debts Butler arranged another. (But Booth had received in the course of the first benefit a handsome trophy, a hand and wrist made of gold, with a diamond held between thumb and forefinger. Or so it is reported. Probably his debts swallowed that, also.) The second benefit put money in the actor's purse. Booth paused in San Francisco for still another tribute and set sail for the East. Ben Baker preceded him, to make arrangements there. Baker, also, was weary of the golden West.

It was August, 1856, when Booth finally set off. He left the coast behind, he said later, "a mere stripling—full of promise (for good or bad) and Bowery rant." He had in his pocket, over his passage money, a draft for five hundred dollars. "After meandering through the gold fields of California and Australia for nearly five years," five hundred dollars. "One hundred dollars a year weren't big average pay, were it?" Edwin inquired, with ungrammatical jocularity, years after.

He voyaged again to the Isthmus and this time there was a train to carry him across it. His father had predicted that, Edwin remembered, and had also prophesied that there would one day be a canal between the oceans. He took ship again on the Atlantic and voyaged north to New York. Benjamin Baker, advance agent and universal uncle, was on hand to greet him.

As Booth's representative—he probably had other interests which prompted his return to the East—Baker had only one specific instruction in addition to his general assignment, which was to find engagements for a tragedian. He was to arrange for Booth's appearance as a star anywhere but in Baltimore. Booth had stipulated against beginning in the city with which his father's name was connected so intimately what he hoped would be a tour of some duration. He preferred to begin elsewhere, so avoiding the appearance of attempting to profit to the fullest by Junius Booth's fame.

Edwin was anxious to rub off as much as he could of his father's method before appearing in Baltimore. It still clung to him. Of that he was conscious. In many parts he felt himself little more than a bad copy. He had every respect for the original, although he was beginning to question whether the elder method was the only one. But he rightly believed that, if he was to make his mark where he wished it, he must bring a new luster to an old name. Not a higher luster necessarily, merely a different. He was by no means cock-sure about it. Inclined to pessimism, he rather doubted his success. He did not wish to fail in Baltimore, or to succeed there, if that was to be his fortune, until he was more surely himself.

Booth did not return from the West in any mood of exalted self-confidence. "The height of my expectation," he told William Winter, long afterward, "was to become a leading actor in a New York theater after my starring tour, which I supposed would last a season or two." He came back to get an Eastern verdict and to rub off the rough spots.

He discovered that Baker had done the one thing he was not supposed to do. Baker was innocently enthusiastic about his success. He had been to Boston, but had failed to make any definite arrangements there, although he had vague promises. William Burton in New York was interested, but not for that autumn. He had suggested a later date. But Baker had not despaired. He had kept up his confidence even when he found nothing in Philadelphia. He had gone on to Baltimore and had closed with John T. Ford for an appearance at the Front Street Theater. He knew Booth would be pleased.

Booth was anything but pleased, yet there seemed no way out. Baker had had full authority and had used it; in any event, Booth had to start somewhere. Meanwhile he could at least go home to the farm for a short rest. He went and the servants shouldered trunks full of costumes, of Hamlet and Mr. Brown-Smith, and nodded to one another.

The trunks were heavy. Doubtless full of gold. "He's from the diggings," they said, which was true enough.

Asia and the others were there to greet him. Wilkes, whom he had left a school-boy in Baltimore, was grown to a handsome lad with an eye to the stage; a boy with a careless swing and the Booth beauty. He was already dear to the ladies. So was Edwin, for that matter, then and after. He charmed even his sister, who writes that he came back, "older in experience only" and looking like a boy still—

and very fragile; his mild dark eyes and long locks gave him an air of melancholy. He had the gentle dignity and inherent grace that one attributes to a young prince, yet he was merry, cheerful and boyish in disposition, as one can imagine Hamlet to have been in the days before the tragedy was enacted in the orchard.

The young prince opened in the autumn of 1856 at the Front Street Theater, playing Richelieu. His appearance roused much curiosity and was successful. He stayed only a short while, however, and then was away on a tour which led him first into the South, then westward through West Virginia, then north through Pittsburgh, and on in a wide circle. His stops, even in the larger towns, were brief; he made many one-night stands. He took what halls were available and played to what audiences would appear.

Baker says he himself went along, and that many odd things happened. Once, for example, the small audience in a second-floor theater crowded so closely around the one stove, which was almost under the stage, that Booth, when he appeared, could see nobody at all out front. Perhaps Baker loved tall stories. Possibly it is to him we should attribute one rather too good to be true, and having to do with printers. Somewhere they billed Booth as "Mr. Booth" —the old form, then falling a little into disuse and in his case undesirable because it was the style employed by his father. Booth shook his head. "Make it simple Edwin Booth," he directed. Apparently the correction was sent to the printer by word of mouth. At any rate, it appeared so: "Simple Edwin Booth, tonight in . . ." The reader is under no obligation to believe.

In Richmond during that first tour Booth found Joseph Jefferson, also a precocious youth, managing a theater for Henry C. Jarrett. They had met some years earlier and it was a reunion of old friends. Jefferson, after the first exchange of stories and when he had heard something of Booth's adventures in California, spoke of the young tragedian's forthcoming appearances. He was particularly interested in "Romeo and Juliet" because he had a Juliet about whom he was enthusiastic.

She was no great actress, said Jefferson, although able enough and well trained. She had played the part to Charlotte Cushman's Romeo at Niblo's, had studied voice, and had been on the stage since she was fourteen. That was not, however, a very long time. Nor was she really beauti- ful: she had a quiet and thoughtful face, from which she drew her heavy dark hair back flatly. Her eyes were large and dark and there was something in them . . . well, something. Her mouth, also, was rather large, a generous mouth. But you could not describe her by describing her. There was something . . . Jefferson threw up his hands. You loved her. You were charmed by her; she was sweet and spirited. She was "slight in figure, but with lovely lines; honest, straight-forward eyes, brown and tender." (That phrase is not Jefferson's, but another's.) She had "an ineffable grace which made even strangers love her." In short, she would be such a Juliet as Booth would not soon forget.

She was living with Jefferson and his wife, and one can imagine that her quiet face lighted suddenly when she was animated. Jefferson introduced Romeo to his Juliet—Mary Devlin, daughter of a merchant of Troy, New York. She smiled at Booth. Jefferson says that at the end of that first week they came to him and knelt in mock submission. "Your blessing, father," begged Mary. "Bless you, my children," Jefferson answered; or so, years later when he was writing his memoirs, he remembered having answered. That is the spirit of their meeting, if not the letter.

They were together only a little time, at first, but they do not seem to have doubted, from the first. They would be married, where and when and how the future would decide. Edwin must go on, now, and leave her; he must tour and make his name and something more solid than a name to back that fading five hundred dollars. He was still an apprentice and she was hardly that. Meanwhile she would go on playing; Booth's boyish determination not to marry an actress went in a heap when he first saw her. They would write and be lonely. But not for long.

They took a grave leave, no doubt, being grave youngsters ordinarily. They talked more of the theater than of themselves, but no shyness really stood between them. Booth went on, a star of the third or fourth magnitude, playing in barn-like theaters, drinking rather too much to keep off the cold and now and then rather too much for playing. He thought of the safe hundred dollars a week he might get still from Laura Keene, and how it would make an immediate marriage possible. He went on through the winter, and April found him in Boston, where Thomas Barry of the Boston Theater was at length ready to try out one more of the young tragedians then so numerous.

Booth made his first Eastern appearance of real importance there, on April 20, acting the rôle of Sir Giles. William Winter, not yet critic of the New York "Tribune," or of anything, was in the audience and was at once captivated. The rest of the audience seems to have responded similarly, if not so earnestly. Booth's first starring venture in Boston was a success, in the box-office and out. Reading the Boston papers, William E. Burton congratulated himself on having signed a contract with Booth a few days before, and began to make plans for an opening which would be an opening. He decided that the new star should begin in "Richard III," although Booth had expressly stipulated against that. Apparently it did him little good to stipulate.

Burton placarded the town with noticeable billings. "Edwin Booth, Hope of the Living Drama," announced one, with a producer's confidence. "Richard's Himself Again," screamed another. And everywhere Edwin was announced as the "Son of the Great Tragedian," which was precisely what he had hoped, rather ingenuously, to avoid. And Burton, further, collected all the favorable press notices he could lay hands on and caused them to be printed in a little booklet, which was widely distributed.

Booth was scheduled to open on May 4 at Burton's Metropolitan Theater. That was a Monday and he left Boston the Saturday night before. As he boarded the train a telegram was handed him.

"Mr. Booth announced for Richard next Monday. Seats going like hot cakes."

Edwin took a long drink and followed it with another. He was a little the worse for several when he reached New York, but the assertion that his opening had to be postponed for two weeks while he sobered up is a canard. He was sober to end his apprenticeship and begin his career on the New York stage.

# V

## "HOPE OF THE LIVING DRAMA"

DURING THE FIRST YEARS OF EDWIN BOOTH'S APPRENTICESHIP his father and Edwin Forrest had shared the tragic throne. Then Junius died and Forrest ruled alone. There were other tragedians, of course, and no metaphor exactly sums up any situation. But Forrest was the dominant mime of a generation which was coming to an end. He stood between Edwin Booth and the top rung. He was a little over fifty years old, which is likely to be past the prime for an actor. It was past the prime of Edwin Forrest. He was, in the words of Nym Crinkle of the "World," "backing slowly out of sight with the dignity and distress of a paralyzed titan." He was to continue that retreat for some years yet.

Forrest was one of the first native-born actors to acquire resounding fame. He was a mighty man; it seemed to his contemporaries that he summed up in himself the might of a young country, the rude might. He was no polished actor, nor subtle. He was a great, rough figure. He did not bend and sway to his rôles, advancing with delicate precision along the line of least resistance. He plowed through them, hoarse and vigorous; and, often enough, the character which stood in his way was dismembered by his progress through it. He had a mighty voice which does not seem to have been often modulated or very frequently musical. He attained his effects—and he did attain them—by sound and fury. He had come down, years before, like some young barbarian of the North upon the classics and he beat them into submission.

When he was a young tragedian he was beloved of a young nation. Prejudice ran high in those days; only in 1849 it had found bloody expression in the Astor Place riots, when the long drawn out wrangle between Forrest and William Charles Macready, the English star, reached its climax in the crackle of musketry; and many who had come to hoot the English actor remained to die on the cobble-stones. They swore by Forrest when he was a Bowery star; and all the loyal American societies backed him to the last man.

But by 1855 or thereabouts the public temper was beginning to grow a little quieter. From the top the virus of softer living was beginning to trickle downward. This virus infected the stage early. The theater is of necessity international and an older civilization filtered in through it. The more cultivated theater-goers were beginning to question the stalwart school. Forrest's style, as noted by Lawrence Barrett, who was himself beginning in those days, was a subject of derision to the new generation. And, to go with this, Forrest himself was beginning to lose his youth, and the vigor of youth becomes easily the harshness of middle age. "Age and infirmity were showing their effects on his once powerful frame," Barrett comments. His voice, never melodious, was growing harsher.

Critics were not lacking to point out this decline of powers, to any who might have missed it. Walt Whitman, writing of theaters for the Brooklyn "Eagle," was among the first to notice it. He had thrilled to Forrest once, but both men were growing older. Whitman lamented his ranting, his noisiness, and doubted he was a good model for young actors. It was very old style, the Forrest method. Some read and nodded: that was just what they had been thinking.

Whitman's voice was not the only one raised against Forrest. It was not the loudest or the funniest. The aging actor was the victim, in 1855, of a direct assault—a furious, angry, punishing attack. He was struck with the pen of William Stuart, born Flaherty or O'Flaherty in Ireland, and in New York for reasons which were much speculated upon. It was generally felt and sometimes said that he had left Ireland very suddenly and with good cause. He was witty, clever, and unscrupulous. In the spring of 1855 the New York "Tribune" employed him as its critic and sent him to the Broadway Theater to notice the appearances there of Mr. Forrest. Within a few days the town was talking, between amusement and distaste, of those criticisms.

It has been often contended that Stuart was paid more than the "Tribune" paid him for those notices. Jefferson in his autobiography speaks guardedly of the matter, reporting that "a certain critic" had admitted to him that he was paid a "large sum of money" to go regularly to the theater and "write down" Mr. Forrest. That certain critic could have been none other than Stuart. The same charge is made by Winter and by many others, although there seems to have been no agreement regarding the source of Stuart's extra pay.

Some suspected Edwin Booth; and Stuart, after his later break with the tragedian of our story, probably dropped dark hints sustaining this theory. It was quite certainly not true. Even Crinkle, who was no adorer of Booth, specifically notices that no one who knew anything of the matter suspected him. But Crinkle, one of the first of the critical play-boys and a leading wit of his time, agreed that the circumstances of Forrest's eviction "were not memorable by reason of their magnanimity."

Stuart had an opportunity to see, and to denounce, Forrest in all his Shaksperian rôles. He began with Hamlet; they both began with Hamlet. Stuart described, at length, what Hamlet meant to him, stressing all characteristics of subtlety and quiet melancholy. He paused to pay a compliment to his readers. "There are many in our country whose time and taste enable them to cultivate fancy, possess perhaps a higher and keener sense of the beautiful than is to be found in any other land," he said blithely. But "there are also some, perhaps even many, whose coarser habits and pursuits may lead them to prefer violent physical feats of voice and attitude to pure and beautiful conceptions." Then he was on Forrest, like a whip.

"To the taste of these latter," he continued, "the animal strength and coarse passion of Mr. Forrest may pander, but surely this would find a better field in such characters as Jack Cade than in the dreamy, melancholy Prince of Denmark." Then Stuart tore Forrest to pieces, line by line. He assured his readers that in the Players scene Forrest "had

73···

the air of some huge gypsy, watching with roguish glance for an opportunity to rob a hen roost." He announced that this large, coarse person "defiled the fairest creations, the beauteous temple of Shakespeare's genius." "Back to the Bowery!" he ordered. "Away, go, get thee to the Bowery."

Forrest tried Richelieu. Stuart pounced upon him. The slender, aging, intellectual cardinal . . . this? This fellow of "harsh voice and coarse knit frame"? "Away, go, get thee to the Bowery!" And in Othello, Forrest looked . . . what? "The inflexible, resolute hangman." The harried actor swore mighty oaths in his dressing-room.

Forrest tried Lear. It was "far less repulsive than his Hamlet, Richelieu or Othello," but it proved again that Forrest was "wholly incapable of rightly conceiving Shakespeare's beautiful creations." Then Forrest turned to melodrama, but Stuart was not to be out-foxed. He was too clever a man to reveal animus needlessly or to spoil his case by overstatement. Forrest as Rolla in "Pizarro" was right where he belonged. Here he had a part "more difficult for an actor to miss than to catch," and he caught it. Nor did Stuart find Forrest so "repulsive" in the title rôle of John Howard Payne's "Brutus" as he had been in the "complicated characters of Shakespeare." Stuart liked his victim well enough, also, in "Damon and Pythias," but when Forrest, perhaps heartened, returned to Shakspere and played Macbeth, Stuart was ready for him. He took the opportunity to point out that Forrest had been very good in melodrama.

It went on for seven weeks, cruel, sometimes witty, abuse. There was enough of truth in it to give a faint color

of fairness to what was undoubtedly a malicious and inspired attack. Perhaps Stuart reached his height when he
recommended Forrest, in his favorite "Jack Cade," to the
attention of the butcher's apprentice "whose ear had become
familiar with the bellowing of bulls and the noises and
sights of the shambles," and who therefore would greatly
enjoy the "facial contortions, the throat-rattles and stamping
of the feet with which Mr. Forrest illustrated his conception
of the character he personated."

It did Forrest no good, all this. A lie may prove a
boomerang, but not a half-truth. It set the old thunderer to
tottering; he was tottering the more two years later. He
was waiting for a push. And at that moment Booth was
coming down to New York for his first great test.

He was "the hope of the living drama"—and of William E. Burton, proprietor of Burton's Metropolitan Theater, which had been Laura Keene's theater a season before.
It had been a long, hard winter for Burton and others.
The panic of 1857 was on them. Burton looked hopefully,
and doubtfully, at a sheet of bluish ruled paper, dated
April 18, 1857, and certifying, with no regard for punctua-
tion, that "an engagement has this day been entered into
between William E. Burton of the city of New York of the
first part and Edwin Booth tragedian of the second part."
Without pause it continues:

> Said party of the second part agrees to perform at said
> Burton's Theater for the term of twelve nights commencing
> Monday evening May 4th and ending on Saturday May 16th
> on the following terms said party of the first part agrees to
> share equally the receipts of the theater each night (after de-

*Darling of Misfortune*

ducting three hundred and fifty ($350) dollars) and to give a clear third of the receipts of the theater on the first Friday night and a clear half of the receipts of the theater on the second Friday night as benefits, said party of the second part's name to be starred exclusively on the play bills of said theater.

Burton found himself in possession of this bit of paper (it is still preserved, incidentally) near the close of an unsatisfactory season at Broadway and Bond Street. He had moved there that autumn from his old theater in Chambers Street and his old patrons had not followed him as he had hoped they would. He had started his season on September 8 with the Davenports, husband and wife, and had come nearest financial success when Dion Boucicault and Agnes Robertson appeared in one of Boucicault's plays entitled "Genevieve, or, The Reign of Terror." But even that did only moderately well, and Professor George C. D. Odell, whose "Annals of the New York Stage" is without a rival for the student of the theater, remarks that his season was "simply frittering away, without a single outstanding success."

Of Burton's misfortune, too, was Booth the darling. In a happier season Burton might not have taken a chance with this comparative unknown. If Booth had not been something of a last desperate card for his first New York manager it is doubtful whether Burton would have used all his skill to "puff" him before his arrival, or have wasted money so prodigiously on advertising. But Burton was ready to take any straw that offered, and Booth was a straw.

The season had been none too prosperous for anybody.

. . .*76*

Miss Keene, who had had the Metropolitan the season before, had lost it to Burton through failure to announce her intention to renew her lease. She had built a theater of her own at 622 Broadway and named it after herself, there producing "Camille," "The Marble Heart" (she could have used Booth in that if he had become her leading man) "Masks and Faces," and other plays, with no great success that season.

The Broadway had had a season prosperous in spots. It had started out badly in the autumn of 1856, with Harry Loraine, "a mediocre provincial actor from England," as Claude Melnotte, but had made money with Forrest, who had played on alternate nights through most of the winter and might have still been playing when Booth arrived if it had not been for sudden illness. Thomas Placide had been prominent in the company which alternated with Forrest; and after him came E. L. Davenport to offer "Richard III" and "Othello," as well as "What On Airth Is Goin' On?" The Broadway opened, on the night of Booth's first appearance, a "magnificent spectacle" called "The Son of Night." That same evening Laura Keene was playing "Like and Unlike," in which she was a favorite.

Wallack's Theater, in early May, was presenting "The Iron Chest," "The Merchant of Venice," "The Wife," "Don Cæsar de Bazan," and other favorites with J. W. Wallack in the leading rôles and his support drawn from the members of one of the best stock companies New York has ever known. Wallack's had had a fair season, aided by E. A. Sothern, who that year appeared for the first time under his own name; Matilda Heron; and John Brougham, who was losing money at the Bowery Theater faster than he could make it by appearing as a star. It was a season when many great names were in the making. There was Jefferson, beginning to attract attention, and Barrett. If a theatergoer had not wished to see the "hope of the living drama" in May, 1857, he might have chosen, in addition to the offerings of Miss Keene and Wallack's and the Broadway Theater, "Fate, or, The Children of Love," at the Bowery; "Cleopatra, or, The Battle of Actium," at the National; and, at Barnum's American Museum, a play called "Neighbor Jackson," which had to do with a runaway slave.

Or he might have gone to a minstrel show, to any of many minstrel shows. One visited Burton's discarded theater in Chambers Street, where Edward Eddy—"Hi, Eddie Eddy Eddie Eddie Eddie Eddie Eddie Eddie!" they used to yell at him on the Bowery, until even their brass throats wore out—was making out none too well. In that season one might have seen plays in which the topics of the day, "slavery, Mormonism, spiritualism, returned Mexican volunteers, crime waves in the cities, the horrible financial crisis"[1] were uppermost.

Then Booth came, and Booth was beautiful. "A slight, pale youth, with flowing black hair, soft brown eyes full of tenderness and gentle timidity, a manner mixed with shyness and quiet repose," as Barrett describes him. He took his place "with no air of conquest or self-assertion and gave his directions with a grace and courtesy which have never left him." Who could stand against him in a

[1] George C. D. Odell: "Annals of the New York Stage." Columbia University Press, New York, 1927–31.

day when, as Crinkle phrases it, they were "a little tired of the thunderous and inarticulate genius of the giants"? "Stalwartism was overdone. Why not let in the milder muse, with poetry and rhythm and thought and sweep away the stage for a new setting?"

The theatergoers were ready for the change, as we have seen. They read with interest advance descriptions of Edwin Booth and, on the evening of May 4, 1857, flocked to see what the elder Booth had left them, what Burton had brought to cap his season.

They drove to Broadway and Bond Street in their best carriages, to see Booth. The gentlemen were at their most gallant and the ladies at their loveliest. New Yorkers had already in those days the habit of gathering in force outside theaters to watch the gentry enter, and they gathered that evening. And the humbler patrons of the drama were there, too, to say nothing of the critics. It was "a very crowded and intelligent audience" which saw the new Richard, played by a young actor whom the "Herald" found "slight, handsome and active." He captivated the crowd from the moment of his first appearance; his voice, while powerful, was thrillingly musical. "An unqualified triumph," the "Herald's" reviewer wrote that night, scribbling for the next day's paper. The acting was remarkable for its "freedom and boldness." But it suggested "his father at every turn of phrase" and, in the considered opinion of the critic, was noticeable for its lack of the "scoffing, sardonic, humorous mockery" suitable to the rôle.

Booth said afterward that his early performances, particularly in Richard, were just so many awkward imitations of his father. He had been trying for upward of five years to eliminate the vestiges of his father's method which still clung to his, and he had been only partly successful. Nevertheless it hurt to find that his failure to create his own technique was so palpable that even a "cricket" (Booth usually called them "crickets" and talked of their "chirping") could notice it. There was bitter as well as sweet in the "Herald's" notice. That of the "Tribune" also was mixed, for the reviewer of that dignified journal found Booth a "most unequal actor." He explained:

His fine, careful acting in one scene is no guaranty that he will not walk feebly through the next and let it go by default. He omits many opportunities for making technical points and slips over many sentences which, in other hands, have seldom failed to gain the audible approval of the house; but, on the other hand, when he takes up a favorite scene with the resolve to make it a sensation, all his tameness instantly vanishes and he renders the passage with a vigorous truthfulness which startles his audience into wild enthusiasm and brings down a perfect storm of applause.

Edwin, comparing these reviews, may have suspected that the "Tribune" reviewer was most pleased with precisely those passages which had led the "Herald's" critic to see him as a copy of his father. He disappointed the "Herald," which wanted a change, but failed to satisfy the "Tribune," which hated to see the good old "points" go unappreciated. But they agreed that he had at least the physical basis for great acting—the physical beauty, the "rich, sonorous voice of unusual compass and flexibility." The "Tribune" reviewer was, summing it all up, "disposed to look upon him as one of the most promising of all the horde of 'young American tragedians' of this latter day." Running through the notices, one detects, for all their gravity, an undercurrent of feeling that something out of the ordinary had happened.

Booth's critics did not realize, nor, in all probability, did Booth himself, that in this acting with its irregularity they were seeing a conflict between old methods and new. The thunders which Booth had heard through the keyhole of his father's dressing-room echoed in him; in him, too, flashed the more subtle lightning of the new ways. He realized what he was doing, but not its implications. He was deliberately playing "down"; the passages that the "Tribune" saw him as "slipping through" were those in which he was adopting the conversational tone that was slowly finding its way to the realistic stage but had not yet gained a foothold on the slippery heights of poetic tragedy. That it never really gained a foothold, perhaps never will gain it, is beside the point. The old mountains are not now frequently attempted, being too slippery for modern methods, but an art as a whole may gain from a study of the technique even of failure.

That his was a conscious effort toward a new method and a definite split with the elder "ranters" is made apparent in a letter written to him by Mary Devlin at about this time.[2] In it she wrote that "the conversational, colloquial school" he desired to adopt was "the only true one for the present day," adding, however, the caution that "too much

[2] From "Edwin Booth, Letters to His Daughter and His Friends." Compiled by Edwina Booth Grossman. The Century Co., New York.

is dangerous." There was Miss Heron who to Mary seemed
to be carrying it to an extreme and giving "too much Mrs.
John Smith." The letter is one of many the two young
actors exchanged after they had met in the South; letters
filled, for the most part, with grave discussion of acting.
They had evidently been discussing at length just the point
that so bothered Edwin's first critics. Richard III is not, of
course, among the rôles in which this method can be used
to its best advantage. If it had been, Junius Booth would
hardly have chosen it as his favorite.

Edwin had a better chance to exercise restraint in the
rôles of Hamlet and Iago, which he also acted during his
first engagement. He appeared in "Richelieu," and as Sir
Giles Overreach, Shylock, Lear, Romeo, Claude Melnotte
in "The Lady of Lyons," Sir Edwin Mortimer, Petrucchio,
St. Pierre in "The Wife"—a favorite of that day's tragedians—as the Stranger and as Brown-Smith in "Little Tod-
dlekins." That last was played for his benefit. His repeated
appearances served to increase his popularity and he was
something of a sensation for three weeks. He did not play
every night; on one occasion, while he rested, Young Hengler, a "rope vaulter from Niblo's," filled in and played
Hamlet for a night only. Young Hengler took it quite seriously, in which respect he was quite alone. Possibly Burton
thought the contrast would be amusing; no doubt it was.
Burton was making money and in a mood to be amused.
Booth played until May 26, the engagement having been
extended by ten days. Then he went to the road, touring
for a good part of the summer.

He returned to the Metropolitan in August, opening with Sir Giles. Of this performance the "Herald" remarked:

Mr. Booth's Sir Giles is one of his very best impersonations and he treads close upon the footsteps of his father, whose performance in the last act we have never seen equalled. Mr. Edwin Booth has the same electric flashes, the same marked inequalities, and achieves almost the same triumphs. He is an actor whose rise has been almost without parallel and who, as we have said before, has his future in his own hands.

In the last act of "A New Way to Pay Old Debts" Sir Giles is undone, his wicked schemes are frustrated, and he falls dramatically in a fit. The play is not a reticent one. Junius probably got out of it all there was in it, and more, and his method could hardly be improved upon. The only way to improve upon "A New Way to Pay Old Debts" is that which time has adopted. Booth played a week on this occasion and went back to touring, wisely using his New York recognition to solidify his success on the road. The canny actor of those days neglected neither. Booth was followed at the Metropolitan by James E. Murdoch and then by Charlotte Cushman, who was heavier than she had been.

He wandered that winter and returned in the spring to act, in April, at the Metropolitan once more. "He follows implicitly the old school of acting," the "Herald" assured its readers. He went to Wallack's a few weeks later and again drew crowds. Times were still bad, but the theater business was picking up. In that year Joseph Jefferson was definitely proclaimed a man of genius. And in that year,

also, Boucicault's "The Poor of New York" was first produced at Wallack's—which was that season, as in the season
preceding, under the management of William Stuart—and
ran for more than a month. Fourteen theaters were open.

Booth's tours, which it would be profitless to follow in
detail even were the records complete, took him to North
and South, to East and West. His began to have the appearance of an assured success. He no longer feared that he
would be forced to take advantage of Miss Keene's still
open offer, and he began to reach a financial position which
made marriage thinkable. The correspondence with Mary
deepened in feeling, no doubt; both grew excited as it
seemed they would not have to wait much longer.

We may pass over the years between the spring of 1858
and that of 1860, thinking only that they saw Booth's slowly
increasing prestige, a mellowing of his art, a gradual escape,
both in method and in the public view, from the shadow of
his dead father. He then, also, began to turn his mind to
the plays he acted and to think of adding to the playing
versions of Shakspere some of the many beauties pruned
by earlier actors. But he was not yet to have an opportunity
to work out these ideas with anything like freedom.

Mary came up to New York toward the end of this
period. Then, on June 30, 1860, her lover wrote a happy
letter to a friend, Captain Richard F. Cary. The day had
come, was coming. "Fear, hope, regret, bliss, love, etc.,"
agitated the heart of the writer. "This day week," he wrote,
"'young Edwin' is no more. A sober, steady, pater-familias
will then . . ." and then, before he finished the sentence, a
hand-organ in the street began to play "Love Not" and he

was so upset by it that he broke off. He was going to be happy . . . and married in a week.

Nothing intervened. On July 7, Mary and Edwin were married in the home of the Rev. Samuel Osgood at 118 West Eleventh Street, in New York City. John Wilkes Booth and Adam Badeau, later a general on Grant's staff and still later Grant's biographer, were witnesses. Some weeks before, Mary had made her last appearance on the stage.

They took rooms at the Fifth Avenue Hotel on the corner of Twenty-third Street and the avenue.

Booth liked acting, but not the actor's life. To go upon the stage, to bend his supple body and his melodious voice to his wishes, to experiment with new readings and new interpretations, to read newspaper praise of his efforts, to be looked on admiringly by people he respected, to attain a great name—these things, except when he was uncommonly depressed, he took delight in. He had, further, a wholesome respect for the cash that flowed into his pockets. He wrote not a little about the "ducats" and almost always coupled news of his receipts with comment on his artistic triumphs. He had a healthy appreciation of money—an appreciation to be expected in a youth whose father died, after many successes, very close to poverty; whose family was never too sure of its financial security and was pretty constantly looking about for aid. If he could have stayed comfortably at home, going to a near-by theater for regular performances, he doubtless would have found his life as satisfactory as one subject to dyspepsia and resulting moods of melancholy is likely to find it.

But that was not, in 1860, the actor's life. There were few long, contented runs on Broadway. Booth could not, like the modern mime, rent an apartment after a few uncertain weeks and settle down for a winter, relatively sure of steady and unvaried employment in one spot. New York was a center, but only a center. It was not, as for all but a few pioneering souls it has become, a circumference as well. In 1860 the actor's life was something to give any one pause. The traveling salesman, by comparison, led an existence of humdrum domesticity; was a fixture, with home and fireside.

— An actor, particularly a rising tragedian, must spend most of his time on trains and boats, in bad hotels and makeshift theaters, in carriages from tavern to show-shop. He might stay for some weeks in New York, or even for most of a winter. He might stay for briefer periods in Boston or Philadelphia. But the actor could not neglect the road. Always it stretched before him, with rewards at the end and ruts in the path. He enjoyed the comparative rest of a New York hotel for a time, then was off again.

A long train ride—and train rides were long, in those days—took him from New York to the first stop of the route. Perhaps it was late in the afternoon before the train jerked into a little station. It was usually winter and one left the car's stove for a windy platform, and left it for a drafty carriage. The hotel was blocks away; perhaps, indeed, the town was hardly in sight from the railroad station. It was desolate and forbidding, whether the actor were a rising young tragedian or no. Perhaps the carriage passed a great barn-like building labeled "Opera House" and suggesting

---

at a glance broken floor-boards on the stage and rats in the dressing-rooms. The front of the theater would be plastered with sheets announcing the arrival of, shall we say, the "hope of the living drama."

But, rattled and tired and cold, the living drama in the carriage was hardly hopeful. Would the hotel be as bad as it was remembered? Almost always. Would the food be heavy and indigestible, leading instantly to a bout of dyspepsia, to headaches and nausea? With hardly a doubt. Would the room be cheerless and the water frigid in the pitcher, the windows rattling in their frames? Oh, surely! And would the hard and bumpy bed reveal, after the first ten minutes of repose, certain industrious small occupants of beds? The chances were not against it.

There was the bad dinner to be eaten in the middle of the afternoon, if the actor was there by then; and the nap to be taken, if circumstances allowed. Then there was the theater, with more drafts and bare board walls and chilly dressing-rooms and a stage with a gale sweeping across it. Then, for a few hours, was acting—lights, applause, cheers, perhaps. The accounting came after, and the comfort of a check. Then the hotel again and perhaps an early call; sometimes, when a long journey intervened, no hotel at all, but fitful naps in a straight seat. Bang, batter, jerk, over the country-side, to a new town and another theater like the one behind; and another hotel, no more inviting; and more meals which disturbed the stomach. And so on . . . and on and on . . . perhaps for months broken only by the greater comforts of some larger city where the population might make a week's stay profitable.

A man must have a romantic love of change to endure such a life uncomplainingly; he must feel the vagabond, the wanderer. He must remember that, not many years before, the strolling player had had not even a slow train for his transportation; that in many rural districts creaking wagons still bore the players to their public. He must feel a part of all the storied vagabondia of the theater and dash at hardships with an unquenchable spirit. The life itself must seem glamorous or be but physical discomfort unbearably prolonged.

⌐ Booth was no vagabond by nature. His feet knew, from the first, no itch. Temperamentally, so far as manner of life went, he would have been quite content to settle in Bel Air, hang up his shingle as cabinet-maker, go home each evening to a warm fire in a solid house. And even if he had been born with that love of the open road so sedulously celebrated by snug poets in cozy houses, it might well have been shaken out of him by the time he was twenty-seven. He had been at it, even then, for fifteen years. He had learned enough about bad hotels, when he was with his father, to last him a lifetime. He had wandered far and seen much and trudged through sufficient snow-drifts. He was no husky Forrest, but a slender and contemplative young man, with a taste for pipe and fireside and loving wife.

In that last picture the attentive reader may find one thing missing. The flowing bowl is forgotten. But Booth had not been forgetting it. He had one thing in common with the actors of his time, at least: a love for that bowl. Already it has been noted how his friends maintained, on that point, a discretion which matched the tall stories told by his enemies. His drinking habits are not important in connection with his life generally; it is not recorded that he drank spectacularly enough to make the habit significant in his career, except on one tragic occasion. But he was by no means abstemious before his marriage, and Mary used all her influence, for a time successfully, to curb what together they called his "devil."

His drinking prior to his marriage had been sporadic. His friends, when they did not hear from him regularly, feared the worst and looked about anxiously for their young tragedian, fearing to find him reeling. They often did, as witness a note from Adam Badeau, a gentleman of high ideals, written about a year before Booth's marriage. "Tis likely as not you are on a spree" Badeau wrote chidingly. "It is nearly five months since one of your performances of this sort and since I have known you you've never missed one in that space of time. You might have waited until I could care for you."

Badeau spent, it may be noted, not a little time looking after his friend Edwin. They had met not long after Booth's first appearance in New York and had struck up a friendship. Badeau was a serious-minded young man, eminently fitted for the eminence he later attained. He found life real and earnest, and God firmly in His heaven. Right and wrong were no vague abstractions to Adam Badeau and he was inclined to preach from his own point of assurance. He was a little rigid but no prig. He might chide Edwin in his cups, but he would see him safe home and in bed and be not too sternly admonishing until the next morning.

Badeau with gratified eyes saw his friend's marriage. So did all of Booth's circle, to whom the coupling of these two seemed ideal. And one of its first results was to end those drinking bouts which had worried others besides Badeau. The two youngsters nestled cozily in their rooms.

There was a heavy bearskin before the fireplace and upon it, as autumn came on, Booth lay at full length, supporting his head on his hands, leaning his weight on his elbows. He stared down at a book, although he seldom needed it. Mary sat near by in a low chair. Then for hours on end, and with such interruptions as we may guess at, Edwin read his parts to Mary's cues, trying new readings, seeking to build up to a new consistency in his interpretations of the rôles of Hamlet and Richelieu and Iago. He and Mary bought a dog and it lay near Booth, looking up now and then to see that all went well, and then dreaming peacefully to the music of the two voices.

For the first months the two young people seldom went out. Now and then there was a dinner at the Century Club, where writers and artists were to be found; now and then such a friend as Badeau happened in. And once the great dog, careening through the hotel dining-room where the two were by accident dining at a table with a young woman not long in New York and friendless, leaped on his mistress with vast delight and upset the table into the stranger's lap. It was disconcerting. Edwin, shy with strangers, withdrew into himself and glared at the dog. Mary was all quick apology, and Lillian Woodman, who had looked with longing eyes at the young tragedian and his fortunate wife,

restrained herself from kissing the offending dog before
every one.

Lillian had seen Edwin months before in Boston and
worshiped him from afar. She was a properly brought up
young lady, so she did not write him, as so many did; it
was not for Lillian Woodman to suggest a rendezvous on
a corner near the theater, like one Mable; nor to send him
a lock of her pretty hair for remembrance' sake. Lillian
merely looked. But some day, she told herself with school-
girl optimism, she would know this beautiful and thrilling
young actor. She may have been a trifle taken aback when
she discovered him married, but one look at Mary eliminated jealousy. Lillian was free then to romanticize the two
happily and to wish, wish, wish that something would happen to bring them together. She patted the dog as restrain-
edly as her intense appreciation of its efforts would allow,
and assured Mary that it really made no difference and that
her dress was not really ruined.

Mary may have been a little lonely, too, knowing few
girls of her own age in the city. At any rate, she and Lillian
were friends in a moment and after a time Lillian was
actually allowed to visit the Booths in their rooms, to see
Edwin on his bearskin rug before the fire and to hear his
voice as he read the appeals of Romeo. Lillian did not mind
that another was Juliet. She was delighted to be there.

She was still more delighted when the Booths began
in the autumn to have more social engagements and she
was included. She met Badeau and Cary, perhaps, and John
Wilkes, who was in town now and then for a few days at
a time, although he was playing chiefly in the South. She

may have met Booth's friend, Dave Anderson, who was on from California and acting with Julia Dean Hayne in "The Lady of Lyons" and heard Anderson and his young friend talk of the wild yesterdays. Perhaps she met Asia Booth, who had become Mrs. John Sleeper Clarke very recently. And it was not long before Lillian met, at a small party, Thomas Bailey Aldrich, poet and wit and editor; a shining, loved boy, prized in conversation. Whatever sentimental feeling may have been mixed with her adulation of Edwin Booth vanished, then, and betook itself elsewhere. She has described it all, most charmingly, in a book called "Crowding Memories." It is signed by Mrs. Thomas Bailey Aldrich.

Booth had, at last, precisely the life he was best fitted for. He could lie before a fire and read and smoke; he had near him some one to whom his profession was of great personal concern, who lived largely, one suspects, for his art. Mary had a vast respect for Edwin's art. And a vast tenderness. For all his friends, he was a moody, introspective young man. He had found now somebody to whom he could talk with utter freedom; whose interests were his interests; who asked nothing better than to sit with him before the fire and read Shakspere, discussing interpretation, joining with him in plans for the future. The strain of adjustment to the outside world, always great for Booth, lessened. It must often have been difficult for him to leave the rooms, even for the short trip to the theater. But an actor needs must act.

When he went back to the stage it was to the Winter Garden, which was really Burton's Metropolitan Theater—

usually called Burton's New Theater to distinguish it from the Chambers Street house—renamed. Stuart, no longer connected with Wallack's, had joined Boucicault in taking over the lease of the playhouse at Bond and Broadway. Boucicault, nothing if not versatile, had seen to the decorations himself, and the interior was generally considered very beautiful. The acoustics had not been helped and the sight lines were not what they had been, but no one thought of that. The managers had been a year at it, opening the season before Booth's marriage. Jefferson had been a star there much of the year, appearing in "The Octoroon," which opened on December 5, 1859, and played some two months on its first attempt. Boucicault had written it quite by himself—for that assiduous collaborator a rare accomplishment.

Laura Keene had put on "Our American Cousin," Tom Taylor's play which is chiefly remembered now for its connection with a national catastrophe, and had made so much money at it that she began to sparkle all over with diamonds. Jefferson, observing with an amused eye, speculated whether they were new friends or old ones returned. She sparkled more than ever in November of 1860, when she offered an extravaganza, not unlike the modern revue in some respects, which was called "The Seven Daughters of Satan." It seems to have been concerned chiefly with the daughters.

It was in that month, on the twenty-sixth, that Booth appeared first after his marriage, opening with "Hamlet" at the Winter Garden. Mary stood in the wings or sat in her box and repeated the lines over to herself as he read them. The "Herald," on this occasion, thought him too violent, E. G. P. Wilkins, its dramatic critic, standing firmly by the official "Herald" theory that he was a very old-fashioned actor. Mr. Wilkins advised melodrama for him, as Stuart had advised it five years before for Forrest. But the reviewer was better pleased when he turned to "Richelieu," which was not generally counted as melodrama.

For the first time, now, Edwin found himself in direct rivalry with Forrest. The old thunderer came back to New York after almost four years; he had last played there in the winter preceding Booth's début. Most of the time he had been in retirement at Philadelphia. He opened in September at Niblo's, playing three times a week. He played Hamlet three weeks, nine performances, and followed it with Lear for three weeks; then Othello. Thus he spread twenty-seven performances out to October 26 and gave himself intervals of rest. After playing Hamlet, Lear, and Othello over again, one after the other, he continued with Macbeth, Richard III, Richelieu, Rolla, and Jack Cade, running through into March. He played to good houses, and the management's problem was in finding something to present on his off nights. It proved difficult; once, Professor Odell reports, a "world renowned horse tamer" was resorted to, and again "Anderson, the Great Wizard of the North," filled in.

When Booth began in opposition, after Forrest had been on two months, he met the issue fairly. After Hamlet, which Forrest had played earlier, he continued with Shylock, Sir Edward Mortimer, Don Cæsar, Richard III, Richelieu, and Sir Giles. The critics had opportunity for direct comparison. There, on the one hand, was Forrest's roaring

Hamlet; on the other, Booth's quieter and more thoughtful prince. Each wore the robes of Richelieu. To Forrest's hoarse Othello was matched the subtle wickedness of Booth's Iago. It is something of a pity, indeed, that those two interpretations were not brought together on the same stage. It is reported that such a plan was once advanced, and that Forrest snorted.

The older generation of playgoers was faithful to Forrest. Now, when the elder recall the good old days, Edwin Booth is certain to be among their memories and, as they measure others by his stature, sneers are usually the portion of the moderns. So, in 1860, those who looked back were faithful to the great native American who shook the scenery with his voice. They smiled in pity at those who followed the sentimentality of a new hero. Those who turned to Booth were the younger: they found poetry there, and culture and no insistence upon the rough, wholesome virtues. "They would accept the Himalayas if they were gilded," wrote Crinkle, cattily epigrammatic.

Booth left his success for a few weeks in mid-season and dashed off to Philadelphia to play with Miss Cushman in "Macbeth." He was back on January 21 and remained until the season was almost over, playing to good houses. Miss Cushman returned to tell of her bon mot. She had observed, in playing with him, Booth's refined and very intellectual conception of the character of Macbeth. She had "begged him to remember that Macbeth was the grandfather of all Bowery ruffians." The Forrest supporters smiled over that and those of Booth were not displeased. They were a trifle sensitive about Bowery ruffians.

Booth heard the story and when next he saw Julia Ward Howe in Boston (she was fond of the young actor and his bride) told her that when Miss Cushman's Lady Macbeth was urging him on to murder he had struggled with an impish desire to inject: "Why don't you kill him? You are a great deal bigger than I am." She was, unfortunately. The critics had noticed it and commented, promptly. There was then no glossing over such disasters. Somebody had watched Forrest in Hamlet and had gone off to write that there was far too much of him for the rôle. "Half of him could play it," commented the reviewer, unkindly truthful.

Having met Forrest on equal terms and come off well, but being unsatisfied with his own work and not indifferent to the criticisms of it, Booth felt that the next step was to broaden his experience. He felt, as so many young artists then and later have felt, that the trouble with him was America. He wrote to Cary that he was considering a trip to Europe in search of art. He wanted to study and inhale enough of it to vivify his future productions with "something of the true and the beautiful." "Art degenerates even below the standard of a trade in America," he bewailed, raising even then no new cry, and continued:

I can go traveling through this country for perhaps five years longer, and make a great deal of money, but money is not what I want—nor position, either, unless I can feel the consciousness of deserving it. Fortune has placed me in (for my years) a high and, many think, an enviable position, but I feel the ground tremble beneath my feet and I am perfectly aware that unless I aim at a larger circumference than the rim of the almighty dollar (which one can't help in America) I'll go down eye deep in the quicksand of popular favor.

And to this he adds, with evident joy, that he had taken in fifteen hundred dollars in "one little week." And again he commented, still to Cary, "I've had the best people and the entire press yields me the palm, particularly in Hamlet," and "my mark is made here, and with the best people too. I'll draw like a blister the next visit." That was from New York, where the almighty dollar ruled and the quicksand of public favor tugged with particular force.

He was delighted, though, when an offer came to appear at the Haymarket in London. He could go to London, where the artist was honored, where the almighty dollar did not rule. "It is the grand turning point in my career," he assured Cary. "I look forward with a heart full of hope that I may achieve all that you desire of me."

Cary desired the best for him, but Cary had other things to think of. Sumter had been fired upon; the war was about them. Cary, Captain Cary, was leaving for the front. "Stick to the flag, Dick," Booth wrote him, "as I intend to, though far away." Cary stuck to the flag until he died under it. Booth sailed to stick to it . . . in London. He was no warrior.

# VI

## THE SEARCH FOR ART

ALTHOUGH BOOTH HAD MADE STRIDES IN HIS PROFESSION BY
1861, he was still catalogued by the critics as "promising."
His was not an overnight leap into fame, notwithstanding
all the elements which favored him. Very young actors did
not, in those days, so quickly advance to the top—largely,
of course, because what has come to be known as "type-
casting" was not then commonly resorted to. Particularly
of the tragedian was variety demanded. He must be able to
do Lear one night and Iago the next, with Hamlet to come
after. And then, possibly, he would be asked to take part
in one of those frolics allowed tragedians and play a
Mr. Brown-Smith for his benefit.

Under such requirements a handsome person and a
pleasant voice were not enough, nor could the measure be
filled by the addition of a few mannerisms. It was not possible, either, for a tragedian to become famous through the
simple personation of himself. A day of long runs and
realistic characterization has simplified matters for all but
the best of the moderns as it was never simplified for any
one seventy-five years ago. Not then could a pretty little
girl with an individual manner of pursing her mouth leap

into stardom in an evening; nor did a quaint way of carrying the head assure success for the aspiring young man. We have lost and gained by the change: greater charm and youthfulness finds its way to the stage of 1932, but less sound acting.

Booth would not, however many trips he might make abroad in an effort to imbue his art with truth and beauty, be fully acknowledged as the greatest Hamlet of his day until he was already somewhat too old to play the part without a wig. It was generally admitted by the time of his first European visit, however, that he had everything but experience; it was even admitted that, in certain rôles, he was already near the top of his profession.[1] He went to England with a reputation; he hoped to increase and refine it there, entering the lists on his return as a "young tragedian" no longer, but a full-fledged knight, wearing his mistress's colors proudly.

In London he signed a contract with J. B. Buckstone, lessee of the Theater Royal, Haymarket, and spent some weeks looking over London, with Mary on his arm. He does not seem to have liked the city as well as he had expected.

On Saturday, September 21, 1861, the London "Times" carried in one of its long, closely printed columns, an advertisement which promised:

Mr. Edwin Booth from the principal American theaters, son of Mr. Booth, contemporary with the Elder Kean, will make his first appearance at this theater on Monday, September 30, in the character of Shylock in Shakespeare's play *The Merchant of Venice.*

By Monday the advertisement had been altered to read "his first appearance in England."

The advertisement also promised an excellent company and explained that Mr. Charles Mathews would continue during the engagement of the young tragedian, playing "The Soft Sex" on Booth's off nights. Booth appeared, at first, on Monday, Wednesday, and Friday. Considerable curiosity was aroused by the announcement, particularly since London had not yet entirely forgotten Forrest, who with his booming voice had been not a little of a sensation.

Booth had not, however, gone at a very propitious time. The animosity which existed between England and the United States during most of the Civil War was already beginning, and the English were not predisposed to think kindly of any one from the States. Then, too, Booth had gone into the wrong theater; he always went into the wrong theater, whenever possible. For some years the Haymarket had not been connected in the mind of the public with classic drama, and the public mind was not quick to change. Shylock was, moreover, probably the last rôle the American actor should have essayed for his beginning: he never liked the part particularly; he never felt either that he was fitted for it or that he entirely understood it. Buckstone, for reasons of his own, insisted that "The Merchant" be first produced, and Booth agreed somewhat unwillingly.

The engagement began as scheduled on Monday, September 30. The "Times" of the next day commented as follows:

Mr. Edwin Booth, who last night made his first appear,
ance as Shylock in *The Merchant of Venice,* scarcely corre.
sponded to the current prediction that he would prove an actor
of the "fiery, impulsive school." Those who, on the strength of
this intimation, expected that old-fashioned rant which still has
its admirers must have been grievously disappointed at witnessing his very steady and well considered performance. Only in
the scene which follows the discovery of Jessica's elopement does
he let go the reins of passion, but even here he retains all
his old self command and, in spite of the force with which
he expresses his resentment of the injuries he has received and
his resolution to take speedy vengeance, he never leads one to
expect that the artist will be merged in the character he represents. . . .

That Mr. Booth will awaken the sort of admiration which
approximates to surprise is not to be expected, if Shylock
is to be taken as a sample of his powers. But as a judicious
actor, gifted with an excellent voice and an expressive counte-
nance, which he turns to good account, he fully merited
the hearty applause with which he was received last night.

This tolerant half-praise was not what Booth had hoped
for, nor were the half-filled houses. He hoped against hope
that enthusiasm would increase, and meanwhile played Sir
Giles Overreach for his fourth performance. The "Times"
looked at it and remarked:

By his performance of Sir Giles Overreach in *A New
Way to Pay Old Debts,* Mr. Edwin Booth has confirmed the
impression made by his Shylock. He is still the sensible actor,
with a good voice and no small knowledge of routine; and
there are portions of the character he brings into high relief
by remarkable vigor and truthfulness.

The critic added that Mr. Booth had again been honored with "considerable applause."

Booth played Sir Giles on Wednesday of that week and Shylock on Friday, and the next week he repeated performances of the two characters. During the week following he did nothing at all, except visit London, make acquaintances, and take Mary to the Tower—unless, to be sure, he had done that earlier. He liked London less and less. He found the people sunk deeply in their ancient ways and lacking the American instinct for change. That habit of the national mind he believed to be, partly at least, responsible for the lukewarmness of his reception.

When he returned to the Haymarket in the following week he played Richard III on Monday and the "Times" appears not to have paid any attention to it whatever, overlooking at the same time the productions of "Fitzsmythe of Fitzsmythe Hall" and "Fish Out of Water"—the latter probably a monologue—which were offered as afterpieces. The "Times" was not even interested when he repeated Richard on the following day. He played five days that week, returning to Sir Giles on Wednesday and to Shylock, for which Mr. Buckstone seems to have had a passion, on Thursday and Friday. The next week he repeated "Richard" and "The Merchant" and then offered "Richelieu," which for eleven years had not been seen in London. And with "Richelieu," at last, he struck it.

He struck it, to be sure, more in the hearts of the populace than in the cool gray minds of the critics. By his second appearance it was evident, even to his manager, that it was with the Bulwer-Lytton play that he should have begun. The crowd, which had remained indifferent to Shakspere and had not even risen to the brightly colored fly of "A New Way to Pay Old Debts," was delighted with the slightly meretricious grandeur of Lytton's cardinal. The box-office was not exactly stormed, even so, but it was filled with the comforting clink of silver. Buckstone decided instantly to play "Richelieu" for the rest of the engagement, and this he did until Booth quit on November 9.

The "Times" did not, however, change its tone. Although it did not review the play until the appeal to the paying theatergoers had been proved, its dignity was superior to such considerations. It admitted:

There is much that is meritorious in Mr. Edwin Booth's performance of Cardinal Richelieu in Sir E. B. Lytton's play. He has formed a general conception of the prematurely old man, still under the influence of strong passion; he sustained the character with dignity and he perfectly knows the telling points to be made.

But—

that there is a comic side to the great cardinal, as depicted by Sir E. B. Lytton, that he can be playfully gallant with Marion, banter with Joseph, and even chuckle over Baradas in the plenitude of the favorite's power, he does not seem aware and, therefore though there is plenty of force in his delineation, it somewhat lacks variety. He appears to the most advantage where there is no doubt of earnestness of purpose and his more powerful scenes find manifest favor with the audience.

The most powerful of those powerful scenes was, of course, the curse. It was always one of Booth's most magnificent efforts. Booth was not a tall man, but in his red robes he seemed majestic. "He was a physical giant, stately and statue-like," Otis Skinner remembers, having seen Booth years later and played with him. He seemed, according to the general report, to be about seven feet tall when he drew around the form of the girl under his protection "the awful circle of our solemn church."

It is always unwise to go behind stage illusion. The trees of the forest are, we know, canvas; the crown of the king is probably only gilt paper; certainly his jewels are glass. The engine which bears down on the pinioned hero? A "flat" supported from behind by stage-hands. Too much study of the mechanics of illusion gets us nowhere. But the trick of Booth's stature, particularly since "Richelieu" is no longer being played, is too amusing to pass over. The simple fact is that when he launched the curse Booth was, if not seven feet tall, well over six.

He wore, of course, robes which trailed the ground. As he stood to begin the curse he rose slowly on his toes, his feet being concealed under the robes. And as he rose, every one else on the stage sank to his knees. The old cardinal seemed, so, to be magnified by the power of the Church which spoke through him; all others were lessened in stature as they knelt within the shadow of mighty Rome. It was magnificent. The audience gasped and, when the spell was broken, cheered. It seemed like a miracle, and they told their friends, who hastened to see it. From the beginning until his retirement from the stage, Richelieu was one of Booth's most successful parts and one always in demand.

Perhaps if he had played it from the first in London his success there—his solid success, at any rate—might have been far greater. It will be noted that he did not appear at all as Hamlet, the rôle which shared with Richelieu the greatest popular favor and which was in later years to be connected indissolubly with his name. It was already so connected in his own country, where Shylock was rightly considered one of his less successful impersonations. His reason for avoiding Hamlet in the engagement which he had at the start believed so significant in his professional career is not entirely clear.

It may be, however, that Buckstone felt London was having at the moment all the Hamlet it could stand. At the Royal Princess Theater, in opposition to Booth, Charles Fechter was playing, in his blond wig, which is generally spoken of as red. And that wig had London by the ears.

Fechter, who was not to come to the United States until some years later, was then at the height of his fame. He played other rôles, to be sure, Othello being a favorite, but it is his Hamlet which is remembered. It was marked by great fire and a French accent, as well as by the wig. Fechter was born in London, but his mother was French and his father German. He was educated in Paris. His greatest triumphs as a tragedian were attained in English-speaking countries. He had notable originality in his readings, and vast force, but it was his wig which caused the greatest excitement when he appeared in London. Always before, Hamlet had been a dark and somber figure, preferably with long black hair. Fechter appealed to ethnology. Hamlet was a Dane, was he not? And the Danes were blond, were they not? Ergo?

Ergo, as it happened, Fechter made a sensation. Probably Booth would have gained nothing by the presentation of his subtle, outwardly conventional Hamlet, against that wig. He did it later, but the time was not yet.

All in all, the trip was anything but what had been hoped for it. The artist did not, on the whole, seem to be welcomed with much greater understanding in London than in the United States. He had learned something, too, of the world's economic preoccupations. The almighty sovereign in England matched America's almighty dollar. There were not so many sovereigns as there had been dollars, which was no intrinsic advantage. The eye for the main chance which he felt was the sharpest eye possessed by the theater-managers of New York was no sharper than the same eye in the head of the Londoner. He had had bad productions at the Haymarket, with inadequate casts; the Haymarket was, moreover, the wrong theater. The English hostility to all things American was much mentioned by his stanch defenders. It must be admitted, however, that that antipathy did not extend to the next occupant of the old theater, E. A. Sothern in "Our American Cousin." Sothern and his built-up rôle of Dundreary were tremendously popular.

Booth went to tour the provinces, both sore and worried. He had fair success there and no less a beginner than Henry Irving, who supported him in Manchester, reports that "he was a star which floated across our horizon, bright, brilliant, buoyant, alert, full of vigor and the fire of genius." Irving did not say it at the time, to be sure, but years after and under circumstances calculated to bring out the most generous words. Booth returned to London after a few weeks, spurred by fears for his young wife.

Mary had not accompanied him to the provinces. She had not even been able, during the final weeks of his London engagement, to sit in her box and say over to herself the lines her husband was speaking. On December 9 she bore a daughter to the young tragedian and the child was named Edwina. "Thank God all is well. A daughter," Booth cabled Lillian Woodman at his wife's request. And all was well.

They remained in London several months while Mrs. Booth gained strength. Edwin wrote Cary that the autumn would find them in Boston again. "A poorer but a wiser man than when I left there, but I do not say aught of that," he added. He was wiser, much wiser. He had discovered that in matters of art and dollars there is less difference among nations than eager young men think. The notion that there was some special appreciation to be found abroad, some special abundance of art, does not seem thereafter to have troubled him.

When Edwin and Mary crossed to France in the spring it was with the tourist's wish to see what was worth seeing. Booth did not act there, but he was given a sword which Frédéric Lemaître had worn as Ruy Blas. And Mary engaged Mlle. Forrnier, *"a voyager aux États Unis d'Amérique en qualité de bonne d'enfant, aux prix annuelle de six cent francs par ans, et susceptible d'augmentation"* and with very exact stipulation with regard to traveling expenses in both directions. That agreement lies now in a trunk at The Players, beside a letter from a little girl who sent Booth a lock of pretty hair and asked him not to laugh, because, at sixteen, she was not very happy. The actor tossed it there, as something he wished to save.

At the time, however, he stowed it away light-heartedly in a trunk as he and Mary packed to return to the United States. With Marie—a name which seems, in one form or another, to be inseparable from the annals of the Booth family—to care for little Edwina they sailed happily, and landed, without incident, at Boston. Mary seemed quite to have recovered, although she was never robust. She had gained slowly after the birth of her child, but the visit to Paris had brightened her eyes and colored her cheeks. Edwin looked at her in happy admiration and they looked together at young Edwina, wriggling in the arms of the *bonne d'enfant*. They were bound home, and anxious to get there.

They had gladly departed from dark, damp London, which had not welcomed them as it might have. They were anxious to see their friends again; Edwin looked forward to discussing with his younger brother, Wilkes, the details of the latter's appearance in New York. He was eager to be back again and busy; to prove to all that he was the Booth of the Booths. He thought with enthusiasm of his appearances in his own country, so much more satisfactory than those abroad, and to audiences so much more receptive.

Edwin had been glad to learn, while he was still abroad, of Wilkes's appearance in New York—his first. The elder brother had been sent newspaper cuttings describing that engagement, at Wallack's Theater, which had been taken over by Mary Prevost. (Wallack had a new theater.) One of the cuttings, snipped from the "Herald" a few months before Booth returned, revealed that Wilkes had "displayed unmistakable evidence of original talent, often crude in its conception, it is true, and unequal in its power of expression, but still developing great future promise." The reviewer continued:

He has had an opportunity of testing before a metropolitan audience the abilities which have won him such a reputation in the provinces. That he has passed through the ordeal with so fair a success is proof that there is the stuff in him of a first class tragedian, if he chooses to correct by study the extravagances that disfigure his impersonations and which, we fear, have been more or less confirmed by undiscriminating applause of country audiences.

Precisely how good an actor John Wilkes Booth was before he quit the stage for finance and speculation in oil shares has never been a matter of agreement. Winter, who may have resented any other talent in the family than his beloved Edwin's, thought him not much—a crude youngster from the provinces, who under favorable conditions might have gone some distance, though not to the top. Opposed to this view is that of other critics who believed that he might have been greater than his brother, if he had lived. He, also, was beautiful, with that slightly unreal beauty of the actor and the Booth; he, also, had a moving voice. He was gayer than his brother and more reckless, on the stage as off. He had much of the dash and fire of his father and acted almost as strenuously.

It may be noted, however, that John Wilkes—he was called sometimes John and sometimes Wilkes in his family and out—had, himself, no illusions. He looked up to his brother as an artist, with respect that was not lessened by the humorous smile with which he paid it. Clara Morris once, while playing with him, expressed her admiration of his Hamlet. Wilkes shook his head and smiled. "No," he said. "No, oh, no! There's but one Hamlet to my mind —that's my brother, Edwin. You see, between ourselves, he is Hamlet—melancholy and all."

Wilkes was a good friend and faithful brother, and popular with all who knew him. Too popular, some said; too much the convivial dram-drinker, too much the pursuer of pretty ladies. He was both, beyond question. Feminine hearts turned to him with enthusiasm, as they turned to Edwin. Both handsome youths received, whenever they appeared, thick sheaves of notes from the susceptible girls of the vicinity. The writers urged meetings, begging for even the slightest hint that their adoration was accepted. Edwin read the notes and smiled, and tossed them into the fire; now and then, with faintly malicious humor, he saved the more amusing and may have let others into the joke. The letters were, it may be added, in all cases signed only with Christian names.

Wilkes was not so Spartan. He made something of a name for himself as a lover, in his few years. After he died Edwin received several anxious requests from young women, who feared they might be compromised, for the return of letters they had written and gifts they had given. He loved lightly and well, did Wilkes. It was argued for him, however, that he never knowingly deflowered virgins.

More worrying to his family than his sowing of wild oats, however, was the wildness of his political views. He had spent the most formative years of his youth in the South. Most of his friends were Southern, and all his beliefs. Given half a chance he would argue for hours about the war, praising the Confederacy, indulging in pseudo-legal defenses of the right to secede, painting bright word pictures of the noble, outnumbered heroes who fought for their homes. He was reckless in his remarks, particularly when only his family listened. He could, and did, denounce in the most violent terms the leaders of the North, beginning and ending with the President.

Edwin, who was a stanch Union man, was annoyed. He did not wish to argue the matter. He would not listen to Wilkes when the latter fumed. Once, to be sure, he went so far as to ask why, in the name of all that was consistent, Wilkes did not go South and fight with his friends if he felt so strongly about it. The young man replied that he would but that he had promised his mother not to bear arms. Edwin snorted and stalked away.

But the Booths were not really worried. Wilkes had always been an excitable young man, prone to shout challenges to the trees and assail the underbrush with his saber. He had never really done anything—and never would do anything. A wild boy, but he would grow calmer; every one sowed wild oats. He seemed to be settling down seriously to his profession and no doubt the New York criticisms would help him. He had much to learn yet; if he set about to learn it he would have less time for women and politics and less energy for dram-drinking.

Edwin was too glad to be at home with Mary and the baby to worry greatly about anything. They acquired a house in Dorchester, Massachusetts, and remained there for a time. Then, in the late summer, they came down to New York. Edwin had already negotiated for a season at the Winter Garden. He followed Kate Bateman in, beginning on September 29, 1862.

# VII

## THE END OF·YOUTH

IF YOU MATTERED IN THE WORLD OF ART OR LITERATURE AND lived in New York in the autumn of 1862, it was almost inevitable that sooner or later you would be invited to the home of Dick Stoddard and his wife, Elizabeth, at Tenth Street and Fourth Avenue. Every one who made pretensions then to poetry or to painting or to the legitimate drama knew the Stoddards—Richard Henry, the gentle poet and journalist, who mixed Italian with the English of his rhymes; Elizabeth, who wrote books and gained some slight fame as a realist before it was time for realism and who was sooner or later heartily detested by all over whom she rode rough-shod.

If you went to the Stoddards' home you met Bayard Taylor and E. C. Stedman, who mixed poetry and business, Fitz Hugh Ludlow, Launt Thompson, sculptor and erratic drunkard, Thomas Bailey Aldrich, who had good family and money and infinite charm. You talked and laughed and drank wine; perhaps you and the rest swooped down on the "studio building" across-town between Fifth and Sixth avenues, in Tenth Street, where Thompson and many others of the circle had rooms. There you found more talk before

open fires, more wit flowing from Aldrich, more unantici-
pated remarks from Mrs. Stoddard, more wine.

On other nights, perhaps, you would go instead to the
Century Club. There again you would find the Stoddards
and the Stedmans and Aldrich and Thompson and the rest.
There the occasion would perhaps be a dinner for some
visiting celebrity of a literary cast; there Aldrich would
charm every one and the wine would flow freely. Wherever
you went, the talk and the drinking would last far into the
morning and be most brilliant. There would be talk of the
latest epigrammatic poem from Aldrich's pen; of the sharp
criticisms of life in general to be read in Henry Clapp's
"Saturday Review." After the theater, actors might drop
in, or even critics. Certain actors, of course. Then the talk
would turn to the stage, and many witty things would be
said at the expense of aging Forrest. You would find it
cultivated, self-conscious, a little precious.

Fewer amateurs would you discover if, instead of the
Stoddard circle, your temperament led you to another which
had its center in Pfaff's Cave, a beer-saloon and café, on
Broadway near Bleecker. There you would find Clapp himself, bearded and mordant, letting the quips fall acidly
where they might. There you would find, almost certainly,
Walt Whitman, large and commanding at his chosen place,
ready to crush the trusting hands of those introduced to
him. While you waited, Charles B. Seymour, stately and
likewise bearded drama critic of the New York "Times,"
might stride to the table under the sidewalk reserved for
the "bohemians." They did not hesitate to call themselves
that, in 1862. And there, for one more, would be

young William Winter, a fledgling writing for Clapp's weekly.

Once you might have seen a serious young man arrive rather shyly and wince perceptibly at Whitman's handshake. You could have seen him sit at the special table and smile a rather strained small smile, as of one who suspects, politely, that he is in the wrong place. That would have been William Dean Howells, looking over New York's literary life after a much more satisfactory visit up Boston way, where he had seen all the best poets and had been dined by them. Howells thought very little of the bohemians, holding that they were both rough and self-conscious, and probably being unfavorably affected by the fumes of beer. The bohemians, on the other hand, thought Howells a prig and mimicked him behind his back after he had turned it on them and returned to the higher thinking of New England.

Wherever you went you would discover both conversation and drinking going on with gusto. At the Stoddards' and the places they frequented the beverage was wine; at the cave it was beer. Everywhere it was plentiful, loosening tongues, making wit seem wittier.

The Booths, wrapped up in themselves in the months which immediately followed their marriage, had had little or no part in this, although Edwin was a member of the Century. They were content together. And Edwin was shy, shrinking from these thoroughly educated gentlemen who tossed Latin and Italian and French into their talk as into their verses. When he was with them he felt raw, school-boyish. He shyly withdrew, so successfully concealing his fear of his fellows as to convince them he was a haughty Hamlet too good for the world.

Two years with Mary had changed him somewhat. She was, on the testimony of all who knew her, possessed of a genius for friendship. People met Mary once or twice and felt that they had never been without knowing her. She was not particularly beautiful; she was not unusually clever or in any way talented. She was merely extraordinarily lovable. She took people on faith and liked them by instinct, as they liked her. She was at home in a world to which Booth, and men like Booth, are always a little alien. And she was precisely the person best suited to aid him in his difficult—and the more difficult because not consciously realized—adjustment to the world outside. She could lead him places he could not go alone; her love for him and her belief in him could give him confidence he never could gain alone. Accustomed to her sympathy, he gained tranquillity and confidence.

He had had time enough by the autumn of 1862 to profit by her companionship to the fullest. Those he met discovered the change in him; he was no longer the tortured young Hamlet he had been. And so, for the first time in his life, he made friends quickly and with comparative ease.

He was striking enough and interesting enough to take his place in the Stoddard circle. He had been for some time in correspondence with the Stoddards, the exchange having begun with an appreciative letter from one of them on his acting. They knew him as a handsome and poetic youth who was rapidly acquiring fame. He was under thirty, but he was the leading tragedian of his country. Behind him was an eventful career. His bizarre boyhood, which had taught him to hold "much of the Hamlet mystery no more than an idiosyncrasy"; his adventursome early twenties in California and Australia; his present success— these gave a background which led Mrs. Stoddard to consider him a very interesting young man.

We find Edwin and his wife, then, suddenly living a life quite different from any they had lived. Lillian Woodman no longer saw them, as she had seen them formerly, aloof and content to be by themselves. The bear rug was deserted. The baby, with its nurse, was securely cared for and the Booths were free to play. After a time they began to take Lillian with them and the three played much together with their artistic friends. After the theater, nowadays, there was usually a party. At first Booth smilingly held his graceful hand above his wine-glass when the servant would have filled it. Then, and Miss Woodman noted it even through her preoccupation with handsome Tom Aldrich, he no longer interfered. His glass, which had been always empty, was now only sometimes so.

Meanwhile he was acting—Hamlet and Othello and Romeo, among others. He was again in conflict with Forrest, but this time there was hardly a contest. Many still were faithful to the older star, but the new was brighter. Even the "Herald" found, in reviewing Booth's first appearance after his return, that his art had been "mellowed and refined," although—

Frankly, we still find in him, though in a greatly modified degree, many of the defects that impaired the merits of his former performances. When not under the influence of strong excitement, he lacks force and dignity, and the management of his voice is not always judicious. On the other hand, when the interest of the piece is strongly marked, he is generally equal to its requirements and at times his genius manifests itself in readings of the text which have originality and freshness not often to be found in the impersonations of his older rivals. His Hamlet is not as even a performance as that of Macready or Forrest, but it has merits of its own that recommend it to people of cultivated taste.

The cultivated taste of the "Herald's" reviewer was even more gratified by Othello, always one of Booth's worst parts, but it reported that "so thorough and complete does Mr. Booth's disgust for ranting and mere play acting seem to be that he seems in danger of running to the opposite extreme." That proved, at any rate, that the "Herald" had at last seen the point: Edwin Booth was not one of the elder ranters. It must have gratified him.

Forrest had begun his Hamlet at Niblo's on September 15 and, a few weeks later, essayed Richelieu. Then when, late in October, Booth attempted Romeo, Forrest appeared as Claude Melnotte, an equally romantic part. Thus did the leading tragedians of the day simultaneously and with eager confidence put forward their worst feet. Booth was never so bad, not even in comedy, as when he essayed the rôles of romantic lovers—he said once that he "hated the whole tribe of them"—and Forrest, whatever he may have been twenty years before, was, in 1862, no heroic youth. But they continued this misguided battle until Booth concluded his first engagement on November 7.

Mary was by that time already a little worried. Lillian Woodman noticed it and kept her own counsel, although she more than suspected the cause. Now and then Mary was forced to remark, with yesterday's formality, that Mr. Booth was not well that day.

It is unlikely that the two weeks and more of rest that Edwin took, after November 7, added anything to his sobriety. Sobriety was difficult enough, in the society he now frequented, even when it was imperative that he be in condition to play at night. It must have proved far harder when his time was his own. It was probably with relief that his wife saw him return to the stage on November 24.

He played through then until December 15, after which he and Mary, whose health had not been improved by worry, went north to Dorchester. Booth played in Boston and, while he was playing, friends in New York were disappointed to receive a note from Mary asking that everything they had left behind be shipped to Dorchester. Her doctor, she explained, had recommended that she remain for the winter in more quiet surroundings and Dorchester was quiet. Still they were not greatly concerned about her health and confidently expected that when Booth returned in February she would come with him, if only for a time. That was, indeed, the plan.

But in the end Booth came alone. The day before they were to have started, Mary had sprained a tendon, and the injury, while not serious, required quiet. "Take care of him," Mary wrote privately to Lillian. When their friend saw Edwin she understood the reason for this plea.

The memory of those days was vivid to Mrs. Aldrich

when she wrote of them, years afterward but evidently from some contemporary record of her own. A glance told them all, as he rejoined the New York circle, that the quieter life of Boston and its environs had not changed the habits of the tragedian, however beneficial it might have proved ￫ to his wife. He was nervous, anxious about Mary, whose strength did not return, lonely without her. To allay his anxiety by the best means he knew was his natural inclination, and he yielded to it. When he began to play on February 9 it was quickly evident that his discretion was not adequate to the emergency.

There was a hurried consultation among his friends and Aldrich and Thompson appointed themselves guardians. It was secretly resolved that they would never, so far as was possible, leave him alone; that, with him, they would make every effort to keep him from drinking. For the next two weeks or so history curiously inverted itself. The Edwin Booth who had once sedulously guarded his father from his father's "devil," was now as resolutely guarded from his own. Thompson and Aldrich, working in shifts, stayed with him almost always. One or the other of them was with him at his hotel until he was safely asleep; one or the other went with him to his dressing-room and remained there.

Now and then, at the theater, there would be a knock at the dressing-room door and Booth's servant and dresser, one of the farm negroes, would appear with a tall glass. Edwin would look at the glass and his guard would look at him, with a shake of the head. A brief struggle of wills would ensue and then Booth would usually succumb to

moral suasion and the promptings of his conscience. The
servant would carry the tall glass away again, wagging his
head thoughtfully. Booth would look cross, and a little relieved. Thompson or Aldrich, whichever it was, would pretend that nothing had happened, perhaps would study with
sudden interest one of those knickknacks with which
Booth usually kept his dressing-room cluttered.

But they were not very successful on the whole, whatever spectacular successes they may have attained on occasion. They failed often enough to let the damage do itself.
Booth began to play when he was not at all himself and the
romantic legend that tragedians are at their best when
intoxicated was rudely jolted. Booth was at anything but
his best. The members of the audience whispered together.
They remembered Junius and his famous drunkenness and
all the wild stories told of him. "Like father like son," they
murmured. "A chip of the old block." It was regrettable,
but it was evident that Edwin Booth was going to let
drink ruin his career. Very early prohibitionists pointed to
him with concealed delight, as a horrible example. They
wagged their bonnets and talked knowingly of the gutter.

"We have seldom seen Shakespeare so murdered," remarked the "Herald." The management, seeing Booth's
condition and understanding his anxiety, should have
stopped the engagement. The "Herald" was very much
annoyed at the management, which did nothing of the
kind. Booth staggered on, drinking now for no reason but
his own thirst. Adam Badeau was at the war and could not
help him. He could not even write chiding, friendly letters.

Matters were not helped when Wilkes came down from

· Boston and reported that Mary was really ill. She had gone in to Boston on a snowy day and had waited long for a horse-car. When she reached home she was taken with a chill. To the maid who put her to bed she murmured that she felt she would never be warm again.

Having conveyed this information, Wilkes added encouragingly that the doctor thought it would prove no more than a cold, after all, and that a few days in bed would see her through it. Already when he left, Wilkes said, she was better; her eyes were brighter and her cheeks had color in them. The doctor was not at all alarmed. So Wilkes told Edwin; to others he may have been less optimistic. Booth was frightened, thought of going to Dorchester, and thought better of it, was advised by his friends that there was no danger and by the physician that all went well—and took another drink. A long drink. That was late in February. The next day Mrs. Stoddard, who did not let any life go unattended if she could help it, wrote to Mary.

"Sick or well," she wrote, "you must come. Mr. Booth has lost all restraint and hold on himself. Last night there was grave question of ringing down the curtain before the performance was half over. Lose no time and come!"

Mary was already worse when this letter came. She needed quiet and peace. But she had to answer.

"I cannot come," she wrote Mrs. Stoddard. "I cannot stand. I think sometimes that only a great calamity can save my dear husband. I am going to try and write to him now, and God give me grace to write as a true wife should."

Booth read these letters, later. He was done with the Stoddards.

## Edwin Booth

Booth was playing Richard the night of February 20. He was, says Mrs. Aldrich, who tells her story with drama, only half himself. He walked through his part; sometimes his lines could hardly be understood; sometimes he swayed. In the wings his fellow-actors watched and looked at one another doubtfully. The audience grew impatient. A few left; more stayed, curiosity not the least of their motives. When he quitted the stage Booth went to sit in his dressing-room before his make-up table, staring unseeingly at the mirror. A fog rose about him and receded, rose and receded. He would fight it down and shake his head resentfully; it would rise again. He was sober enough to know that he was drunk and to wish not to be. In his struggle with himself all outside things vanished. A call-boy laid a telegram before him and thought Booth saw it. But Booth stared into the mirror. He had not opened the envelop when he went to the stage again.

When he returned to his dressing-room there was another telegram beside the first. Booth shook his head, wonderingly, and made no effort to pick either from the table. He raised a glass and drank again. The gas-light played queer tricks with his made-up face. The call-boy came once more and left something and went away. Booth paid no attention. He went on and off the stage, and sat in front of his mirror and stared at his face and pushed down the fog. Then the stage-manager came in and stared at Booth and held a telegram in front of him. Booth waved it aside. The manager had read it, and persisted. Then, slowly and carefully, he read it aloud. It was from a doctor in Dorchester.

" 'This is the fourth telegram. Why does not Mr. Booth answer? He must come at once.' "

The manager read it over, and again, and Booth understood. His friends were told.

They gave him strong coffee to drink and roused him, finally. It was long after midnight, when the last train for Boston had gone. There was nothing to do but wait for morning.

Booth was sober enough at eight o'clock on the morning of February 21 when he boarded a train with Stoddard. Sober—and he could have killed himself. The train started at eight o'clock. It was hardly outside the city before Mary died in Dorchester.

Edwin sat a long time by Mary's body that day. When he came out he was composed. He was composed when Mary's body was buried in Mount Auburn Cemetery in Boston. He was composed as he gave up the Dorchester house and canceled his engagements for the rest of the season. Then, with all those things done, he must have sat long and stared at nothing. He did not drink after that. In those days his youth ended. In the spring he went to live with his mother and his sister Rosalie in New York.

His friends wrote many letters of condolence. He responded. The clergyman who had married them wrote, hoping that Booth's art might prove his consolation. "I cannot repress an inward hope that I may soon rejoin her who, next to God, was the object of my devotion," Booth replied, answering formally a formal letter. But when he wrote to Badeau a few weeks after Mary was buried there was no formality. He wrote on and on, page after hurried

*Courtesy of the Albert Davis Collection*

MARY DEVLIN BOOTH

page, telling of his grief. It is a broken, stammering letter, with sentences ending nowhere.

"This blow renders life aimless, hopeless, darker than it was before I caught the glimpse of heaven," he wrote. "She was the sweetest being that ever made a man's home something to be loved." His heart was crushed, dried up and desolate. "I have no ambition now, no one to please, no one to cheer me."

He tormented himself with memories:

I left her in the bloom of health and hope. I left her joyful and loving, throwing kisses to me as I parted from her. Two tiny weeks slipped by and I was summoned to her bedside. *I came too late.* The baby wife lay dead, after one week's illness. Can you believe it? I can't. I think she is somewhere near me now. I see her, feel her, hear her, every minute of the day. I call her, look for her every time the door opens. In every car that passes our little cottage door, where we anticipated so much joy, I expect to see the loved form of her who was my world. . . . Two tiny years, Ad, and the bright future is a black and dismal past. . . .

God and she and I only know the depths of our devotion. My acting was studied to please her and after I left the theater and we were alone, her advice was all I asked, all I valued. If she was pleased, I was satisfied; if not, I felt a spur to prick me on to attain the point.

He told of the letters he had received. There was one from Henry Ward Beecher, who had met Mary once at Mrs. Howe's. "Like all who came within her atmosphere, he loved her," Booth wrote. He remembered a vision he had had two days before her death. "Come to me, darling,

I am almost frozen," she had said then, holding out her arms. Why had he not gone? Why had he not gone? But she must be living somewhere, still. Did not Badeau believe she lived? "Oh, my married life has yet some touches of the real in it, has it not?" he asked. She must be living, somewhere. "Be brave and struggle, Ad," he wrote, "but set not your heart on anything in this world."

Then, as always in war, thousands were turning to vacancy with the same stunned plea for assurance. They must live somewhere, all these young men fallen. They could not have quite gone out. Their voices must still be in the air, if only we could hear them. Then, as always in war, men and women appeared to announce that they could hear those voices quite clearly. They were the voices of spirits. Mediums, believers and charlatans alike, promised that they could pierce the veil.

Booth wished to believe that. "She is living and is with me now," he wrote to Badeau, later. "I believe she is near me, I believe she hears me, I believe she understands." In Philadelphia he found a group interested in "psychic phenomena." He received communications from Mary and from his father. He tried hard to believe. They were "almost convincing." "But I want something beyond a doubt," he wrote. He could not get beyond a doubt. A Miss Edmunds almost made him believe, but never quite.

Badeau was wounded that spring. He was taken to a hospital and Booth wrote him there. Edwin expressed the conventional hopes for his quick recovery, hopes which it cannot be doubted he felt. But . . . but if Ad did go, Edwin wished to make a bargain. "Come back to me and assure me of the reality of what perplexes me so often," he begged. Edwin would do as much for his friend, if he went first —of which, it must be added, there seemed then little likelihood.

But Badeau did not die. Instead, after a summer in the hospital, he was brought back to New York in the autumn of 1863 and went, at Edwin's urging, to the Booth house at 28 East Nineteenth Street, where he was cared for very tenderly, and where he and Edwin talked long of God and art and spiritualism. Wilkes was there and helped care for Badeau; but, because he was there, not much talk of politics was possible.

Booth was then a little past the first bitter sting of his wife's death. He was thinking of acting again. Perhaps he might yet make his career a monument to Mary, who had so often planned it with him. He could remember what she had said and try to please her. Perhaps she would be pleased.

# VIII

## A HUNDRED NIGHTS OF HAMLET

WHEN HIS WIFE WAS NEWLY DEAD AND HE SEEMED TO HIMSELF crushed by misfortune, Booth thought for a little while of abandoning the stage. But that thought passed quickly. Even if there had been no other reason for his continuing, even if he had been as hopeless as he felt himself, he could not afford to retire. He had managed to make himself indispensable to too many. He was, in short, head of a family. His own infant daughter was but one of many who looked to him for support.

Wilkes who, at about this time, had begun to make money by stock speculation, was almost the only one who did not come to him for aid—Wilkes and Asia, whose husband, Clarke, was prosperous and had not yet ventured on too many of those ambitious projects which were later to send him also to Edwin for help. Of the rest, Junius was acting, with some success, but was likely to turn up at any moment with a request for a loan; Joseph seemed to be getting nowhere; Junius, indeed, was inclined to think that Joseph had inherited his father's mental instability. He was a doctor, licensed, but could not quite make up his mind whether he wished to go on being a doctor. Meanwhile he could usually find a place for a few dollars, if Edwin could let him have them, temporarily.

The titan with the broken nose who died on the Mississippi had left his family little besides his fame. Mrs. Booth had, apparently, a small income, but Edwin supplied most of her wants and the wants of Rosalie, who did not marry but remained with her mother. The dwelling in Nineteenth Street which Booth purchased housed mother and daughter and Edwin, with Wilkes now and then brightening the rooms with his presence and clouding the air with his tirades.

During the summer which followed the death of his wife, Edwin had seen much of Asia, to whom he was deeply attached. She and Clarke were living, for the most part, in Philadelphia, and Booth visited them there. On one visit he found Clarke filled with enthusiasm and a project. The comedian had just heard that the Walnut Street Theater was to be sold. Why should not he and Booth scrape together the funds to buy it? There was money there, Clarke was sure, particularly if the theater could be made the Philadelphia headquarters of both his comedy and his brother-in-law's tragedy.

Booth thought over Clarke's plan, saw in it a means of so increasing his responsibilities that he would have no time to remember, and agreed. In the autumn they did buy the playhouse, sharing its management thereafter. The project, to run a little ahead of the story, proved profitable. They paid for the theater (it had been purchased on mortgage, of course) in three years, which was far better than they had expected. This success gave both men new confidence in their executive ability, without, unfortunately, noticeably increasing that ability.

The Philadelphia enterprise did not, however, interfere with Booth's return to the New York stage. He made his first appearance of the season of 1863–64 on September 21, still at the Winter Garden, which was then under the management of T. B. Jackson. All the town knew of the tragedy of the winter before and his return was made the occasion for the expression of warm sympathy. More girls than ever wrote letters to this poor, beautiful young man, who was a spectacle to stir their hearts; so young, so handsome, so unhappy. His misfortune gave him a new standing in the affections of his countrywomen. And he played Hamlet, a rôle for sorrows.

The "Herald," to be sure, considered Hamlet "almost his worst part, from an artistic point of view," while admitting that it drew money. That newspaper still insisted on thinking of him as a promising young actor, who might go far if he heeded good advice, such as the "Herald" was ready to give him. The reviewer was by no means "blind to his great merits." If he would, thought the "Herald," he might become the greatest actor in the country. The "Herald" did not name an alternative candidate, but perhaps was thinking of Forrest, who had begun three weeks earlier, at Niblo's, being as melancholy, in the rôle of the Dane, as his increased bulk would allow.

Forrest, on his three-nights-a-week schedule, played longer than did Booth, whose first engagement ended on October 17. Clarke came after him, and after Clarke came "The Ticket of Leave Man" with Mr. and Mrs. W. J.

Florence, who were always popular. They stayed for a run, remaining until March 26; and Booth stayed on the road, playing in Philadelphia, Boston, and elsewhere. The season saw the first play by Augustin Daly, who had been a dramatic critic previously. It was excitingly called "Leah, the Forsaken," and had Kate Bateman for its star on its first production. Later in the season his second play, "Taming a Butterfly," was produced.

In the spring Booth returned, but not to the Winter Garden. Instead he went to Niblo's, which therefore had the honor of being the first home of his long-popular play "The Fool's Revenge," which was Booth's variation of Tom Taylor's variation on the Rigoletto theme—a play based on Hugo's "Le Roi S'Amuse." It had been produced in London for the first time in 1859 and was sent by a friend to Jefferson. Jefferson took one surprised glance at it, wondered what on earth the friend was thinking of, and sent it on to Edwin. Edwin tinkered with it and tried it out; but not until March 28, 1864, was it publicly played by him under the management of William Wheatley. The central character is that of Bertucchio, a court jester. At the opening, Rose Eytinge played the only important female part, that of Fiordelisa, Bertucchio's daughter.

Long gone is the day of such plays as "The Fool's Revenge," which was "theater" unalloyed; melodrama without reticence. It lived even then for its star part, as did so many plays; "The Bells," which started Henry Irving's success, is a similar drama. Bertucchio was long one of Booth's most popular rôles. Bertucchio, court fool but an intellectual none the less, is defamed by a nobleman and plots revenge. He joins with others in what he believes their scheme to steal the wife of his enemy. Gloatingly he watches while they invade the castle and come down a ladder with the bundled form of a woman in their clutches. He dances with glee, little dreaming that it is . . . his daughter!

Imagine his rage and terror, then, when he discovers the truth some hours later. Then he is standing outside a locked door, behind which are his fellow-conspirators, and the woman. He rubs his hands . . . and there enters the anteroom the wife of his enemy, quite obviously un-abducted. Consternation! And a chance for the actor. Booth took that chance to its fullest and the audience was en-raptured. Seldom had they seen, gathered in one spot, so much emotion. The "Herald" was quite won over. Its re-viewer (quoted by Dr. Odell) remarked:

> Mr. Booth has made the part of the jester in this play another of those grand dramatic studies which justly entitle him to rank as the greatest actor of his time. Such a minute attention to all the proprieties of the part as he employs in every scene and such terrific intensity of dramatic power as he arose to in the third act have not been seen before by the present generation.

And to this tribute Dr. Odell adds on his own behalf: "Nor by any subsequent generation up to the time my pen writes this sentence, except in the work of Salvini, Ristori and Sarah Bernhardt."

The "Herald," it may be noticed, herewith handsomely abandons qualifications. "The greatest actor of his time," no less. They were coming into line, now. They liked him best, of course, in his worst plays, but they admitted his greatness. We wonder whether it may have been his ironic sense which led Booth to follow "The Fool's Revenge," which ran until April 16, with "The Iron Chest" and, of all things, "The Marble Heart." Very likely not. Booth was no ironist. But he did get out of his system in this one engagement his three worst plays. For variety, on April 23, he turned to his worst part in a standard play, enacting Romeo to the Juliet of Avonia Jones. After this dissipation, he returned to the Winter Garden and for a space left melodrama to the Bowery.

Melodrama was in full bloom there, as it had been for years and was to be for years to come. But "Bowery melodrama" was a generic rather than a specific term and there was much of it on Broadway and elsewhere, as there was much Shakspere and "classic" melodrama on the Bowery. It was on the old street, however, that one was in those days most likely to see the most spectacular exhibits of what may be called pseudo-realistic drama.

There, for example, it was that the girls disported themselves in what was, to paraphrase Winter, the equine no less than the mimetic art. There, according to a recent biographer of the street,[1] Charlotte Crampton was one of the first of leading ladies to play from a horse, appearing on January 3, 1859, at what had been the National Theater, where Booth had supported his father in 1850. Miss Crampton played Mazeppa. Mounted on her trusty steed, she galloped excitingly over the stage and finally charged up a

[1] Alvin F. Harlow: "Old Bowery Days." D. Appleton and Company, New York, 1931.

runway which led her and the horse in the direction of the flies, to the nervous tension of the onlookers.

Many others followed Miss Crampton in the ensuing years, each with her horse. It was the custom, once started on horseback, to play one after another those dramas which required Dobbin—"Dick Turpin, or, The Highwayman's Ride," "Jack Sheppard," and others—before turning the co-star back to pasture. In those days, also, the "quick-change" artist was famously popular, particularly at the New Bowery, and the appearance of one actress in five parts became almost a commonplace. Adah Isaacs Menken had, in 1862, played no less than nine characters in "The Three Fast Women, or, The Female Robinson Crusoes," and had given her competitors something to shoot at. The Davenports, the Wallacks, and the Conways were, meanwhile, defending the standard of poetic melodrama on the same stage. And all the Bowery theaters were chilling their audiences with ghost stories. Great days.

They had not been such great days, however, for Jackson of the Winter Garden, and at the end of the season of 1863–64 he gave up his lease. Clarke, who would keep biting until he choked, suggested at once that it be added to the Booth-Clarke holdings. Certainly, as he pointed out, the purchase of the Walnut Street had been a wise move. If he and Booth had been successful there, why not at the Winter Garden in New York? Both actors could be certain of drawing money to the box-office; it would be hard if they could not find other attractions which would prove profitable for at least a third of the year. Booth agreed with him; they made an offer for the Winter Garden and it was accepted. But since neither could, of course, be continuously at the playhouse, they took in William Stuart, who had had experience as a manager, to act as resident director. He was given a suite of rooms in the theater and there he lived happily and, probably, without too much exertion.

They planned to proceed in a systematic fashion. Clarke should be the first in a season divided roughly into three parts. He would play through the autumn. Booth would follow him at the turn of the year and play until spring. Spring and summer would be filled in as seemed advisable at the moment. In accordance with the plan, Clarke opened the house under its new management on August 18.

It was a handsome house, or at least a highly decorated one, Boucicault having seen to that. It was a popular house and was already connected in the public mind with such players as Edwin Booth. And it was, although no one knew it, entering on the last stage of a long career which had begun with Tripler's Hall, erected at Broadway and Bond in anticipation of the Jenny Lind concerts. It had burned before she arrived, but a new theater had at once been built on the plot and named, with fine simplicity, "The New York Theater and Metropolitan Opera House." Under that style it opened in 1854, with Henry Willard and Harry Eytinge managing and Julia Dean as star. The next season it was known as the Metropolitan Theater, merely, but Rachel played there; the year following, Laura Keene leased it and named it after herself. Then she lost the lease and Burton took it over, presenting Edwin Booth for the first time as a star.

Burton retained control, to continue a recapitulation,

until the autumn of 1858, when Stuart and Boucicault took over and opened with a grand new title, "The Winter Garden, a Conservatory of the Arts." Jackson was the next lessee; and then it came into the hands of Booth and Clarke, with Stuart as a sort of resident liability.

Booth had, he afterward told Winter, "no desire for gain," but his hope was rather "to establish the pure, legitimate drama in New York and by my example to incite others, actors and managers, to continue the good work. We would take our chance of making money outside New York and be satisfied with the glory of the good work we accomplished there."

Booth's plans were indeed ambitious. He was weary of "commercial" management, which entailed bad casts, scrappy scenery, and slashed plays. He determined, as Charles Kean had determined in England, to bring Shakspere to the stage in all, or almost all, his glory. He planned settings and properties which would match the majesty of the Shaksperian line. He was intent on bringing to the stage a scrupulous historical accuracy in all things, the counterpart of the inspired realism of décor which David Belasco was somewhat later to bring to the modern stage.

Booth would, at the Winter Garden, dash aside all makeshifts. And, in a very large measure, he did just that. Then began what Crinkle has called "the simultaneous gathering together of the best elements of the community into the theater"; then Booth "came to mean for us the patronage of the best elements of that intelligence and good taste which the theater elsewhere vainly and intermittently struggled for."

During the years of Booth's control, although he shared it with less determined idealists, great plays were given in the grand manner. His labors at the Winter Garden, and later at his own theater, are often forgotten by those who sum him up easily as an actor and nothing more. That was the habit by the time he died; many specifically lamented that he had "done nothing for the theater"; that he had been content with the traditional incompetence of supporting companies, the traditional hacking of Shakspere's plays. At his prime he was far more than a mere "star" taking his fifty and sixty per cent of the gross. He was a producer of vision.

If Booth had sought to bury his sorrow under work, he was in a fair way to succeed as the summer ended. It had been generally a pleasant summer. Junius was at home for the first time in two years; Wilkes, in June, had come to Nineteenth Street for the summer and with his appearance the mother's anxiety for "the younger boy—strange, wild, and ever moody," the boy who "caused them all some degree of anxiety"—abated. Mrs. Booth was pleased when her brilliant sons, who had been going their own ways, began to talk of making at least one appearance together, in "Julius Cæsar." She liked them all around her. Edwin was for the plan heartily; perhaps he was not sorry for an opportunity of contrast with his brothers, for some of the papers now called Junius "the Booth of the family."

Edwin was still the mainspring of his family, of course. He would not have had it otherwise, but it was a responsibility that never left him. Added was the strain of managing two theaters; driving them, too, as the mainspring. He had little time for memories. But, on the other hand, the strain began to tell on him physically.

It is at about this time that there appear in his letters the first references to the enemy of all his later years. At irregular intervals he was the victim of attacks of violent indigestion; dyspepsia, he called it. At such times, in addition to abdominal pains, he was incapacitated by headaches. Days he spent in darkened rooms, to stagger out at night, pale and suffering, to act. An attack would pass away only to be followed, after a time, by another which would leave him unable to eat, dizzy, showing every symptom of auto-intoxication.

The recurrence of this ailment is found to parallel the irregular strains of his profession. When he was resting it almost vanished. When he began to play it returned. At any moment of particular strain—when he was making a first appearance, offering a new production he had labored over, or, in after years, when he was striving again in London—his physical condition was at its worst.

Evidently he was a sufferer from nervous indigestion; his viscera reacted sharply to the strain of public appearances. He was a man of instinctive shyness, forcing himself to a life of constant exhibitionism. He said often that he never knew stage-fright and he was undoubtedly perfectly honest in that statement. But his digestion knew stage-fright, for years. His mind adjusted itself to his profession, but his intestines always cringed. He learned to go on anyway, of course, and only once or twice did his body play him utterly false. But those critics who, looking around for a word, spoke of his complexion as "bilious" were good diagnosticians.

Edwin left the new theater to Clarke in the early autumn and played outside New York, but he returned to vote in the exciting election of 1864. He cast his ballot, the first of his life, for Abraham Lincoln and was overjoyed when Lincoln was reëlected. Wilkes was cast down. He grew excited when Edwin told him of the vote. "Lincoln will be king of America," he said, violently. Edwin shook his head and left the room, to avoid argument. He always avoided it, when possible, on that subject. Knowing this, and being unable to keep off it, Wilkes avoided the house, visiting it only to see his mother, "when political topics were not touched on," at least in Edwin's presence. Elsewhere Wilkes talked freely. Many did; his words were no wilder than those of hundreds who had never sympathized with Lincoln's beliefs or with his actions.

The brothers got together, however, to talk of their joint appearance and managed to keep off politics long enough to make definite plans. So, after the election, the following advertisement could appear in the newspapers:

Mr. Stuart has pleasure in announcing that, owing to the generous zeal and untiring devotion of Mr. Edwin Booth, a performance will be given at this theater on Friday evening, November 25, 1864 (Mr. J. S. Clarke having kindly ceded the evening for the occasion) for the benefit fund to raise a statue of Shakespeare in Central Park, being the second benefit in this theater. The evening will be made memorable by the appearance of the three sons of the great Booth

JUNIUS BRUTUS

EDWIN AND

JOHN WILKES BOOTH

who have come forward with cheerful alacrity to do honor to
the immortal bard from whose works the genius of their father
caught inspiration and of many of whose greatest creations he
was the best and noblest illustrator the stage has ever seen.

Stuart paused for breath at this point. Another sentence
or two crawled down the column to reveal that the brothers
would appear in "Julius Cæsar"—Junius as Brutus, Edwin
as Cassius, Wilkes as Antony. Yes, Wilkes as Antony,
avenger of the murdered despot.

Prices were raised for the occasion, the highest to five
dollars. Admission to the "beautiful parquette" was a dollar
and a half; to the family circle half a dollar. The house was
crowded and the statue fund gained appreciably. Mrs. Booth
sat in a box and saw her three sons play to an audience
which applauded lustily. She was very happy and proud of
the boys.

The event went off splendidly except for a slight disturbance. Fire-engines stopped outside the house while the
play was on, with great clanging of bells and much shouting. There was a commotion in the lobby, and excited voices.
The play faltered for a moment; the audience stirred un-
easily. Men stood up and looked back; a woman screamed
apprehensively. Edwin Booth stepped forward out of his
part to assure the crowd that there was no cause for alarm.
A police inspector rose in his seat and shouted: "It's only a
drunken man! Keep your seats." The audience evidently
accepted this explanation, possibly on the theory that the
drunken man had arrived on the fire-engine, and kept its
seats.

The play went on. The firemen trooped through the lobby to the small fire in the Lefarge House, next door, and the blaze was quickly extinguished. The incident was of no consequence and the audience resigned itself to wars of long ago—to assassination and the addresses of the conspirators and of the bright youth who, in his rôle of Antony, cleverly led the populace on to seek vengeance; to mimic battle and the clash of harmless spears.

But it was not a little incident. The newspapers the next day were excited. There had been, the "Herald" revealed, "a vast and fiendish plot to burn the city." Fires had been set in twelve hotels, being discovered in each in a room just vacated by a man whose subsequent movements were impossible to trace. Another fire had been started in Barnum's Museum. An audience at Niblo's had been even closer to panic than that in the Winter Garden. Next Niblo's the Metropolitan Hotel had begun to blaze. The actual damage was not great as fire damages went in those days. No lives were lost. But the evident plot made the city nervous and uneasy. The enemy had struck close home; no one doubted it was the enemy. The first effort had been ineffectual, but who could foretell what might come?

The newspapers loudly denounced this dastardly act, although pointing out that it was precisely what one should have expected from the forces of rebellion. "Atrocity!" shouted the newspapers. "Atrocity! The work of fiends!" Men met in little knots on street corners and cursed the Rebels. Those whose fidelity to the North was suspect held their tongues. Wilkes held his tongue in public, although at home he made some defense of the act as one of war.

Edwin walked out of the room. He had no time for such incendiary nonsense. He wished Wilkes would grow up. Wilkes was, after all, nearing thirty.

Edwin Booth had no time for politics. For several weeks before the joint appearance, he had been preparing a new production of "Hamlet." He had brought to it, for the first time, his new determination to present in the grand manner. He was pleased with the result: the grandeur of the sets, the accuracy and beauty of the costumes, the fullness of the text, the skill of the supporting cast. He opened on the day after the three-Booth "Cæsar" and the press was enthusiastic. So, too, was the public.

Stuart took time from the composition of long sentences beginning, "Mr. Stuart has the honor," to look at this new "Hamlet" in rehearsal. He was delighted with it. "It will run six months!" he promised. Booth, tired but polite, gave it four weeks. Stuart thought it over and decided that he had perhaps been too optimistic.

"He gave it eight weeks," Booth said, afterward.[2] "At length he agreed with me that if we got four weeks out of it we should be satisfied."

It started off briskly, with good houses. And then it continued briskly, with good houses. The four weeks came and went. At first Booth was delighted. Then he grew tired of the nightly repetition of one part. He wanted to go on to something new. "I was heartily sick and weary of the monotonous work and several times suggested a change of bill, for I felt that the incessant repetition was seriously

[2] In a note to William Winter, published in "The Life and Art of Edwin Booth." The Macmillan Company, New York, 1894.

affecting my acting." He discussed a change with Stuart, who would not think of it.

"No, no!" he exclaimed. "Not at all, my dear boy. Keep it up. Keep it up. If it goes a year, keep it up."

Booth sighed, but in all logic Stuart was right. After all, Booth was not only the star of success. He was the manager of a theater which that success kept prosperous. He was more or less bound to consider his associates, who naturally felt that, having a safe thing, it would be folly to abandon it. So they kept it up. It ran through December and through January. The crowd still came. There may have been, as was unkindly hinted, no little "paper" in the house by February, but there was money in it, too. Booth was bored, but every one else was delighted. "Hamlet" had never run so long before.

"This terrible success of Hamlet seems to swallow up everything else theatrical," he wrote to Emma F. Cary, a sister of the dead Richard Cary. "I believe you understand how completely I 'ain't there' most of the time. It is an awful thing to be somebody else all the while."

The engagement became a wonder of the age. A group of gentlemen with the good of the legitimate at heart felt that it should be made the occasion of some special ceremony. John T. Hoffman, Governor of New York, George Bancroft, Charles P. Daly, Charles A. Dana, Professor R. O. Doremus, Bayard Taylor, and many more put their heads together. They decided on a medal which would celebrate the hundred nights' "run" of the play. It then, of course, became necessary to run it a hundred nights. And that, of course, did make a long free list necessary. These details attended to, Tiffany was commissioned to make the medal.

Booth thought it should be given to Stuart. "He was certainly responsible for the run of the play," he said afterward. But the medal was for Booth, with his head embossed on one side. The plan was to give it to him as the run ended. But unfortunately it was not completed at that time. It was still at Tiffany's when on March 22, 1865, Stuart announced a benefit at the Winter Garden for "Mr. Edwin Booth on the occasion of the one hundredth and last night of Booth's Hamlet." The doors opened at "½ of 7," the performance began at "7½." The house was crowded and Edwin made a brief speech. It was, like most of his speeches, inaudible beyond the first few rows.

Booth went to Boston almost immediately and began an engagement there. He was in Boston when the glad news came that Lee had surrendered. The bells of all the North rang and hearts everywhere were lightened. In Washington there was a great "illumination." Wilkes was there to see it. He had been in Washington most of the winter, although not acting with any regularity. He had not, indeed, acted much for the past two years. His oil shares had proved profitable. Wilkes saw the illumination, but was not one of those who delighted in it. He went to a boarding-house in H Street, and there there was no jollification.

Edwin was happy in Boston. Peace had come, and victory. Now it would not matter what Wilkes said or thought; the war was over. The boy would take it badly for a time, naturally, but he would get over it. And now, perhaps, that youngest Booth would really settle down to cultivating his talents. Edwin wished Mary could have been there to see peace come again; but he played Sir Edward Mortimer with a light heart, in Boston on the night of April 14, 1865.

# IX

## "WRETCHED AND UNWORTHY BROTHER"

JOHN WILKES BOOTH HAD BEEN IN WASHINGTON MOST OF THAT winter. In the South the forces of the Confederacy were stubbornly yielding. Only some miracle could save those forces, with which was Wilkes's heart. And Wilkes met at a boarding-house in H Street with some others and plotted a miracle. Mary E. Surratt, who owned the house, was there; John H. Surratt; strange, ugly little George E. Atzerodt; muscular, stupid Lewis Thornton Powell, called Payne, who had, at any rate, fought with the South; David E. Herold. A young man clerking in Washington lived in the house and was puzzled by the actions of the other roomers and their visitors. He was none too bright in deduction, but he had a long memory. Sometimes, he said, Mrs. Surratt and Atzerodt and the rest would go into a room when Wilkes Booth came, and close the door carefully after them. The young man was rather hurt at being excluded.

There was little nobility in the group which plotted at Mrs. Surratt's. If Wilkes Booth thought of himself as a modern Brutus, striking to free his nation from an ambitious despot, he must have closed his eyes hard to Atzerodt.

If he dreamed himself a William Tell, heroic against a tyrant, he must have found it difficult to fit Mrs. Surratt into the picture. They were dark people meeting in a dark room to plot darkly—all save Booth. He was young and beautiful for such a business. He had galloped through the woods, heroically sabering trees and assailing the leaves with eloquence. But there was nothing heroic about Mrs. Surratt's musty boarding-house.

It was contended afterward by those of the plotters who remained alive that assassination was not dreamed of in their scheme. Abduction—that was to be the thing. A sudden sortie, the forcible seizing of a tall, gaunt man who would, after the first shock, go with them peaceably; flight into the South with their captive and his deliverance to the leaders of the South; Lincoln a hostage, then, and a forced, favorable ending to the war; places of heroes for themselves in the country they had so brilliantly saved. So it was argued, publicly, afterward. Not murderers, they, but saviors of their cause. Humanitarians, really, ending bloodshed. Great things were to come out of the shabby room in which Wilkes Booth, tragedian, stood out so oddly by contrast with his fellows.

The plotters met for the last time the night of April 14. They had learned during the day that Abraham Lincoln and his wife would be that evening at Ford's Theater, where Laura Keene and Harry Hawks were reinforcing the resident stock company in a performance of "Our American Cousin." By that time they knew that Lee had surrendered. Wilkes had seen the fireworks. Wilkes, at least, had no longer any thought of abduction. The others, when they were pleading for their necks, insisted they still thought the first plan held. Nobody believed them, really. It was murder when they met before the theater hour on the evening of April 14. Double murder, if they could manage it. Seward, Secretary of State, was to go too. Wilkes would see to Lincoln. They may not have known, then, that General and Mrs. Grant had found themselves, late in the day, unable to join the Lincolns at the theater. Major H. R. Rathbone and his fiancée had taken their places.

The President's party had a double stage box; and when they entered, Lincoln showed himself gravely to the audience, bowing to a ripple of applause. It was a gala occasion; the front of the box was hung with flags and there was a picture of George Washington in the center. Lincoln sat back to watch the play.

Wilkes Booth had left the Surratt house for the last time. He had had a drink or two with friends. Now he sauntered into the theater, nodding to the door-man. He merely nodded. He was free to come and go as he pleased in Ford's Theater, where he had often appeared as leading man. The door-man, who liked him, nodded back. Booth walked in at the rear of the house and stood for a moment watching the play. Then he moved to the side and walked slowly, indifferently, down the aisle. He clutched a small pistol in his pocket. He paused and leaned against the wall, nonchalantly. No one noticed him; the audience had eyes only for the stage.

— A guard who was to have stood in the corridor behind the President's box, between its solid partition and the side wall of the theater, had slipped away, unnoticed. He had

*Courtesy Library Theatrical Hall of Fame*

J. WILKES BOOTH  THE ASSASSIN

gone to the gallery to watch the play. There had been, apparently, only one guard. Not long before, there had been good grounds to believe only accident had thwarted a plot to kidnap the President, but there was only one guard. And he was in the gallery, watching the play.

The house was dark, as Booth went slowly down the aisle. Only the stage was light. But the light from the stage reflected into the box in which Lincoln sat, hidden from the audience and visible only to the players. Booth stepped out of the open aisle into the corridor.

Then, after a moment's pause to make sure he had not been observed, he must have moved very quickly.

Hawks, as Asa Trenchard, was alone on the stage, well down toward the front and ready with his exit line. In the wings, up stage, Miss Keene waited with a boy, W. J. Ferguson, to go on. Ferguson had a line or two to speak. From where they stood they could look into the box. But, for a moment, they were not looking into the box.

In that moment the door of the box opened and Booth slipped in, quietly. He had fired before he was noticed. The bullet entered the back of Lincoln's head. The President leaned back with his head against the wall, as if he were very tired. The report of the pistol rang through the theater. A tendril of smoke floated out from the box.

Rathbone rose to grapple with the assassin. He seized Booth as he rushed toward the front of the box. Booth stabbed him in the arm. Perhaps, turning, he whispered hoarsely, "*Sic semper tyrannis.*" Perhaps he only thought he said it. The theater was still quiet as he leaped for the stage. His foot caught, by his dangling spur, in the flag. He could

Darling of Misfortune

have made the leap easily, otherwise, for he was an athlete, but he fell heavily.

Still the house was utterly quiet. Then there was a sudden, desperate scream. It followed Wilkes Booth as, though his leg was broken, he strode across the stage. He passed between Laura Keene and young Ferguson, who stood frozen. Mrs. Lincoln leaned out of the box and began to cry something. Most of those in the audience could not understand her. Whitman says she cried, "He has killed the President!"

Booth was at the stage door before the house went mad behind him. He was swinging into the saddle as the audience rose up and men shouted hoarsely. He was pounding away over the cobbles, iron clattering against stone, as the stage suddenly filled with noisy men, women screamed in the audience, and some were trampled in the panic. He was away at a gallop when soldiers filled the theater, shouting and pushing to clear it. And the President sat with his head against the wall of the box, as if he were too tired to notice all this uproar.[1]

Lincoln was taken across the street, to die at seven o'clock the next morning without having regained consciousness. The news spread through the city and through the nation. It was first a wild rumor. In the first accounts the name of the assassin was not given, although Wilkes Booth had been recognized by many; there was no time for that in the surge of the dreadful news. Later accounts

[1] The description of the scene follows the account of W. J. Ferguson, embodied in his book, "I Saw Booth Shoot Lincoln." The assassination has been variously described, but Ferguson's account carries conviction.

named Booth tentatively. One of those reached Philadelphia, where Edwin Forrest was living bitterly in retirement. A friend hurried to tell him. "And they say Wilkes Booth killed him!" the friend gasped. "I don't believe it." "I do," said Forrest. "All those god-damn Booths are crazy."

In Boston, Edwin had played Sir Edward to the end and gone to a friend's home and to bed. He heard nothing until the next morning. Then his negro servant, eyes popping, told him that Lincoln was shot. The negro hesitated a moment, and told him the rest. Booth sat stunned and stared at his breakfast as it grew cold in front of him.

"IMPORTANT!" announced the New York "Herald" that morning, at the top of column one, page one. The editor who wrote it must have stared at that word, as it stood alone, with abashed surprise. But he had no time to fish in his vocabulary for something which would less palely suggest the import of the account which followed. He could only write on down the column, line after line, telling his story in the head-lines. The separate accounts were set in the order they came over the wire, building oddly to a climax. The despatch which told of Lincoln's death was well down in a pillar of close-set type.

It was maddening news, although not all, even in the North, loved Lincoln or set him so high as he has been set by succeeding generations. They were too close to see him. But they were not too close to see his martyrdom.

A hot fire swept over the country, burning away doubts and qualifications. A gigantic reward was offered for the murderer, who fled through Maryland with a broken leg. The murderer's brother sat that morning in his room in

Boston and stared at his cold breakfast. After a time a letter came, by messenger from the Parker House. Henry C. Jarrett, manager of the Boston Theater, at which Booth was playing, wrote carefully. The letter had to be worded for the newspapers.

EDWIN BOOTH, ESQ. MY DEAR SIR:

A fearful calamity is upon us. The President of the United States has fallen by the hand of an assassin and, I am shocked to say, suspicion points to one nearly related to you as the perpetrator of this horrid deed. God grant it may not prove so. With this knowledge and out of respect to the anguish which will fill the public mind as soon as the appalling fact shall be fully revealed, I have concluded to close the Boston Theater until further notice. In great sorrow and haste I remain, yours truly . . .

To Booth this letter must have come as the first concrete entity in chaos. It gave him something to do. He must answer in kind. He wrote:

With deepest sorrow and great agitation, I thank you for relieving me from my engagement with yourself and the public. The news of the morning has made me wretched indeed, not only because I have received unhappy tidings of the suspicion of a brother's crime, but because a good man and a most justly honored and patriotic ruler has fallen in an hour of national joy by the hand of an assassin. The memory of the thousands who have fallen in our country's defense cannot be forgotten by me even in this, the most distressing day of my life. And I most sincerely pray that the victories we have already won may stay the brand of war and the tide of loyal blood. While mourning, in common with all other loyal hearts, the death of the President, I am oppressed by a private woe not to be expressed in words. But whatever calamity may befall me or mine, my country, one and indestructible, has my warmest devotion.

Booth's friends, by letter and telegram, advised him to remain for the moment in Boston. His friends were loyal; they rallied around his mother and sister in the Nineteenth Street house and assured Edwin of their safety. His mother, of course, was almost prostrated by grief. Junius, who had been acting in Cincinnati, disappeared on the day after the assassination, but turned up shortly in Philadelphia, where he joined Clarke and Asia at their home. Asia, not well before, became seriously ill from shock and her mother was sent for. Aldrich wrote Edwin from New York:

Is there anything I can do for you here or elsewhere? God knows my heart is tender for you this day. The nation's woe is great; how inexpressible must yours be! I wish you were here with those who have loved you these many days, but I think it best you remain in Boston a little while longer. You could do no good here and it is quieter where you are. Launt and I called at the house to see your mother. She had gone to Philadelphia that morning. We saw Rose.

You must keep a brave heart in your bosom. That is the utmost man can do in calamity. The rest is with God.

Booth was notified by the Federal authorities in Boston to hold his luggage in readiness for search and himself in readiness to be questioned. Meanwhile, the whereabouts of Wilkes was unknown. A great hue and cry was raised and the result was, naturally, a swarm of false reports, rising like gnats from disturbed weeds. Wilkes had been captured in Pennsylvania; he was seen in Virginia; he had escaped to New Orleans. These stories ran parallel with accounts of the funeral. Much space was given to the Booth family; the story of Junius Booth's marital difficulties was raked up and so garbled that many later historians have assumed it cut from the whole cloth. The press also rummaged, with glee which modern tabloids could not exceed, through the "love life" of the nation's villain, telling with suitable moralistic throwing up of hands but with all possible detail of the prostitutes he had supported, the mistresses he had left.

Edwin did not know how he stood, even with his friends. Badeau is one of the first to whom he wrote; one can detect in the letter a fear that even Badeau might desert him:

My dear Ad:

For the first time since the damnable intelligence stunned me, am I able to write and hasten to acquaint you of my existence, as it has been so long a time since I last wrote you, making me afraid my silence . . . You know, Ad, how I have labored since my dear Mary was called from me to establish a name that my child and all my friends might be proud of. You know how I have always toiled for the comfort and welfare of my family—though in vain—as well as you know how loyal I have been from the first of this damned rebellion and you must feel deeply the agony I bear in thus being blasted in all my hopes.

Alas, how frightful is the spectacle! What shall become of me? Poor mother! I go to New York today expecting to find her either dead or dying. I've remained here this long at the advice of friends who thought it necessary I should be set right before the public of Boston to whom I owe so much that is dear to me. You know our friends who loved and appreciated my Mary so well and as many who have ever been—even in this most awful hour—my firm and staunch friends. Abraham Lincoln was my President for, in pure admiration of his noble career and his Christian principles, I did what I never did before—I voted and *for him*. I was two days ago one of the happiest men alive—Grant's magnificent work accomplished and sweet peace turning her radiant face again upon our country. Now what am I? Oh, how little did I dream, my boy, when on Friday night I was as Sir Edward Mortimer exclaiming, "Where is my honor now? Mountains of shame are piled upon me!" that I was not acting but uttering the fearful truth. I have a great deal to tell you about myself and the beautiful plans I had for the future—all blasted now—but must wait until my mind is more settled. You will be pleased to know that the deepest sympathy is expressed for me here—and by none more sincerely than dear old Gov. Andrew. God bless you.

Ned.

Booth was still at Boston when deputy United States marshals searched his trunks and found nothing incriminating in them, or in his correspondence. Some time after that he went to New York, muffled in a black coat and with a hat pulled low over his eyes. Friends met him at the station and he was taken home without being recognized. It was probably as well. Feeling ran high, the newspapers fanning it.

Characteristic of the editorial tone, which was far more

temperate than that of the news columns, is the following excerpt from comment in the New York "Times." The reader may amuse himself by making such slight word changes as are necessary to bring this outcry up to date—or up to 1914-18:

> Every possible atrocity appertains to this rebellion. There is nothing whatever that its leaders have scrupled at. Wholesale massacres and torturings, wholesale starvation of prisoners, firing of great cities, piracies of the cruelist kind, persecution of the most heinous character and of vast extent and finally assassination in high places—whatever is brutal, whatever is fiendish, these men have resorted to. They will leave behind names so black and the memory of deeds so infamous that the execration of the slaveholders' rebellion will be eternal.

This bitterness seems to us now, as we look back sentimentally on the gray-clad army and hold the memory of Robert E. Lee high in knighthood, not a little absurd. So, doubtless, will our fulminations during the World War appear after another fifty years have passed. It was dangerous to be a Booth in 1865; it would have been hardly more nerve-racking to be a relative of Wilhelm von Hohenzollern in 1917. It is amazing, indeed, that the citizenry kept as well as it did its temper, its sense of fairness. It is to the credit of the "Times" that it could find space— if not very prominent space—to observe that it was "only thoughtful and honest to say that the Union has had no stronger or more generous supporter than Mr. Edwin Booth. From the commencement he has been earnestly and actively solicitous for the triumph of our arms and the wel-care of our soldiers." It was more than thoughtful and honest. It was one of the brave decencies of journalism.

Such decency stood, one suspects, somewhat isolated from the general public attitude. It was, however, reflected in the New York "Tribune" which, while its leading articles repeated shrilly the most violent of epithets, still found an opportunity to observe:

We learn from Boston that Edwin Booth, who had just terminated an engagement there, has declared in his grief and affliction that he will abandon his public career forever. There will be no occasion for such action. No community would be so cruelly unjust as to allow the stigma of Wilkes Booth's crime to tarnish the fame of so true and loyal a citizen as Edwin Booth. The intended engagement at the Winter Garden, which was to have commenced in a few weeks, will doubtless be relinquished, but Edwin Booth's friends will not consent to his sharing the odium or the disgrace which must be visited upon his wretched and unworthy brother.

Against these kindly expressions of sympathy were set in the New York "Herald" denunciations of the whole family and a steady flow into the Booth household of denunciatory and threatening letters, advising instant flight, change of name, and renunciation of citizenship, with death as the alternative. One, fairly characteristic, is signed a little sweepingly "Outraged Humanity." It reads:

You are advised to leave this city and this country forthwith. Your life will be the penalty if you tarry heare 48 hours longer. Revolvers are already loaded with which to shoot you down. You are a traitor to this government (or have been until your brother's bloody deed). Herein you have due warning. Loose no time in arranging for your departure. We hate the name of Booth leave quick or remember!

It was all very well for his friends to assure him that the letter was from one mentally unbalanced. Such nice considerations would not matter if "Outraged Humanity" had the revolver, as there was every chance he had. For several weeks Booth went out only at night, and walked along the darker streets. William Bispham, whom he had met a few years before in Philadelphia and who was within a few months one of his closest friends, visited him daily and walked with him almost every night. "Nothing but the love poured out for him by his friends saved him from madness," Bispham said later. "For days his sanity hung in the balance."

For days after the crime many things hung in the balance. The search for Wilkes was carried on with more enthusiasm than direction for almost two weeks, while he lay in agony from his unset leg, which by the time of his death was so infected that, without Boston Corbett's bullet—or his own, if it was his own—he could hardly have survived. Wilkes Booth was trapped on April 26 in a Virginia barn, which was fired. He died from a bullet wound in the head, which may have been self-inflicted. His body was taken, with every precaution for secrecy, to Washington and buried in the Federal prison there.

At about the time of his death, or shortly before, both Junius Booth and Clarke were arrested in Philadelphia and taken to Washington for questioning. Junius had, some little time before the murder, written Wilkes a letter in which was a recommendation that Wilkes abandon the "oil business." An astute Secret Service, which had protected Lincoln with one guard—and had not even picked a man who had seen "Our American Cousin" and so might be trusted to mind his guarding—was instantly very knowing about the "oil business." It took Junius some time to convince the authorities that when he had written "oil business" he had meant oil business.

Clarke was arrested on general principles and because Wilkes had left with him a long, aimless screed, addressed "To Whom It May Concern" and revealing the writer's determination to do something—it is not quite clear what. It suggests that Wilkes Booth's mind was affected and is the best evidence of those who argue that he was insane at the time of the murder. This letter, evidently written the previous November, was left with Clarke, sealed, and Clarke opened it only after the assassination. He was held for a time while this fact was established; then he and Junius were both released. Ford also was arrested, as were others connected with the theater, including Miss Keene, and also released.

The announcement of Wilkes's capture and death ended a long siege of suspense for the Booths, and with it came a certain relief. They were at least to be spared the slow horror of trial and execution.

Before that suspense was ended, however, Booth issued his proclamation "To the People of the United States: My Fellow Citizens." It was published, although not widely, in the newspapers on the advice of a friend. The original draft, still extant and preserved at The Players Club in New

York City, shows many changes and interlineations. This was apparently its final form:

When a nation is overwhelmed with sorrow by a great public calamity, the mention of private grief would under ordinary circumstances be an intrusion, but under those by which I am surrounded, I feel sure that a word from me will not be so regarded by you.

It has pleased God to lay at the door of my afflicted family the life blood of our deservedly popular President. Crushed to very earth by this dreadful event, I am yet but too sensible that other mourners are in the land. To them, to you one and all, go forth our deep, unutterable sympathy; our abhorrence and detestation of this most foul and atrocious crime.

For my mother and sister, my two remaining brothers and my poor self, there is nothing to be said except that we are thus placed without any agency of our own. For our loyalty as dutiful, though humble, citizens as well as for our consistent and, as we had some reason to believe, successful efforts to elevate our name personally and professionally, we appeal to the record of the past. For our present position we are not responsible. For the future—alas! I shall struggle on in my retirement bearing a heavy heart, an oppressed memory and a wounded name—dreadful burdens—to my too welcome grave.

In the existent draft the words "in my retirement" are written in heavily. Below is a paragraph signed by John B. Murray, a financial leader of some prominence. It states that he had composed and written the proclamation, except for the words quoted, under Booth's direction. The style is reminiscent of Booth's, however, and he probably had more to do with the composition than Murray realized. It is in any event a fair, if eloquent, statement of the case. It made Booth friends. It was the right note.

His whole attitude struck the right note. With the exception of this one statement, he made none throughout the affair. Without appearing to hide, without undignified protestation, he kept himself reticently from sight. He was called upon to go to Washington at the time of the trial of the conspirators, which began on May 11 and continued until June 30. He did not testify. He made, otherwise, no public appearance. With no hope for the future, with decent self-respect in the present, he waited. He waited while Lincoln's body was borne in state to its burial; while his brother died; while those who had plotted with Wilkes in Mrs. Surratt's boarding-house were tried for their lives.

Herold, Powell (or Payne), Atzerodt, and Mrs. Surratt were condemned to death. A sentimental plea that the woman's life might be spared swept the country but was ignored. On a hot July day a week after the end of the trial the three men and the woman were made to sit for horrible slow minutes on a scaffold in Washington. The jailer believed and hoped that a reprieve would come for Mrs. Surratt and that he would not have to hang a woman. None came. The traps dropped noisily.

The newspapers were filled with detailed descriptions of that last scene. Booth did not read them. But it was over, finally.

Booth foresaw no such change in the public mind as actually came about. He retired from the stage, believing that he would never return to it. "All my friends assure me that my name shall be free, and that in a little while I may be where I was and what I was," he wrote. "But alas! It looks dark to me." Booth thought people remembered and did not forgive. He could not see that for innocent victims the sentimental sympathy of the public sweeps away all other considerations. He thought only of the monstrous shame which had come upon him. He did not feel, as his friends felt, that his sorrow and his manner of bearing it increased the love of the people for him.

Thousands to whom he had been only an actor now felt him a suffering friend. They wished to offer their hands to him and say, "There, there, old fellow!" Thousands to whom he had been hardly a name now extended their sympathy to him. And when an opportunity to extend sympathy without cost to self and an opportunity to satisfy curiosity by looking on the brother of a "monster" knock together . . .

Booth, seeing nothing of this change, lived in close retirement in New York. Even in sorrow, curiously enough, his health improved. Sorrow in private made no such demands on his nervous force as did triumph in public. His dyspepsia improved and he gained weight. Friends noticed it. "I'm a little Byronic in my dislike of such compliments," he wrote Miss Cary late in the summer. "I don't feel as I look."

Edwin's friends did not realize how far back the pendulum was swinging from the attitude which had prompted those threatening letters in the spring, but they did believe he might in time return to the stage. They argued with him during the summer, and his friends of the press joined with them. Under this urging he abandoned his intention to retire permanently, although he was still doubtful. He permitted definite plans to be made for his return. To Miss Cary he wrote:

You have doubtless heard I will soon appear on the stage. Sincerely, were it not for means I would not do so, public sympathy notwithstanding; but I have huge debts to pay, a family to care for, a love for the grand and beautiful in art, to boot, to gratify, and hence my sudden resolve to abandon the heavy, aching gloom of my little red room, where I have sat so long chewing my heart in solitude, for the excitement of the only trade for which God has fitted me.

Similar needs had driven him back to accept the sympathy of the public after the misfortune of 1863. Now his return was set for January, 1866.

# X

## RETURN FROM EXILE

NEWS OF BOOTH'S PROJECTED RETURN TO THE STAGE WAS greeted, generally, with expressions of pleasure. There remained, however, many who extended no welcome. Immediately after Wilkes's crime, his brother was urged by not a few intent advisers to abandon his profession entirely, most of them adding that it was not in any case a profession suitable to a gentleman of his high personal standards and unusual gifts. The ministry would be better, far better, counseled a number who preferred to remain anonymous. He saw what came of play-acting. Let him no longer risk his immortal soul by traffic with the devil, nor let him doubt that the devil was in the playhouse. See what the theater had done to his brother, who, the writers suggested, was quite typical of the players. You cannot touch pitch and escape defilement, they argued;• you cannot wallow in a sink of iniquity and come out clean. Satan will find some mischief still for the actor's hands to do; repent while there is yet time.

And all this because, of course, the crime of Wilkes Booth had given the moralists a new whip to beat the theater with. They cried out to the people to witness how prophecy had fulfilled itself; they had told every one that the theater was an evil, a demoralizing force, a foster-mother of crime and all indecency. And now see what had happened!

Actors and others in the theater could only keep quiet and bide their time, a course which has, incidentally, always served the theater well against its detractors. It was useless to seek to match the moralists, shout for shout; to explain to deaf ears that the acting profession is not one which produces assassins more than another; that there have not, on the whole, been many mimes who were murderers. So the actors kept out of the way as much as possible for the first few weeks, particularly in Washington, where an eager Government was seeking to lock the barn door, preferably with the actors in the barn, after the horse had been stolen. They agreed publicly that Wilkes was a monster, and privately thought that he was a "poor, crazy boy." Those of them who had known him were unable to reconcile the careless, rather noisy lad with the dark plotter of bloody deeds.

And the theater regained its popularity while the moralists still thundered—if, indeed the theater had ever lost popularity. A strangely durable thing, the theater. In the autumn, production went on briskly and in September there opened at Niblo's a frolic which frightened the professionally holy almost out of their wits. It was called "The Black Crook." In it, for the first time—for the first time in a reputable playhouse, at any rate—the girls wore tights, without skirts. Some of the protectors of morals came near dying of apoplexy; and "The Black Crook" ran for four hundred and seventy-four performances, bringing new prosperity to Niblo's.

About Booth himself, however, the question was still unanswered. Public opinion had exonerated the theater as a whole from complicity in the crime of Wilkes Booth. It remained to be seen what its attitude would be toward Wilkes's brother. Edwin's friends, and Edwin himself, were hopeful. Still, it was something of an experiment. One madman with a gun might outweigh all those who sympathized, who sought to restate their regard for an innocent member of an assassin's family. Stuart must have felt some trepidation when in December he announced the return to the stage of Edwin Booth, who would appear in his favorite rôle of Hamlet on January 3. This advertisement was duly printed in the New York newspapers—with the single outstanding exception of the New York "Herald."

It had pleased James Gordon Bennett, some little time before, to fall out violently with the Managers' Association, of which Stuart, nominal head of the Winter Garden, was a member. For months the "Herald" had frothed at the editorial columns. It accused the managers of all the sins it could think of, and it was singularly capable of thinking of sins. The managers were of foreign birth and foes of the American spirit. The eagle screamed. The managers put on plays which incited to crime and wantonness; their productions were lewd and indecent. They had fouled their own nests. They had brought disgrace on the living drama. They led small boys and girls into paths of unrighteousness. They demoralized grown men and women. They had made it impossible for respectable members of Society—members of Society, for example, who showed their respectability by reading the "Herald"—to go to the theater at all. They insidiously plotted against the American commonwealth. They were upholders of the Continental Sabbath and of wearing tights without skirts. And, further, they did not advertise in the "Herald."

That last charge, at least, could be demonstrated. They did not advertise in the "Herald"—not the Olympic or Wallack's or Niblo's or Fox's Old Bowery or Barnum's or the Winter Garden. The "Herald" offered its readers, in the advertising columns, a choice only among the smallest fry. The readers might entertain themselves at several minstrel shows with the sanction of the "Herald's" proprietor. The other productions current were connected with the infamous managers.

The houses which were not represented were the leading houses of New York. They advertised elsewhere: in the "Sun," the "Evening Post," the New York "Tribune," and the rest. And over each single advertisement in each newspaper appeared the line "This Establishment Does Not Advertise in the NEW YORK HERALD."

Bennett grew more angry every time he saw it.

Nor did he have the satisfaction of seeing the productions in these theaters wither before his scorching wrath. Possibly all his outcries against indecency merely whetted the curiosity of the unregenerate playgoers; certainly "The Black Crook" went all the better for the denunciation of it, which was not, however, limited to the "Herald." And

Wallack's continued blithely, in that season producing forty-nine plays, of which "It Is Never Too Late to Mend" was the most popular.

Some of the other titles may prove interesting. "Lost in London" was a favorite, with twenty-three performances. "The Serf" and "The Needful" ran fourteen each; "Don Cæsar de Bazan" was good for ten. And among the others, which ran from nine performances to one apiece, were "Dreams of Delusion," "The Double Gallant," "Still Waters Run Deep," "Ici On Parle Français," "A Wonderful Woman," "To Marry or Not to Marry," "How She Loves Him!" "Miriam's Crime," "Married Life," "Single Life," "Deaf as a Post," "Rural Felicity," and "High Life Below Stairs."

The "Herald" particularly despised Wallack's, which bore up rather well. It was frantic every time it thought of Stuart, Irishman born. And it found its best target when Stuart announced the return of Edwin Booth. "What!" wailed the "Herald." "Can Such Things Be?"

Or, more specifically, thus:

Is the Assassination of Cæsar to be Performed?—The public must be surprised to learn that a Booth is to appear on the New York stage the coming week. We know not which is the most worthy of condemnation, the heartless cupidity of the foreign manager, who has no real sympathy with this country or the feelings of the American people, in bringing out this actor at the present time, or the shocking bad taste of the actor himself in appearing. Will he appear as the assassin of Cæsar? That would be, perhaps, the most suitable character and the most sensational one to answer the manager's purpose. Shame upon such indecent and reckless disregard of propriety and the sentiments of the American people! Can the sinking fortunes of this foreign manager be sustained in no other way than by such an indecent violation of propriety? The blood of our martyred President is not yet dry in the memory of the people, and the very name of the assassin is appalling to the public mind; still a Booth is advertised to appear before a New York audience!

The "Herald" paused for a reply. It was not to be the reply expected. Mr. Bennett's "Herald" did the memory of the public too much credit—or its sense of justice too little. The public was not so readily taken in as the "Herald" had hoped. It could, with the wind in any direction, tell one Booth from another Booth. The Booth who was to return to the stage on January 3 was not the Booth who had killed Lincoln. The public resented this effort to kick a man when he was down, particularly as it was not the right man. The "Herald" succeeded chiefly in arousing increased sympathy for Edwin Booth, making him appear an under dog and the victim of unfair tactics. Its attacks, which drove other newspapers to Booth's support, enlarged public interest in Booth's return and increased public emotions. Booth's appearance became more than the return of an actor to a stage: it became an opportunity to acclaim an under dog; a martyr to another's sin; a gentleman who had suffered unjustly.

The other newspapers perceived this aspect of the event. The "Tribune" moved its editorial comment to the first page on January 3 and felt it "safe to predict that the Winter Garden will be thronged tonight as it has rarely been thronged before." "Since the golden days of Rachel," it added, "this theater has not witnessed an event so important and so interesting as the reappearance of Edwin Booth." It continued, lengthily, in a vein of adulation. Other newspapers responded similarly to the "Herald's" attacks. Men and women who had thought nothing whatever about the whole affair passionately took sides and discovered that great things were at stake.

For days in advance tickets sold rapidly. Stuart warned in his advertisement that the supply was limited and that, although the management was anxious to keep tickets out of the hands of speculators, prompt action was necessary on the part of prospective patrons. They must run, not walk, to the box-office. They did so, in numbers, but speculators are not so easily outwitted. Blocks of tickets were purchased and held for an advance, which came. The "Herald's" complete silence regarding the whole matter on the day it was to come to a head—the belated silence of dignity, no doubt—was broken rather amusingly in one of the advertising columns. There appeared this note:

EDWIN BOOTH—A Few Choice Seats may be obtained for this evening by applying at the bar at Buckland's Hotel, corner of Twenty-seventh Street and Fourth Avenue.

A great crowd, only a minority holding seats, choice or otherwise, gathered that evening in the streets around the Winter Garden. Special details of police were on hand in the event of trouble. Men and women had come from Boston and Philadelphia and Baltimore and even Washington to witness the event. Long before the doors were open, hundreds were ready to burst in and other hundreds swarmed outside, with the chance of trouble their only hope for entertainment. The crowd shouted and booed and cheered. It broke up into little arguing knots, and the knots degenerated into battles which the police broke up. There were threatening shouts and loud announcements of projected violent activity, followed by more shouts and more announcements, but very little activity of any kind. Those who actually had tickets and wished to enter fought their way through the lookers-on, aided as much as possible by the police force.

Long before the hour set for the beginning of the performance, at "7½ o'clock," the house was filled. The crowd was a talkative, uneasy one, with policemen evident in it. Back stage, Booth could hear it murmuring, and then, no doubt, he regretted a hundred times that he had submitted to the pleas of friends and of his own necessities; that he had returned to the "excitement of the only trade for which God had fitted him." The trade had never promised half so much excitement as this. The curtain rose and Horatio listened to the story of the frightened watchman.

Then Booth's cue came. He was pale when he went on the stage and a burst of noise met him. Cheering. Booing. Which was it? What was the temper of his crowd? What danger was he fronting? He waited. The noise slowly resolved itself. The crowd . . . the crowd was cheering! Boos and hisses and threats, all were drowned out. They cheered him. It was minutes before he could proceed. Then he went on into the rôle. The melancholy of Hamlet deepened. He played calmly and well; the crowd forgot its emotions in the play. They forgot Booth in Hamlet. All was as it should be. He was an actor once again.

Next morning the "Tribune" reported, in evident glee, on the riotous scene. It was particularly pleased to report that the New York "Herald" had been roundly hissed. It had space for little about the play. But Hamlet was himself again.

Or almost himself. He was never afterward quite the same. No expression of the public's affection could wipe away his own feeling of shame. Too close together had come the tragedies of 1863 and 1865. He shrank back still further into himself. Now the withdrawal which had begun as a mask to hide a boy's shyness was fixed. In the months, and in the years, which followed, "the labor I underwent, with the domestic afflictions weighing heavily upon me, made me very unfit for social enjoyment of any kind and I was forced to shut myself up a great deal. This, of course, made people think me haughty, self-conceited and 'Hamlet-y' all the time, whereas I was very weary and unhappy."

The murder of Abraham Lincoln was too enormous a weight to put aside. Booth was too weary and too unhappy to rally under it. It was easier to retreat into himself, to put on a mask, to hide. He retreated from that catastrophe. His friends never spoke of it. Only the portrait of Wilkes which hung in his bedroom, kept there doggedly as a symbol of pride or of futility or of man's destiny to unhappiness, remained as a thorn in his spirit. Only that and accident.

He never played in Washington after Lincoln's murder, although in later years he was often begged to visit the capital. When he played in Baltimore, Washington lovers of tragedy went there to see him. But he could not always avoid memories. Once in the home of an acquaintance, years afterward, Booth found a plaster cast of a hand. He had been wandering about the room while the others talked. He picked it up—the cast of a great hand, powerful and knotted.

"Whose hand is this?" he asked his host.

James Lorrimer Graham pretended he had not heard.

"Whose hand is this?" Booth asked again, a little louder. Conversation was broken off and there was a moment of waiting.

"That is Lincoln's hand," Graham said, his tone expressionless. Conversation began again, flurried and eager.

"The man to whom it meant such unspeakable things put it down softly without a word," says Howells, who reports the incident.

Work was the best narcotic. Booth plunged into it, making ready new and even more grand productions for the Winter Garden. He joined Clarke in taking over the lease of the Boston Theater, so that they controlled houses in Philadelphia, New York, and the city which was no longer quite the hub of culture. In New York, he played Hamlet, received the medal, opened "Richelieu," which had been in preparation at the time of the assassination and was to have been offered in the spring of 1865. It was, from all accounts, a magnificent "Richelieu," mounted extravagantly. He went, afterward, to Boston, where another enthusiastic audience welcomed him on the occasion of another return to the stage. Late in the spring he went to Philadelphia, to play there on April 23 "in celebration of the birth and death of Shakespeare," as it was at the time somewhat anomalously worded.

The next autumn they swung back into the rotation agreed upon, Clarke opening the season. But with his wife by no means recovered from the shock of Wilkes's crime, and with other obligations pressing, Clarke found his co-management of the Winter Garden inconvenient. He proposed that Booth buy him out and Booth did so, paying ten thousand dollars for his share in the business. Clarke, a few years later, went to England and the latter part of his career is associated with the London stage.

Booth and Stuart continued with the Winter Garden and in January gave a lavish production to "The Merchant of Venice." It ran its course amid much applause, and was followed on March 22 by a spectacular version of Payne's "Brutus, or, The Fall of Tarquin." Special efforts were made to have the final scene, "the destruction of Rome," realistic beyond anything usually seen on the stage. It was a beautiful and impressive pyrotechnical display, bringing gasps from the audience. An even larger audience, however, gasped the next morning.

At a few minutes before nine o'clock that morning, stage carpenters reporting for work smelled smoke and, an instant later, saw flame. There was the sound of running on the stage, and hoarse shouting. In his apartment above, Stuart was roughly awakened by the noise; he ran in his nightshirt to peer from a balcony into the auditorium. Then he leaped wildly back to his room and into trousers and overcoat. After one or two false starts and encounters with walls of smoke and flame, he managed to escape from a building which was burning furiously.

Firemen dragged their engines through the streets; Broadway was blocked off; thousands gathered to see the Winter Garden go up in smoke and flame. From the adjoining Southern Hotel scantily dressed occupants were driven to shiver on the streets; the guests of the near-by Tremont Hotel looked out in horror and hastily got their belongings together. Nothing could stop the flames in the theater, but the hotels were only slightly damaged. The "Herald" of the next day notes that part of the roof of the burning building fell upon a saloon, crushing it and destroying eleven of twelve barrels of whisky stored in the rear.

No one ever knew definitely what started the fire, but it was always assumed that a spark from the last act's realism had smoldered through the night in the scenery, perhaps bursting into flame when an opening door set up a draft. Booth lost everything he had in the way of costumes, and many mementos which he had carefully protected for years. His loss was estimated at about forty thousand dollars. Stuart had less to lose, the fire terminating the lease.

Booth had planned to continue indefinitely at the Winter Garden, although it was not located to the best advantage in the rapidly changing city; he had planned to continue with the organization he had built up, although Stuart was not the partner he would have chosen if the choice were to be made again. Stuart was already acknowledging, to every one who would listen, the great debt owed

Darling of Misfortune

to him by Edwin Booth, and was more than hinting that
the tragedian would have remained a minor star but for
his timely aid. But the fire ended old plans and opened the
way to new ones. The "Herald" summed the matter up
well enough—although on the assumption that Stuart, not
Booth, was the guiding spirit of the enterprise—in an
editorial article on March 24:

At the Winter Garden, he [Stuart] used a very creditable
exertion to sustain the legitimate drama and render it as it
was before the stage became confused by the apparitions of
the woolly horses, stuffed monkeys, fat women and cosmo-
politan giants and dwarfs and before public taste was outraged and palled, almost to insensibility, by scenic glare, blue
lights, the rattle of gongs, tin plates and the demoralizing
posturing of the ballet, lowered in some instances to positive
indecency. The performances which were arranged at the
Winter Garden by Manager Stuart had a tendency to neu-
tralize the poisonous effect of these exhibitions; but the place
was entirely too small, situated too far down town and inadequate to accommodate even the refined audience which the
great city of New York can furnish, not to speak of it as a
metropolitan dramatic school for the cultivation and enlightenment and consequent refinement of the vast middle and
working classes and the rising generation of every rank of life.
Winter Garden, in fact, held within its walls the living principles of art, which is inextinguishable, but was insufficient
to afford it healthy development. Out of evil comes good.

The good was, in the "Herald's" view, that now the
way was cleared for Stuart and Booth or for some others
to build a more stately mansion for the legitimate some-

....176

where farther uptown, so providing cultivation, enlightenment, and the consequent refinement to larger numbers in happier surroundings.

The idea appealed to Booth. Why not build for himself a theater—an ideal theater, dedicated to the living drama; a theater in which he should be master and responsible to no one, free to work for truth and beauty with no financial obligations to partners? He began, at first idly, to investigate the possibilities of such an undertaking. Then his enthusiasm and determination grew. He would build a great theater.

# XI

## "VERY BIG PUDDLE"

MAN CONSOLES HIMSELF WITH LOVE AND FRIENDSHIP AND DRINK
and work—all agreeable narcotics. Combined and recombined in varying patterns, they provide his occupation, his means of escaping thought. To these some men add religion and many seek in music and books and pictures an impersonal approximation of them. When one is lost man turns with redoubled eagerness to those which remain; if all vanish he shoots himself or goes mad in one fashion or another or sits profitlessly regarding his navel, escaping in self-hypnosis from the constant threat of the indifferent external world.

Now for thirty-four years life had been wrenching from the hands of Edwin Booth these essential drugs. Early, while he was still a shrinking boy, feeling himself an outcast as he guided the erratic footsteps of his nonconforming father and contemplated miserably the irregularity of his own birth, it had made unconstrained friendship very nearly impossible for him. He took, then and after, what he could get of friendship; but although many loved him, it was none too much. There was built, very early, an icy wall in Booth which baffled his friends, and only one or two, if, indeed, any, attempted to scale it. But that wall had melted to let love in.

The warmth of that narcotic was hardly in his veins before life snatched it away from him. He was not a man to love twice. His was that deeply monogamous instinct which more often than is generally admitted—tradition insisting otherwise—permeates the male. He did not love again, although, as we shall see, he married again. And while love was lost to him, Fate utilized conscience to strike a double blow, withdrawing at the same moment the warm confusion of drunkenness in which he might have found amnesia. Allowed two years in which to recover, he was then stricken cruelly by his brother's crime, which completed his retreat into himself, making friendship the more impossible.

He was never, although he talked often of God, a deeply religious man. He was convinced, with his generation, of the essential truths of Christianity, but there is no evidence that he found the mystic's solace in faith. There is nothing to indicate that he was greatly touched by music or that he could use books as an escape. He had, in short, very little left but work.

Life left him that, by way of consolation. After 1866 he turned to it furiously, seeking to make it everything. He was still young, still untired, and in that one thing still confident. He had reason for his confidence; if his own good sense did not assure him of that, he could point to his tangible fame. Grant that outside circumstances had heightened it, although one doubts whether that possibility occurred quite clearly to Booth, it was still sound in itself. No ballyhooing which Fate might be pleased to offer in recompense for what she had taken could have made Booth what, professionally, he was in the spring of 1867, if there had been no spark of genius for ballyhoo to fan. He was an actor.

Nothing remained to distract him from his acting. And chance played him in good stead when the Winter Garden went spectacularly up in smoke and flame. It forced him out of an old groove in which he might have remained. It forced him to devote his energies deliberately and consciously to something larger than the outmoded Winter Garden could contain. It drove him to the construction of a theater which he dedicated to the highest thing he knew in the art he served. He went about the new task with an idealistic determination to give the city what he and others a little glibly called a "temple of dramatic art." But Booth did not think of it glibly. Of course he hoped to make money from it; of course he sought to enhance his fame. But there is no reason for the most cynical to believe that he lacked less personal dreams. Doubtless he would have been far better off in the end if he had had none.

He did not hesitate after the Winter Garden burned. He was at the head of his profession. If the destroyed home of the "legitimate" were to be replaced by a home more permanent, more majestic, plans could hardly be made in which he did not figure. He was the incumbent of the tragic throne. He was more. He had, in his brief and interrupted rule at the Winter Garden, proved himself America's foremost producer in the grand manner. He mounted Shakspere, and no Cibbered Shakspere, with a magnificence which his country had not seen before. Charles Kean in London was doing as much, perhaps, but not more; and it is doubtful whether the son of Junius Booth's earliest rival brought to the stage the creative spark which was in Edwin Booth.

In remembering Booth we often forget this aspect of his career. He was outstanding as an actor; during the latter years of his life he was nothing more. Then he was very weary and did not care. But before that he had done much, more than any of his predecessors, to bring Shakspere suitably to the stage in the United States.

Before him, as far as the national stage was concerned, Shakspere had been haggled into strips of poetic silk with which the tragedian might enwrap himself at will. Things were little better in England. Edmund Kean, Junius Booth, Forrest, and the dynastic rulers they succeeded wanted parts, not plays. They were entirely undisturbed in their artistic conscience as they chopped small, scarcely recognizable, chunks from the dramas, throwing aside as useless debris almost everything which did not appertain directly to the leading rôle. They left the pundits to worry over Shakspere; they grabbed such bits as they needed and strutted on.

Now, very early Edwin Booth seems to have resented this cavalier treatment of the poet to whom so much labial homage was paid and so little fairness shown. Almost before he was in his own right a star, and certainly before he was at the pinnacle of public favor, he had begun to revise the Shaksperian plays in his repertory so that they would at least approximate the originals from which they came. Given in the Winter Garden greater powers, for then he began to direct as well as to act and to plan the mounting of the productions, he found greater fidelity to the originals possible.

He was one of those who made "Cibber," as applied to Shakspere, an expression of contempt.

Very likely his productions would to-day appear old-fashioned. They carried fidelity, actuality, into the last detail. They scamped nothing; they suggested no more and no less than they revealed. They made no mountains out of shadows, wrapped no symbols in canvas. The thought that some day an irregular pile of cubes might serve a Norman Bel Geddes for all the interiors and exteriors of "Hamlet," and serve him so well that Hamlet was scarcely visible against his background, would have seemed to Booth quite mad. The throne room of Booth's "Hamlet" was a throne room, complete with throne, pillars, walls, and velvet draperies. When his watchmen observed the ghost from the battlements, no imagination was necessary to conceive of their vantage-point as a castle wall. And when Juliet dreamed on her balcony—but we shall hear more of Juliet's balcony.

One might lean against the pillars on Booth's stage and they would not tremble; the steel of Booth's swords flashed like steel and chattered like steel, because it was steel. He believed in magnificence and solidity on the stage; in those same virtues in plays. No hanging drapery was, in the theater where he produced, asked to suggest more than a hanging drapery. Perhaps he was uninspired. Perhaps he knew subconsciously the ache of the human heart for veritable magnificence; its insistence that play-acting be play-acting, not intimation. Less would have seemed to him cheating.

As, in the summer of 1867, he proceeded with the preliminary negotiations for his new theater, it was with these ideals firmly in mind and unquestioned. He planned a theater of the most solid granite and of unashamed theatricality. If he had been informed that a theater should look like something else; that entering it should be as uneventful as entering a haberdasher's, he would have stared in blank amazement ... and probably strode away, looking Hamlet every inch. But there was nobody there to inform him that restraint and reticence were advancing, with politely opened mouths, to swallow everything.

He intended it for a Shaksperian theater. There, he wrote, "I intend to go even beyond Charles Kean in my devotion to the sacred text of the late W. S. I intend to restore to the stage (to mine, at least) the unadulterated plays of Shakspere. His *Romeo and Juliet,* not so performed since the days of Betterton, I fancy, unless Barry, in opposition to Garrick, revived it; *Richard III,* which Charles Kean failed to attempt and offered a weak apology for retaining the Cibber version."

He was to do grand things, grandly. On that he was determined, even before he found a backer and financial adviser. For the actual management of the project he engaged, rather quickly, Richard A. Robertson of Boston, a successful business man—or a "commonplace tradesman," as Winter considered him. Robertson was willing, even eager, to enter the world of the theater. He saw money in it, being an indefatigable speculator and optimist. He saw fame and a chance to associate his name with that of Edwin Booth; he had perhaps, underneath, a real love for the art. He always said he had, at any rate.

So, with his ideals, his freedom from other interests, his confidence in his own professional star, which was at least still shining in the bare heavens, and Richard A. Robertson, Booth waded in the summer of 1867 into what he was later to describe as a "very big puddle." He and Robertson discussed the matter and drew up working plans. They estimated that the theater would cost half a million dollars. They agreed that of this sum Robertson would provide at once seventy-five thousand dollars. Later, as the need arose, he would add to that sum until his total investment rose to a hundred and fifty thousand. Booth, meanwhile, was to put in what he might have and, by acting while the building was being constructed, make the balance.

The property, it was agreed, would remain in Booth's name. The partnership would continue for five years after the theater opened, and during that period the Boston tradesman was to receive three sevenths of the profits, Booth taking the remainder. At the expiration of that period Booth was to pay to Robertson a bonus of a hundred thousand dollars and any additional sums which might be needed to make up the difference between what Robertson had been paid in profits and what he had invested. At any time, even before the expiration of the five years, Booth might obtain clear title by paying the hundred thousand and repaying whatever part of Robertson's original investment had not been returned to him, up to that time, in profits.

It will be noticed that Robertson stood to lose nothing, provided Booth lived, earned, and did not default on his obligation, regardless of the success or failure of this particular venture. He was assured a profit of a hundred thousand dollars, as a minimum. If his profits exceeded his investment the excess also was his. Booth took all the financial chances.

J. Henry Magonigle, husband of one of Mary Devlin's sisters and a close friend of Booth, was delegated to decide upon a site. He found one that seemed to him ideal, at the southeast corner of Sixth Avenue and Twenty-third Street, far enough uptown in 1867 to eliminate the "Herald's" objections. The property had a frontage of one hundred and eighty-four feet on Twenty-third Street and of a hundred on Sixth Avenue. The site, consisting of several plots, was controlled by J. A. Page and W. Murray and—once they discovered Magonigle's purpose, which was not difficult—they fixed the price at one hundred and sixty-five thousand dollars. Of this sum Booth paid, in May, something over fifty thousand in cash, leaving a balance due, on mortgages, of a hundred thousand to Murray and fifteen thousand to Page. A memorandum showing the details of this transaction is still extant.

Excavation was begun on July 1, after the ground had been cleared of other buildings. After the top soil had been cleared away, a ledge of rock was discovered and unexpected blasting operations proved necessary, increasing the price of the work. The "Herald" later estimated that the excavation cost sixty thousand dollars.

To supply his share of the money, it was necessary for Booth to wring from the road all the "ducats"—he always spoke of "ducats"—it could be made to contribute. So not long after the digging was started he was off on tour. Then he began to send back money. It went to Joseph Booth, who had been called in to act as treasurer and in that capacity to keep an eye on his brother's interests. Joseph would be loyal. And Joseph was loyal. He had, of course, no idea of handling money or of keeping books. He went from complication to complication, floundering deeper as the complexity of the financing increased, until he had quite lost himself.

Some years later an accountant was called in to follow Joseph into the labyrinth he had made for himself. After prolonged study the accountant reported that Joseph had, apparently, figured into the cost of the building the cost of the first two productions in it. It was impossible to tell where the stone-masons left off and Juliet began; not man or God could find a dividing line. But Joseph was loyal. And it was a brotherly thing to give him the job. He needed a job, as Edwin knew.

Booth went on the road and began to send back checks. For two years the checks flowed, through Joseph to Robertson, who remained to give the building his full attention. When the checks were not sufficient, notes were used. Booth had left behind, when he first went out for ducats, a sheaf of notes, signed in blank, for Robertson to use at will. Robertson had the will. The cash, although it came in rapidly (on December 2 of the first year we find Joseph acknowledging the receipt of two checks, totaling eight thousand dollars, which had come so close together that the first was not noted before the second arrived) was never enough. Edwin could make money, but not so fast as Robertson could spend it. The building rose rapidly. "It is getting along fast enough," Joseph reported to his brother on that same December 2.

But before he got this letter Booth had something else to think about. He had played in Chicago that autumn and there met Mary McVicker, a small, vivacious, sturdy young woman, full of energy and nervous force. She was the step-

EDWIN BOOTH AND HIS DAUGHTER, EDWINA

daughter of J. H. McVicker, theater-owner and manager, and had taken her second father's name in preference to that of Runnion, which was legally hers. She was described by a later reviewer, with the frankness so remarkably indulged in by the newspapers of that day, as "no delicate geranium, rising from a Sèvres vase, but a strong, practical Western woman, with but little artistic training but a good deal of rude vigor and force." Down through sixty years that description floats tantalizingly. She was no "delicate geranium."

She had fallen in love with Edwin almost at once. Many women did. But her force, her confidence, made a special appeal to the lonely actor. He did not deeply love her; he had done with loving. He liked her, grew fond of her. He needed a mother for his little girl, who could not be left always in school or with her grandmother. As Booth thought of her he gave himself "up entirely to the contemplation of what was to be of greater import and far more real than the theater or acting or fame or dollars." So Edwin himself predicted. And in McVicker's Theater Edwin and this new Mary played Romeo and Juliet to each other, professionally, and she, at least, played the rôle off the stage as well. When he left Chicago she accompanied him as a member of his company, acting Juliet in Baltimore and elsewhere; acting also Desdemona to his Othello and Margaret to his Sir Giles.

"I traveled West and South that season from September 4th 'til June 9th," Booth wrote afterward, summing up the season of 1867-68, in its professional aspects. "I made lots of money and paid it out as fast as I could count it."

He was back in New York after the close of his tour and had a look at the repository of all that money. The walls were up and Robertson was full of confidence. Booth went over the accounts, solved them as well as he could, and whistled. Already, and only half completed, the building had cost the whole of the amount originally fixed. He discovered that he owed tremendous sums on the notes which had been discounted. He was unable, for all his study, to see where the records showed that Robertson had put in any real cash, although the manager was certainly active and zealous as a paymaster.

But Booth was not a business man; probably, he told himself, he merely did not understand the figures. At any rate, there was nothing to be done about it; he was in for ten shillings and might as well be in for a pound. Four walls, alone, were of no value to any one, so there was no alternative to continuing. Robertson let more contracts and vigorously expressed his complete confidence. It was costing a pretty penny, but what could one expect? They had underestimated, evidently. But it would be a magnificent playhouse. "Booth's Theater," Robertson murmured over to himself, loud enough for Booth to hear.

Booth went away again, somewhat dazed. It was more complicated than he had thought, this business of building a home for the living drama. Perhaps he wished he had brought into it some other of his business friends—E. C. Benedict, for example, or even Stedman. But neither had the money to put in. Of course there was nothing to indicate that any money was being put in, except by himself; still . . . It was very confusing. Clear out of it, however, stood one thing. He must get him back to the road and make more money. He admitted:

The enterprise swelled gigantically in my hands. It has attained such proportions as would frighten anyone whose bump of "don't-care-a-tiveness" was less than mine. I'm in a very big puddle; if I can wade it, well; if not, why, as Bunsby would say, well, too. Certain it is, I have had enough vexation regarding this same theater to drive me mad, and yet I am calm and careless as though the ultimate success were a fixed fact.

He was careless enough whatever may have been the extent of his calm. And it was exciting, uplifting, to see the hole which had been at Twenty-third Street and Sixth Avenue transformed into walls and into the rude shape of a theater, his theater. His name would be carved over the door. The flags which would float from the towers would be lettered, "Booth's Theater."

And that autumn, before he went back to the road, the roof was on. A little later the playhouse was nearing completion, and had cost in excess of a million dollars. Booth himself seems never to have known exactly what it cost. Once he wrote the sum down as "over a million and a half" and then crossed out the word "half" and substituted "quarter." But really all he knew was that he had a theater; he was in debt, but he had a theater. He began to plan, returning to New York, for the first magnificent production. He left the rest to Robertson; left him to know how deeply the theater was mortgaged to Oakes Ames and others.

Perhaps even Robertson was a little confused by that time over this madly financed ideal. Most of the money had been obtained, McVicker afterward deduced, "on the credit of Booth's name, by a system of shaving on short term loans," which, McVicker rightly added, was "entirely wrong in an undertaking so large." There was never afterward anything to indicate that Robertson had put in one penny, but no one ever knew. Robertson subsequently insisted that he was at least obligated by the notes.

The building was floating on paper, but it looked solid enough by the first day of 1869. Then it was done save for the finishing touches, and the construction of scenery for "Romeo and Juliet" was under way. Joseph figured it in, resolutely. The opening was set for February 3, 1869.

And it was a fine building, that granite temple. It lifted three stubby towers a hundred and twenty feet above the sidewalk. Ornamental iron rails ran around each tower, flags floated over two of them, and there was a vast deal of mansard roof. The building fronted for the full length of the plot on Twenty-third Street, although the theater itself had a frontage of only a hundred and fifty feet. Between the theater proper and Sixth Avenue was a narrower building, uniform architecturally but separate. It contained offices and studios. Through it, to Sixth Avenue, was cut a secondary entrance, hardly less elaborate than the other.

Entering from Twenty-third Street, one came first into a lobby magnificently faced with Italian marble. From one side of it a winding staircase, also of marble, rose toward the balcony and, in a niche at the stair landing, there was a handsome statue of the elder Booth. From the lobby one entered the auditorium, domed, capable of seating almost eighteen hundred persons, profusely decorated with busts of Shaksperian characters, bas-reliefs of the muses, paintings and carved decorations. It was considered very beautiful and was at least magnificent.

*Edwin Booth*

The stage was unusual in capacity. From the foots it ran back fifty-five feet and was correspondingly wide and high. Underneath was, invisible of course, a deep pit filled with hydraulic machinery and sets. The machinery poked the sets up through slits in the floor, very little of it being "flown," hauled up to the fly loft above. The old device of the slotted stage, with the flats set into the slots and pushed out from the wings, was done away with. The hydraulic system, leaving less to man-power, made possible the utilization of far more massive scenery than could have been handled by the old method, so leaving Booth freer to make his settings match his dreams of grandeur.

It was, all in all, a theater to make the audience gasp; however unstable it may have been financially, architects and builders had worked well. It was possible to push up through the floor of that stage a wall for Juliet's balcony which was sixty feet high and had, yes, two balconies. Asia so reports. There was, however, only one Juliet.

Booth had had time to see it in its full magnificence, and be thrilled by it, when, on January 13, he received a letter from Robertson. He carefully saved that letter, and it survives both writer and recipient. It began, familiarly, "Dear Ned," and continued:

I know how unhappy it makes you to undertake the looking into of business matters. Such is the nature and magnitude of this between us, however, it may be arranged in some way. I will state as briefly as I can my situation and what I want.

Enclosed please find mem'd of the amt. I have invested, also a mem'd of notes of which I am as liable as yourself. Think for a moment, Ned, of all this and of all I have done and what must yet be done to carry this enterprise through and what do I really own? I own a right to make some money providing the building stands and you live. With all this amount of money in this enterprise, what can you imagine my feelings must be when I enter the building or think of it to know I do not own a dollar there. What should stimulate me to go on?

The proposition made to me by Harry [Magonigle] has nearly made me sick—i.e., a third interest upon the present valuation. This to me was so far from being just that I felt that my assistance had been but poorly appreciated and proposed to say nothing more to one who has regarded me in the enterprise about as he would his auxiliary corps—very necessary, but not of much consequence. I do not speak of this with any feeling. Harry's intentions are undoubtedly good, but he is far from being liberal and looks under the circumstances entirely on one side. I have been liberal in this affair. I have done whatever has been called upon me without referring in any way to the documents between us. And I have done what money would not get me to do again. No amount of money would tempt me to go through my experience in Nov. and Dec. just passed.

Why should I not be a fair owner in this building? Why, Ned, should I not have something which I can feel a pride in as much as yourself? Must the mere chance of making money be my reward? Must I lose sight of what has stimulated me from the first, your advancement as well as my own—must I place myself in a position when the most money can be made out of the enterprise?

If it had not been for your desire to have all this in your name—it would have started right in the first place—we should have bought the land together and divided the profits accruing from your advantages in a proper proportion. This is the way the enterprise should have been commenced and it is the way it should be treated now.

It is impossible for me to say in what proportion the profits should be divided. It would depend something upon what the profits will be.

Now, as I view it, I should have not less than 3/7 of the estate conveyed to me and 3/7 of the profits for our seven years. You are far from being deprived of the privilege of acting in other places. There will always be a good proportion of the year for you to dispose of your time as you please. At the end of seven years[1] the property is yours entire if you choose to buy my interest it will be put upon such cosy terms of payment—say 1 to 5 years—if you continue in health—and at the end of seven years you can draw your check for the amount, if you choose.

Now what I have here written you can decide on. My fine idea is that we should own equally together, but if this cannot be allowed then make it 3/7, if this cannot be allowed then a mortgage must be made out and I fall back upon the original document.

I believe fully that this letter will place the matter before you as you desire to have it enabling you to act justly and clearly. I would here say if you feel as if you could not do so, I would be perfectly willing to leave it out to any three disinterested parties.

Try and see me tomorrow,

Yours ever,

D<small>ICK</small>.

This curious blend of business and sentiment is indorsed, in Booth's hand, "Infamous, lying villain!"

But Booth might think as he chose; and the inscription was, in any case, added later. When he received the letter he was deep in his first production, anxious, engrossed. The last

---

[1] This period evidently includes the two years of construction.

thing he wanted was further entanglement, further argument. He consented to the demand and conveyed to Robertson the three sevenths he asked. He believed that he made his partner a "free gift" of it, but he made it, none the less.

Booth was, it may be added, then darkly suspicious of the world. He was overdriven, tired, worried. Possibly he was quite wrong about Robertson. Less probably he was wrong about Stuart, who, enraged at being left out of the new venture, was talking angrily behind Booth's back and making charges of all sorts. Booth paused in the turmoil of readying his theater to write to Jervis McEntee, an artist who was then painting him in various rôles and, with the best intentions in the world, borrowing money from him. Booth asked McEntee to get into touch with Thompson, who lived in the same studio building in Tenth Street. He continued:

> I want him to make a point of seeing Will Winter, and explaining to him clearly the villainy of that d—d rascal Stuart. He of course will, and has already set to work thereat, move heaven and earth to injure me with newspaper-men. I know that he has told a lot of infamous stories about me, in hopes of gaining their sympathy and inducing them to abuse me. He can't do much—there are a few people in the press—and only a few—(I allude now to the corps dramatique)—that I have some respect for and who do not know me personally and only form their notions on Stuart's report, and among these Winter ranks first. Their good opinion I wish to retain, not that I fear their ill—but my good will toward them demands it.
>
> Stuart is black at the core and will kill himself in time, but he can spit venom yet and should be hanged.

Poor overworked tragedian, with so many thorns in his crown! But the thorns' pricking was not felt as he looked up at his magnificent theater, observed the working of the hydraulic machinery, saw the sets for "Romeo and Juliet" rise smoothly from their cavern. All annoyance vanished when, on the day of the opening, he at last read in the "Tribune" and elsewhere his own announcement:

MR. EDWIN BOOTH
respectfully announces that his theater
will open
This (Wednesday) Evening, February 3,
introducing
MISS MARY McVICKER .
as Juliet,
MISS FANNY MORANT
as the Nurse,
MR. EDWIN ADAMS
as Mercutio,
MR. MARK SMITH
as Friar Lawrence,
MR. EDWIN BOOTH
as Romeo.

With a full and efficient company. The tragedy will be produced in strict accordance with historical propriety in every respect, following closely the text of Shakespeare.

The full cast was listed, and named also were all connected in any capacity with the construction of the building. So we learn that the Messrs. Renwick & Sands were the architects; that John A. Robertson had acted as superintendent of construction; that Magonigle was business manager and J. A. Booth treasurer; that Mark Smith was stage-manager and Edward Mollenhaur leader of the orchestra.

And the doors were opened wide.

# XII

## "WORTHIEST TEMPLE OF DRAMATIC ART"

THE OPENING OF BOOTH'S THEATER WAS A THEATRICAL EVENT TO bring out all adjectives from their lurking-place in thesauruses. It was—but let us turn back the pages to find that upon which William Winter, constructive critic of the "Tribune," devoted a column and a half of six-point type to an essay on the subject. Three columns of a modern newspaper would scarcely suffice to contain Mr. Winter's first hurried impressions; and remember that then the critic crouched over a desk with pen in hand and erudition in head to scratch out his views in a neat small hand. Mr. Winter's hand must have ached when he finished. Thus he began:

There had been a vile storm prevalent of rain and snow, and the streets were in a condition that was powerfully hostile to the pedestrian. Nevertheless, a great company of people— representing the culture, the magisterial dignity and the fashion of the city—assembled to witness the inauguration of the new dramatic house. Human creatures, at their best, excited by an intellectual impulse, and gathered amid surroundings that are worthy of their high mood, always present a majestic spectacle. Such a spectacle was seen last night at Booth's Theater. Glancing over the varied and animated throng, you saw many a face that study had paled and thought exalted. Grave judges were there and workers in the field of literature and patient, toiling votaries of science and artists from their land of dreams. The eyes of beauty, too, shone there with unwonted lustre, bespeaking at its heart the influence of unwonted emotion. It was an audience that would have honored any occasion in the world and its presence gave to this one an irresistible charm of intellect and refinement.

It is perhaps a pity to cut Mr. Winter short here, hardly launched on a description which went on from audience to theater, from theater to play, from play to Shakspere and from Shakspere to recognition of sublimity in general. But the reviewer of the "World" must be heard from, the composer of four solid columns (Winter must have felt he had scamped his job when he saw those four columns) on what was later, and far too briefly, to be known as the "Page Opposite Editorial." With simple finality the "World's" reporter began:

No such temple consecrate to the drama has ever been reared before. It was reserved for this latter generation and the New World to unite all the arts in a lasting testimonial and splendid monument. The individual efforts of the young American actor, so worthily shown in the building of a theater unlike any other in its perfect adaptiveness to the one purpose of dramatic art, was met by the unprecedented payment of nearly ten thousand dollars by the public to be present on the opening night to see Shakespeare's tragedy of *Romeo and Juliet,* which they had all seen many times. It was a privilege to help in the inauguration of a Shakespearian theater, and the flinging open of the white portals last night was to let a flood of new glory out upon a sodden city, in which was a promise of lasting radiance, reflecting with increased intensity from a wonderfully resplendent age. It seemed very like a wedding to the crowds of idlers that stood along the walks in Twenty-third Street and huddled together on the Sixth Avenue, forgetting the wintriness of the outside in the faery glow from the interior—warming themselves in the ardor of the scene. And so it was—the wedding of immortal genius and young enthusiasm. All the town had contributed to grace the nuptials. It was all very pretentious and showy.

One supposes it was, rather, while supposing also that the reviewer hardly felt it to be. In full flight of young enthusiasm, if not of immortal genius, he continued to a discussion of tragedy in general, pausing to note that the tragedy of the modern day was a "sickly affair" and that "Romeo and Juliet" was the "most Shakespearian of Shakespeare's tragedies."

Near the bottom of the second column, it is disturbing to notice, he becomes, without typographical notice, somebody else and returns sharply to a discussion of the theater itself. The unparalleled temple to the drama becomes "by no means an ideal theater," which, the writer notes with regret, "has been allowed to be defiled by imitated wood and imitated marble and the other little lies which cast discredit upon what is really honest and thorough in the work." What the readers of the "World" thought at this about-face one may only guess. Perhaps they suspected that the last two columns were written first, possibly by the architectural critic, and tossed happily into place as the drama-reviewer finished.

The "Herald," which had returned to the fold, at least

to the extent of realizing that there was a new theater, had time only for brief mention of "the opening of Booth's Theater—the worthiest temple which has been dedicated to dramatic art in this country since the burning of the old Park Theater." The "Herald" noted it down as "an event as gay and festive as such an event should have been," but permitted a suggestion of cattiness in its pious hope that "the premature extinction of the lights of the collossal chandelier can hardly be regarded as ominous." The "Herald" reviewer admitted his was but a hurried note and that he lacked time to give to the opening the consideration it deserved. Of the play itself he found time to write only a handsome admission that *Romeo and Juliet* has never been more magnificently produced than it was last evening."

It was natural that in the excitement of the scene and amid efforts to describe glowingly both the new house and its first audience, the play itself was somewhat neglected. In all its space, the "World" found room only to observe, "It were impossible in this notice to do critical justice to the acting of Mr. Booth and Miss McVicker." Nor did Mr. Winter, in his perhaps more scholarly critique, contribute information more exact. He permitted himself to see that Booth's performance was perhaps lacking in the "whole hearted passion and in a certain dashing manliness of personality which the Romeo of Shakespeare seems to us to possess." The "Herald" felt that both Mr. Booth and Miss McVicker had showed nervousness at first and had somewhat overacted, but that the latter was full of "rude vigor" in the balcony scene.

We must turn to another account, culled from a clipping

gone astray,[1] for a report more explicit on this interesting point. This report, doubly anonymous, reads in part:

> Mr. Booth's stately structure was inaugurated on Wednesday evening last with all the solemnity of fashion and intellect. . . . The great fan, worked by steam, slowly but surely agitated the atmosphere of the house, the massive scenery, worked by cunning machinery, set the wonderful square in Verona. Mr. Booth made the usual little speech in a beautiful suit of Sunday clothes, evidently prepared for the occasion, the hidden orchestra struck up "Hail Columbia" to fire the American heart and then amid a buzz of expectation, the grand curtain rose magnificently and revealed the most superb effective scene ever done on the American stage. The opening scene, with the loud alarm, the ringing of bells and the rush of fighting Montagues and Capulets down the frightened street, was the most vivid picture ever presented of those turbulent days when Romeo loved, Mercutio railed and Tybalt fought. The scenery throughout the piece was equally grand and impressive.
>
> The balcony scene was a gem as perfect as the soul of a poet could conceive, but it was the face of nature marred by the presence of man. Mr. Booth's inability to conceive the character of Romeo, still less to play it, was here most painfully apparent, and as Mr. Booth, after all, was the feature of the evening, despite the splendid theater, the great fan (worked by steam), the tessellated pavement, the delicious act drop and Miss Mary McVicker we will take the liberty to strip off the gauze and illusion which has veiled the central figure, upon which the future of Booth's depends, and show our readers

[1] The clipping is not identified in the Robinson Locke Collection of dramatic scrap-books, where it is preserved. It may have been taken from the New York "Clipper," files of which are missing for most of the year 1869.

what Mr. Booth knows as well as we do, viz:—that he can't play Romeo. It is a shock to see him come on with a student's stride, a slaty, bilious, self-tormenting, selfish face, which the brightness of a large massive eye cannot relieve of mingled meanness and cruelty which those uncontrollable indices, the mouth and chin, express. . . .

In such characters as Iago, where a good knowledge of stage business and a cold, passionless, icy nature are the essential dominants, Mr. Booth finds his true sphere. His elocution is unstudied, natural and attractive. He has a keen eye for stage effects and without any of the effeminate notions of ribbons and small delicacies of detail which belong to other artists, has a large graceful idea of coloring a picture which is essentially artistic and far more imposing on the public sense. But of the characters he represents he forms no conception, not even a wrong conception, for great artists may make a wrong conception so complete and pierce so thoroughly into details as to become great as a fact in art. Mr. Booth merely drifts through excellent stage business and wonderfully manœuvred machinery with hackneyed notions, caught or conveyed, without any regard to the character as a whole—

Miss Mary McVicker, for whom Mr. Booth thus gallantly sacrificed himself, we are pained to say, is in no way worthy of the sacrifice. She is no delicate geranium—

But we have already learned that she was no delicate geranium.

Stripped of its surplus of personal animus, the view here staged is approximately that held by all of Booth's detractors, who were never few. The charge that he had no real conception of his parts, that he relied chiefly on stage "business," that he merely drifted, was the charge generally made by those who could not see him as his admirers saw him.

And the view of his Romeo, so violently stated here, is not far different from that held even by his most friendly critics. Booth could not play Romeo. But the statement that he knew he could not, made in this instance with the obvious intention merely of reinforcing the writer's own view, is sober truth. On that point Edwin had no illusions. He was no stage lover. He preferred to play villains. He believed himself very bad as Romeo and probably was right in this belief. Once he seems to have said as much, explicitly. J. Rankin Towse, whose lucid criticisms bridge the gap between Booth's century and this, heard of it, at second hand. Mr. Towse himself perhaps rather hoped than believed it was true when he wrote it down in his "Sixty Years of the Theater."

He had it from E. A. Sothern, who had himself once aspired to tragedy, but who had found his place elsewhere. Mr. Towse, several years after he came to the United States in 1869, and after he had been for some time play-reviewer for the New York "Evening Post," visited Sothern in his hotel in Gramercy Park. He found Sothern chuckling reflectively and, learning that Booth had just gone out, was curious. One did not associate Booth with a reminiscent chuckle. Pressed, Sothern explained that he and Booth had been talking of Stuart—of his trickiness, his backbiting, his frequent bitter cleverness. Sothern had remembered, wryly but with amusement, how Stuart had written of his Claude Melnotte that it exhibited "all the qualities of a poker except its occasional warmth."

"I suppose," Sothern said to Booth after he had quoted that quip against himself, "that my performance of Melnotte was as bad as anything ever seen on the stage."

"Ned chuckled," Sothern said, telling the story to Towse. Then Booth spoke.

"You never saw my Romeo, did you?" he asked, simply.

But, however Booth's Romeo may have failed artistically, it drew prodigiously—aided, of course, by curiosity. Hundreds went that they might see the Italian marble in the lobby and feel the gentle currents of air set in motion by the fan (worked by steam). But most went to see Booth as Romeo and, afterward, as Othello. The receipts show it. During the first month, $43,751 came across the counter and the dip which came as "Romeo and Juliet" ran out its welcome brought the gross down only about $8,000 in March. Then, with "Othello" on the boards, the intake rose again in April, touching $44,495 and held up well in May, being only a few hundred dollars under March. It fell sharply, however, after Edwin left the stage temporarily and was followed by Edwin Adams, who played in June and July in "The Lady of Lyons," "Narcisse," and "The Marble Heart," which was still beating.

Only once during the first months of his theater did tragedy echo in Booth's life. Since the death of Wilkes and the burial of his body, rather hastily identified, under the floor of a cell in the Federal prison in Washington, the Booth family had sought to recover it. For some years their efforts were unsuccessful, but finally the pleas of the family were heard. It was arranged that representatives should go to the capital and claim the body, and Booth asked John T. Ford in Baltimore to represent him.

The last stage of Wilkes Booth's progress is recorded curtly in a telegram from Ford to Edwin, dated February 15, 1869. It is cryptic, reading merely, "Successful and in our possession." On the back the folded sheet, still preserved, is endorsed in Edwin's hand: "John's Body."

The body was again identified, so far as was then possible, and the family was convinced it was really that of Wilkes. It was buried in the family lot in Baltimore, where the grave is not marked with a headstone. The incident, which was kept from the public, brought the tragedy of 1865 flaring up again briefly in Edwin's mind, but it died away. His work, his financial problems—these would have been enough to crowd out memory of that old sadness if there had been nothing else to occupy his thoughts.

But there was something else to occupy them. On May 29, when Booth's first engagement at his own theater ended, Mary McVicker quit the stage, not to reappear upon it. On June 7, Mary and Edwin were married at Long Branch. Booth spent the summer with her there and then took to the road again. Once more checks began to flow from Chicago, from Philadelphia and Baltimore and Boston, toward New York, where they poured gently into the financial pit of Booth's Theater and seeped away.

Booth, before he left, established his wife and himself in a studio in the building which adjoined the theater, and there, for the next year or two, their life centered. Mary then began those careful ministrations to his wants which were to occupy her life for some years. She looked to his diet, supervised his bedtime, tried to curtail his consumption of tobacco and coffee, laid out each day the costume he was to wear that night. He stood it remarkably well.

The new Mary Booth and her stepdaughter did not, during the first few years, meet frequently. Edwina was in school near and afterward at Philadelphia, and she and her father kept up a loving correspondence, although they did not often meet. Some of his letters to her were among those she later published and not a few of them are touching in their revelation of Booth—shy, restrained, and harassed—trying still to write to a little girl with understanding and sympathy and lightness. One letter, written at about this time, is peculiarly touching. In it he urges that she learn to skate, that she let none of the games of childhood go untasted. "When I was a little boy," he wrote to her, "I had no opportunity to learn the different games and sports of childhood, for I was traveling most of the time, spending my winters in the South." There was no ice to skate on.

He was doing then, in fact, just what he was doing now—trailing that long and weary road. He was on it that autumn while Joseph Jefferson, with "Rip Van Winkle," played at Booth's, collecting $500 a night and still profiting the theater; while Miss Bateman acted Leah, and Hackett acted Falstaff; while Emma Waller played Meg Merrilies. Among them they kept the theater open until Booth was back. The total receipts for the year of 1869 at Booth's were $380,437, only about $1500 less than Niblo's Garden, the box-office leader of them all, had taken in with a full twelve months. Booth's, of course, had missed the month of January, always one of the best in the theater. Winter estimates the profits of the first year of operation at $102,000. It went back into amortization of debts, of course, but it had been made.

Most of the seventeen theaters in Manhattan and the four in Brooklyn were prosperous that season.[2] One newspaper estimated that the average daily attendance at Booth's alone was close to two thousand. Then there was "a theatrical fever for first rate pieces and performers which has never been equalled before since the days when Peter Stuyvesant smoked himself into undramatic slumbers." This diagnostician attributed the welcome fever to the ending of that "reign of the naked drama" which for a time had threatened to drive decent people from the theater. The "naked drama" was "The Black Crook" and tights without skirts.

Mr. Towse, who had just come over, was less optimistic. Looking around, he found as he later wrote, that in the United States—

as in the mother country, the old order of the stage was quickly passing away; the higher drama, both tragic and comic, was falling into deeper disrepute for lack of adequate interpreters and the boards were more fully occupied by modern or "social" farce or melodrama of no literary or dramatic consequence, even when entertaining.

Booth was excepted from this condemnation, of course; although Towse did not, then or after, give him the fullest meed of praise, considering him a "great, but not a very great, actor and a most accomplished artist." And when Charles Fechter came in January to play Hamlet at Niblo's,

[2] Late in December, 1931, Manhattan had only twenty-three theaters open.

...*206*

Towse excepted him, too, yet pointed out to his friends that it was not the Fechter he had known in London. Fechter had grown fat, overcome by the curse of actors.

Fechter's appearance, long after his fame had reached the American scene, was another event. When he opened, with his famous blond wig, the "World" sent not one but three reviewers: "An Admiring Critic," "A Sceptical Critic," and "A Gossiping Critic." Fechter was moderately successful, despite stiff competition. Not only was Booth playing Hamlet, his most admired rôle, but the city was full of burlesque Hamlets. At the Olympic, George L. Fox, who was one of Booth's favorite comedians, was burlesquing both the tragedians; at the Bowery, Tony Pastor had another burlesque running; the San Francisco Minstrels were being very funny about it at the Tammany; Jem Mace and John C. Heenan were presenting the duel scene hilariously, or so it seemed to their audiences, with boxing-gloves. And Charley Backus was adding to the merriment by caricaturing both Fechter and Booth, in his "Impersonations." Fechter must have found it somewhat confusing. So, for that matter, must New York.

Booth was the victor, if it was a duel. He played "to the most crowded houses which have been witnessed in any establishment in this city," according to contemporary reports. It was difficult to find standing-room; speculators sold tickets at large advances. He was gaining on his debts, slowly. "All flourishes well—only the infernal expense is perfectly barbarous," he wrote James E. Russell, critic of the "Sun." "It is overwhelming, and the devil of it is, I don't see any possible method of reducing it, now or ever."

The trouble was with those debts, with the financial foundation upon which the theater stood. Expenses of operation, although they were high, were still satisfactorily under receipts. The venture was by no means a losing one, and that thought gave consolation to the actor who continued to pour money into it; who continued to meet notes and issue new notes, and go on and on in a dizzy pursuit of solvency. Jefferson, looking at the theater, and receiving his richly earned five hundred a night, thought it a splendid affair. "It is conducted as a theater should be," he observed, "like a church behind the curtain and like a counting house in front of it." But he was wrong. In the front office it was conducted like a revival meeting.

Robertson held on grimly. He held on to Booth's checkbook. All during the autumn of 1870 he wrote for money. In September, Robertson was straining his partner's every sinew to reduce the Oakes Ames mortgage. He was writing:

. All looks well ahead and to know that we are drifting along steadily toward peace and comfort makes me contented and both of us have much, very much, to be thankful for. Can you picture the situation if our enterprise had collapsed? I dare not think what our condition would have been. Now we are beyond all chance of failure. The monument is there without a stain upon it, honorable to us both.

And would Booth hurry along with payments?

Booth's reply to this confident epistle is lost to history, but it may have been caustic. After all, "drifting" is hardly the word to use to a man who feels he is pulling a canalboat, and suspects, moreover, that the path is needlessly slippery. At any rate, Robertson was, on October 4, even more hopeful. "Five years from our starting day will see us free from debt," he promised. Meanwhile, he was going into a new enterprise, about which he was vague, but he would save Booth a slice of it. Meanwhile, also, Booth was to be "a good boy, and keep happy, bright and cosy every minute of your life." He was also to "send all the dollars you can by the 17th, as I have promised Ames $20,000 more on the 20th." He thought that, with what Booth could send and the theater could make, they would have enough. But the next week he reported bad business and even greater need for as many dollars as Booth had. Ames needed the money, wrote Robertson. Ames was associated with Robertson in the new enterprise.

Early in 1871, while Booth played Hamlet, Robertson was asking that three more notes, totaling $9,000 and made payable to himself, be sent at once. The theater had then swallowed the whole of the first year's profits, together with everything Booth had made on the road. It swallowed the second year's profits as easily. They were $85,000. The debts were, to be sure, a little reduced. Booth still did not waver in his plans for the theater, although Robertson began to urge more popular attractions as the profits went down. In January of 1871, Booth brought in a truly magnificent "Richelieu" and, although the critics complained of his supporting cast, the play ran well into March.

Later in the spring "Othello" was revived, with Lawrence Barrett as Iago, and after it "The Fool's Revenge." Barrett thereafter continued alone into April with "The Winter's Tale" and then went on to "The Man from Arlie." The house closed on July 4, however, its first summer darkness. When it reopened two months later Robertson had had his way temporarily and a distinctly popular star, Lotta, came in with "Little Nell." Although she was a profitable visitor, Booth resented her presence and the descent from the classics she implied. He was happier late in September when Charlotte Cushman emerged from ten years' retirement to play Meg Merrilies, Katharine in "Henry VIII," and Lady Macbeth. But not so much money came in.

The partners came to the parting of the ways on this question of policy. Booth had consented once, but when Robertson urged a new effort to popularize the house, he refused. They then began to discuss an ending of the partnership. Robertson suggested that Booth buy him out, as provided in the agreement, or that he buy out Booth and run the house as a variety theater. He offered Booth lands valued at $250,000 and heavily mortgaged. It was then that the accountant was called in, struggled for a time with Joseph Booth's accounts, and emerged to acknowledge himself beaten. The real estate was worth $250,000, he estimated, and as for the rest . . . who could tell?

Perhaps, with what he considered a fair offer and a promise that the house should be kept artistically as he planned it, Booth might have been glad enough to shift his burdens to other shoulders that autumn. But not for what Robertson offered; not with his beloved temple facing prostitution. He refused the offer and exercised his option to buy out his partner. According to Winter, whose estimates were checked by Booth himself, the tragedian paid $100,000 in cash and gave property valued at $140,000. He also, according to McVicker, who came into the picture later, assumed all outstanding liabilities, which even then amounted to more than the theater was to have cost in the first place. Booth lamented:

> I made him a free gift of it and now I must buy it back at this figure merely to get rid of him. He managed to get every foot of real estate out of my possession, except for the Twenty-fourth Street property, which he could not touch, it being in Edwina's name.[8]

Booth returned to his stage in December, 1871, present-ing "Julius Cæsar," and he ran it well into the early spring, at one time or another playing all three parts. Barrett played with him and was a hit as Cassius, and they made money but not enough. Booth went on through summer and autumn, acting where the money was. During the year the theater made $70,000 and Booth again gained a little on his debts. It is hard to see, looking back—it was hard for McVicker to see at the time—where all the money went; why the theater did not finally pay itself out. Perhaps it would have done so if economic conditions had remained normal. Continued general prosperity, however, would not have accorded with the luck of Edwin Booth.

It continued for a time, however, and Booth was alternately depressed and confident. One day he discovered a printing bill of $30,000 and was aghast. "This is damnable and, I think, wrong," he assured Russell. And another day, when Clarke wrote to him from London that the lease of the Lyceum there was going cheaply, he considered joining his

[8] "Life and Art of Edwin Booth." Foot-note by E. B.

brother-in-law in taking it on. Clarke painted a rosy picture and Edwin was more than half convinced, but while he still thought of it H. L. Bateman, also an American, stepped in and snapped up the lease. Bateman struggled along for a time, failing repeatedly, and then allowed an actor who had just dropped his real name, Brodribb, to persuade him that a play called "The Bells" was worth doing. So Henry Irving appeared in "The Bells" and went up to fame like a sky-rocket.

Booth confided to William Bispham that he was deadly weary of the struggle. "When that pile of granite is paid for, I'll retire and act only once in a while for recreation," he said. But it was not paid for. It occurred to him that if he could lease the house, so removing from his shoulders the tasks of management, he could devote himself utterly to paying his debts. Once clear, it would be time enough to return to producing.

This idea revolved in his mind for a time and then he consulted Junius, his brother. Would Junius care to take the theater, on lease, with the understanding that its standards were to be maintained and that, one supposes, terms would be generous? Junius thought it over and, being a confident man, decided that he would have a try at it. So, on January 30, 1873, Edwin turned the theater over to his brother for a period of five years. It was a relief to have that off his shoulders, although the shifting was really of details. "Now I play the part of a hard-hearted landlord only—and star occasionally," he explained to friends. Now he had nothing to do but struggle with his debts, play at every possible moment, and care for his wife. For Mary was not well.

A year after the marriage Mary had borne a child, a boy. Of an extremely nervous temperament, never far from hysteria, she found pregnancy a torment. It was protracted four weeks beyond the normal time and her labor, when it began, was prolonged. At length the child had to be removed with the aid of instruments and was so injured that it died within a few hours. Mary did not rally, and for days her life was despaired of. She was kept, Booth wrote a close friend, "stupefied with chloroform." Finally she began to recover and after a time regained a measure of physical strength. But her nerves did not recover fully; in her ordeal was the beginning of a disorder which, a few years later, began definitely to manifest itself. Her nervousness increased; her fits of hysteria were frequent; only Edwin could soothe her. The marriage, which had seemed to promise comfort and affection if not high romance, became another problem to be solved.

# XIII

## "THIS STUPENDOUS FIZZLE"

"NOW," SAID EDWIN BOOTH TO HIMSELF, "I CAN SIT BACK. NOW
I can take it easy. Now I am on Easy Street."

It was for some one else to worry his head about management and its thousand and one details. It was for some one else to stew over printers' bills, to listen to the complaints of actors, to gesture and direct in a world of canvas and paint. About all those details let Junius bother. Now Booth had a clear and simple, and single, problem—to pay his debts. It was complicated by no artistic burden, doubled by the protests and commands of no Richard A. Robertson. He would work and pay his debts and have his theater; and then, perhaps, he would take it over once more and produce in it. One thing at a time, said Booth, confident that he had at last found the way of life.

"It is my lookout," he wrote Jervis McEntee, in whom he sometimes confided—in return, it may be noted, for a veritable avalanche of confidence—"to quietly withdraw and draw with (!) an easy rein certain little 'ponies'—in the shape of rents, etc., etc.—into my trough." He visualized rents coming in regularly, and nothing, so far as the operation of the theater was concerned, going out. He sighed in relief and congratulated himself that his first difficulties were surmounted.

That his life had been up to then a series of premature self-congratulations very likely did not occur to Edwin. Only to one deeply imbued with pessimism can the thought come recurrently, with undiminished force and personal application, that man is born to sorrow as the sparks fly upward. Most of us keep our heads unbowed, however bloody, not so much as a result of superior endurance as because we cannot believe that bad luck is going on indefinitely overtaking us. No bad run of the cards lasts forever, we assure ourselves, and trot around our chairs for luck. Even if the next hand prove bad in turn, we are only temporarily discouraged. Another deal, we cannot but believe, will straighten things out again. To the thoroughly optimistic mind, indeed, each new evidence that misfortune dogs is but an evidence that good fortune has come nearer. Booth, for all his outward somberness, had that belief; was yet to have it for some years.

He had believed his troubles were over when he married Mary Devlin and began sky-rocketing upward toward fame; he had believed it once again when, after recovering from the first pain of his wife's death, he settled to his steady climb as an artist; his optimism came back, not a great deal weaker, when he had again recovered from sorrow, this time after his brother's crime. On each occasion he believed that his path, if less sweet, less exciting, was nevertheless clear before him. After the Winter Garden burned and he had recovered from the shock of losing so much money and so many prized possessions, he saw his path clear and free from obstacles to his new theater. Now that Robertson was eliminated, and the worries of management laid aside, the future was fair again. He could rest and go forward steadily.

The new régime at Booth's started well enough, with a production of "King John" in which both Junius and his wife, Agnes, appeared. It played to moderately good receipts; and moderately good receipts, together with payment of the rent, continued into the summer. Edwin nodded to himself with satisfaction as he toured. It was working out.

He was no financier. Stedman might have told him that all was not rosy on the economic horizon, if Stedman knew. Remembering the sustained optimism in high quarters which persisted, even unto debacle, in 1929, one questions if he did. Bispham, who was then a partner in the firm of William H. Wallace & Company, iron merchants (Bispham was the company), might have noticed a falling off in orders. Perhaps they did know and did tell him; perhaps he worried and disbelieved them. The country at large clung to its optimism. It did not realize until September 18, 1873, that another period of panic had arrived. Then the firm of Jay Cooke & Company failed; then the country was in a panic waist-deep.

The autumn of that year was one of stress and strain. Banks and brokers failed, and mercantile houses failed, and financiers found themselves in desperate need of funds. The public, alarmed, began to stay away from the theater. During the year, Booth's was to show a net loss of forty thousand dollars, although it had started well enough. Rents stopped coming in. Junius could not pay what he hadn't got.

Booth's creditors descended. They must have money. They could not renew. They were infinitely sorry; they appreciated his difficulties. They hoped that he would find others who could take over his notes and give him time. They were confident of his integrity and quite sure that he was fundamentally sound. Nevertheless they would like their money.

The business at Booth's might have been better, might even have been good enough to help its owner tide over, if Tommaso Salvini had not taken that precise moment to set the United States by its artistic ears. He came on September 16 to the Academy of Music, and almost at once, by his electric art, made himself the observed of all observers. He put Booth—yes, even Booth—in the shade for a time.

He wore his Shakspere with a difference, did Tommaso Salvini, speaking only a few words of English and playing in Italian. The critics began instantly to quarrel over him. He was, said Mr. Towse, "incomparably the greatest actor and artist I have ever seen and one who has never had an equal, probably, since the days of Garrick." He was, countered Mr. Winter, "radically false to Shakespere in ideal." And the theatergoers, if they went anywhere, went for a time to see Salvini. He was ready for them. He had felt invigorated when he first set foot upon the New York streets. "Within a few days my energy was redoubled," he observes in his memoirs. Isolina Piamonti, who played Desdemona to his Othello, probably gasped when he repeated this thought to her.

She had reason to feel alarm. Salvini's ordinary energy was quite enough. Consider, for example, Mr. Towse's description of the Lady Desdemona's death, as enacted nightly at the Academy of Music. Picture her, after one glance at her enraged lord, fleeing to the corner of the stage, holding fast to the base of the proscenium arch, and cowering. Consider:

Salvini, convulsed with fixed and flaming eyes, half crouched, slowly circled the stage toward her, muttering savagely and inarticulately as she cowered before him. Rising at last to his full height, he pounced upon her, lifted her into the air, dashed with her across the stage and through the curtains which fell behind him. You heard a crash as he flung her on the bed and growls as of a wild beast over his prey.

Even Mr. Towse admitted that this was probably not Shakspere. It was, however, "supremely, paralyzingly real." It must have been both to Signora Piamonti. Bernard Shaw, who had seen Salvini in London, says that he really stood almost still and merely suggested violent movement. But Shaw was not playing Desdemona. Young American actresses in the audience looked at one another in shocked surprise, and swore then and there that they would never play the Desdemona to such an Othello. Better, by far, the orderly interpretation of Mr. Booth, who approached the murder as a priest preparing a sacrifice. And, indeed, when Salvini returned much later to act with English support, he could not find an American actress to play with him until he promised to modify his transports.

Booth had, then, in addition to his financial worries, a new rival, his first great rival. Fechter had been aging and fat, but Salvini . . . Salvini was a redoubled Salvini. Booth observed him, chiefly from a distance, being on tour at the time, with some anxiety. Salvini, running across Booth as their travels willed, saw him and thought him admirable as Hamlet and Richelieu and Iago. He did not like him in Macbeth, pointing out: "Macbeth had barbarous and ferocious instincts and Booth was agreeable, urbane and courteous. His nature rebelled against the portrayal of that personage and he could never hope to transform himself into the ambitious, venal and sanguinary Scottish king."

Booth had no desire, at the time, to transform himself into anything but a solvent man. That was the problem of the moment and although Salvini's appearance did not help, or conduce to ease of mind, it was a drop in a bucket already full to overflowing. Where was he to get money? "Everybody wanted the money due, then and there," observes McVicker. "And Booth yielded to bad advice . . ."

McVicker goes no farther on that line, but the bad advice was contributed by one T. J. Barnett, known as "Judge Barnett," always in inverted commas, attorney-at-law, sometime dramatic critic, who had introduced himself to Booth in 1866 as the former reviewer of the "National Intelligencer" and had made the dramatic reviewer's first request—for tickets. He got them and a few days later wrote a flattering letter, discussing at length the play and Booth's acting. Booth retained those letters; it is hard to say why. Later he endorsed the envelop in which he tucked them: "First letter I remember to have received from this damned scoundrel—would to God it had been the last." The notation is dated 1875.

Any one reading the letters over finds it hard to understand what moved Booth to save them, unless he saved everything. They were wandering letters, proceeding from a cluttered mind, and no amount of flattery should have disguised from an astute recipient that their author was hardly worth taking very seriously. Booth was simply not astute. He proved it when that autumn he turned to Barnett for aid. Why he chose Barnett is not evident. No scrap remains to reveal the motivation of this curious choice—made the more curious by the fact that Booth did not lack friends who were at home in the world of finance and hence able to advise, at least to a competent attorney. But Booth employed Barnett, apparently, as a general man of affairs, empowered to sell the theater if possible, to stave off bankruptcy if he could, to save what might be saved.

What he did do, so far as can now be ascertained, was to interview every one within reach and write letters. He wrote the letters to Booth. He wrote in 1873 and 1874 and 1875. He was negotiating. The progress of those negotiations, and their exact purpose, is hazily obscured by Mr. Barnett's laborious mind, to say nothing of his laborious chirography; to say nothing of his habit of writing up and down, across and back, on both sides of dozens of sheets of paper, numbered blithely, obscurely, and frequently incorrectly. Booth never seems to have known precisely what it was all about; as Barnett bombarded him with explanations, he grew, understandably, only the more confused. But he followed Barnett's legal advice, whenever he got a glimmer of what the advice was.

Study of one of these letters—hardly characteristic, because of its brevity—will give some idea of Booth's problems. This is dated October 21, 1873, which was near the beginning of Barnett's labors. It may be well to remember, in starting, that this is a business letter, from counselor to client. It reads:

I do not think that you are drooping even, much less crushed, in your spirits; and I always supposed you to be more assured under a heavy blow than under "little annoyances."
"Better to sink beneath the shock,
    Than moulder, piecemeal, on a rock"
is ever the motto of brave souls. All experience must be bought. It is the rudder of life and is often its best treasure. Youth don't listen, won't heed. When the blood burns and hope is high and ambition strong, the gallant mind, restless as the wind and aspiring as the eagle, sweeps to its point, reckless as impulse itself, presently the "golden mean" of life is reached; which is its safe channel.

It comes to almost every adventurous man to sink, now and then, in the sea of existence—but not to drown, until the third plunge comes; which is said to wind up the charm. You have had your winter of troubles with Stuart—now this; beyond must be clear, safe sailing, if you keep your health and popularity.

Barnett industriously played Polonius to Booth's Hamlet for several more pages, which shall be forgotten, before he reached the matter of business which had prompted him to write. He then lapsed into a discussion of mortgages, efforts to sell, notes due, conferences with Robertson and Ames and a dozen others, compared with which his philosophical outpourings are succinct and expressive. It was evident that he had failed to sell the property. A few weeks later he suggested that Booth give it away. Booth may have swallowed

once or twice. Then he did give it away. McVicker, who is a
tiny light in the darkness, notes that "on November 14, 1873,
Booth conveyed the entire property for no consideration,
being led to believe that it would be protected and carried
until a favorable sale could be made and the property pay
the debts."

The actual date of the conveyance was November 12;
the recipient of Booth's generosity was Clark Bell. Clark Bell
thereafter wanders through Barnett's letters as vaguely as
the lawyer's poetic quotations. Booth finally believed Bell a
"villain"; "Old B has given him my measure and he knows
all the business is a muddle in my brain and tries to make
me think he has made a sacrifice in my behalf—the villain,"
Edwin later wrote; but whether Bell was another of Booth's
misfortunes or a good friend cannot even be guessed. It
is only certain that the transfer of the property, whatever its
purpose, did not solve matters. In December, on the contrary,
we find Barnett again writing:

> Since the middle of last September I have devoted myself
> to the single object of carrying over your property—until final
> sale to Mr. Bell. The Wormsers threaten every day.[1] The dan-
> ger to you is the deficiency judgement which the Ames estate
> I fear would get if the property were sold on this market. They
> have dawdled on strangely. Today I write them a letter of
> which the enclosed is a copy—if they still act the dog in the
> manger, you must go into bankruptcy.

The inclosed letter, in Barnett's best style, pointed out
that Edwin Booth was a great actor and an ornament to the
Shaksperian stage.

---

[1] Simon Wormser was one of the mortgagees.

Barnett was right about one thing, at least. On January 26, 1874, Booth, still on his lawyer's advice, filed a voluntary petition in bankruptcy in the United States District Court. The newspaper summaries of the petition show liabilities totaling something like two hundred thousand dollars, most of it owed to the estate of Oakes Ames, part to Robertson. Assets consisted almost solely of personal property. The "Herald" lists jewelry, books, pictures, chandeliers, objects of vertu, stock and professional wardrobes . . . and a pair of dumb-bells. The total value of all this was under ten thousand dollars. The "Tribune," not mentioning the dumb-bells, estimated the assets at about thirty-five hundred dollars, but contributed a eulogy by Winter, in which it was remarked that Edwin Booth was a great actor and an ornament to the Shaksperian stage.

Junius operated the theater until April 7 of that year and went bankrupt in turn. He conveyed his lease to Jarrett & Palmer (Henry C. Jarrett and Henry D. Palmer), William M. Pritchard, referee in bankruptcy, and Clark Bell concurring.

But this did not end it. Barnett continued to straighten things out. The point now seems to have been to keep the theater in the hands of Bell, from whom it might be reclaimed, and the referee. One more letter from Barnett, although it has, characteristically, not overmuch to do with the case, must be published, if merely as a literary curiosity. It is dated March 9, 1874 and reads:

DEAR EDWIN—
Much has been gained today. Things now brighten. I think Bell is forcibly disposed of. All that remains now on that

score is to arrest the foreclosure. Then we will see how far the
theater will go for us. All which then remains will be to wholly
conciliate Ames if possible; and to fight R. A. R. in the courts
if need be. As to the Bank, if we reduce the debt to them, we
are all O. K. Don't forget the squib I suggested for the Chicago Times. Now the gist of the battle is on the foreclosure.
D—n them!! They begun those foreclosures last September.
They ain't through yet, with all their cash, conspiracy and skill.
Advance our standards now! No whine, no skulk! As to
R. A. R., duplicitus and false, still bait him on. He has done
his spite. He has even gone so far as to tell the M & M [Mer-
chants and Mechanics] Bank that he has got the official figures
of your receipts in Boston and Philadelphia. He is a low spy.
But calm, slow, cool, sure, patient *time.*

"Time! Time!
Tomb-builder and avenger!
Soother, watchman, nurse!
Unraveller at last of skeins
And knots. Father of patience,
Next to God, the Judge, who slowly sees
And patiently doth watch,
Upbraid not Time! He is God's
Outlook on our tower; on the outer work
T'wixt Earth and Heaven."
In real good spirits,
Yours ever,
B

Love to Both.

Barnett retained his spirits, and Booth his debts, through
the spring and summer, neither being perceptibly diminished. Barnett did worry a little in August, while continuing
his vague interviews and endless meanderings, his flow of
cheery advice and quotations from Shakspere and Talley-

rand. He heard that McVicker did not believe he was doing well by Booth. McVicker probably thought that that conveyance so soon before bankruptcy had an ugly look, and regretted Booth was in it. Barnett could hardly believe McVicker thought that.

But Booth, at last, was beginning to be disturbed. He turned to McVicker, and his father-in-law, being naturally interested, particularly as Mary's money was going with her husband's, entered the picture. He threw out the first plank of a raft on which Booth was finally to float to shore from the turbulent waves which had, to him so mysteriously, come into being on the "puddle" he had first essayed to cross.

But Booth, in the autumn of 1874, was still utterly confused. He wrote to McEntee from Cos Cob, where he had spent the summer, apparently in answer to a request from the artist to be told how matters stood. Booth said that "were we lounging in hammocks, I might give you some idea of how I stand with the world." He continued:

> But to put it on paper in an intelligent shape would require several sheets and more patience than I can control—for the mere recital of the details of this complicated business puts me into such a torrent of vowels and consonants, so oddly placed, as don't look well on paper—tho breathed to the gentle winds are not of much consequence.

He agreed that it was a relief to be no longer managing. All would have been well, he thought—

> had the thousands I sent home every year been properly applied. But it's all up, now. I will be forced, doubtless, to pay the debts of another in addition to my own. It does not break

my sleep, however; I care too little for the world's jabs and knocks—I'm used to the severest kind of them.

But it was all, he added, "a stupendous fizzle." The loss of the wealth and labor was the least of his disappointments. His beautiful plans had gone, too. Still, so he told Bispham, "it is by no means the heaviest blow my life has felt," which was the truest of simple statements. What was bankruptcy to Booth? He had the consciousness that he had done what seemed to him to be his duty. To Bispham he wrote:

Since the talent God has given me can be made available for no other purpose, I believe the object to which I devote it to be worthy of self-sacrifice. I gave up all that men hold dearest, wealth and luxurious ease; nor do I complain because that unlucky slip twixt cup and lip has spilled all my tea. With a continuance of health and popularity the good Lord has thus far blessed me with, I will pay every sou and exclaim with Don Cæsar—though in a different spirit—"I've done great things. If you doubt me, ask my creditors." I see some years of hard work before me, all for a "dead horse," too. Not a very cheering prospect.

But he did mind the slip. He was bitter—bitter at Robertson and Bell and Barnett. It was not softening the blow to realize, as McVicker probably pointed out to him, as McVicker certainly explained to Winter, that it was all unnecessary. McVicker writes:

There is no doubt, had Booth been in the hands of proper attorneys, his property could have been saved for him, for such was its true value it could have been bonded for all the indebtedness, but Booth had no faculty for such matters. Had Booth's financial affairs been conducted with anything like the ability he displayed in artistic matters, only success would have been the result; but, unfortunately, he was of a confiding nature.[2]

With McVicker taking a hand, the affair was finally wound up the next spring. The theater went, on foreclosure, to the Ames estate in February, and McVicker bought up Booth's debts. In March Booth was discharged from bankruptcy and although there were, for some years afterward, occasional squabbles about notes, the slate was washed very nearly clean. Booth and the slate together; he had nothing left except his profession, his health (which was not too good), his daughter, and an ill wife. Those things, and debts to McVicker, which he eventually paid. He had put in a large sum of money and limitless enthusiasm. Now he had nothing of it left. His dream of a temple to the theatrical art was gone; his dream of a theater dedicated to Shakspere. He had quite lost his interest in management. It was a stupendous fizzle.

The theater which was to have meant so much remained as a monument to the fizzle for about ten years longer. It continued to bear Booth's name, although in the autumn of 1876 he sought an injunction against Jarrett & Palmer, restraining them from using the name further, contending that he had an exclusive right to it. The Court of County Pleas listened and held against him, so the theater continued as Booth's. Jarrett & Palmer paid $40,000 a year for it to the Ames estate and made money, keeping up its tone fairly well until near the end of its life. Booth played there himself on several occasions, and so did many others: John McCullough,

---

[2] "Life and Art of Edwin Booth." Foot-note by J. H. McV.

Charlotte Cushman, Jefferson, Clarke, Matilda Heron, Adelaide Nielson, Clara Morris, E. L. Davenport, Boucicault, Barrett, Agnes Booth; the roster is long.

The theater was sold by Ames in 1881 to the same Page who had sold the site to Booth. Page paid $550,000 for it, and two years later, shops took the place of the "temple."

# XIV

## DUCATS—AND A DESTRUCTIVE CRITIC

AND NOW AGAIN BOOTH FELT THE WORST WAS OVER. HE EMERGED from another engulfing misfortune, once more with the sympathy of the public, once more called to its attention by forces outside his art. Now he would end his days peacefully, playing and making money, paying his debts, smoking his pipe; now he might grow serenely old (he was only a little over forty, but it was an old forty) with his wife beside him and his young daughter growing up. Nothing more could happen to him, surely. That summer he went to Cos Cob and rested, and that it was over and done with was a relief. Even acknowledged failure, even the complete fiasco to which it had all come, was better than the endless struggle. He knew where he was, at last, as he stretched in a hammock at Cos Cob and got his pipe going well.

His wife was better that year, her nervousness less acute. A friend of his who knew about such things— Dr. A. O. Kellogg, head of the Hudson River State Hospital for the Insane at Poughkeepsie—dropped in for a short stay late in the summer. His visit was not professional. He and Booth had struck up a friendship some time before, in connection with an essay by the psychiatrist on insanity in

Darling of Misfortune

Shakspere's characters. They had become great friends; and very likely Booth was glad of a friendly word of advice now and then about Mary. But Mary was growing no worse and her condition was merely unfortunate, not alarming. It was not such as would keep Booth from the restful peace of his hammock.

The two men were talking together, pleasantly enough, one day in mid-August when one of them suggested a turn behind a lively mare which Booth had recently acquired. It seemed a pleasant way to spend the rest of the afternoon. They trotted off, Booth driving. They reached the top of a hill; then something blew close to the nose of the skittish three-year-old. She reared and plunged. Booth took a firm grip of the reins and tried to quiet her. The other half of the team observed for a moment the queer antics of his partner and then was nervous in his turn. Suddenly the two dashed away, downhill.

Booth dragged angrily at the reins. The light buggy swayed from side to side of the road. He tugged harder. Then the head-stall broke. The mare and her team-mate plunged on at new speed. The buggy swayed perilously; it missed a ditch on one side, swayed toward that on the other, missed it by the fraction of an inch, swayed back . . . was over! Booth flew out of it against a telephone pole. Kellogg held fast to the wreckage and went plunging on down the road. At the bottom there was a final crash and the doctor hauled himself out of splintered boards and broken wheels, not much hurt. He looked around for Booth. There was no Booth. Horrified, he began to plod up the hill, scratched and bleeding.

"Booth! Booth! Are you dead?" he shouted.

Booth was not dead and even in his battered state almost chuckled over the cry. Then he answered feebly. Dr. Kellogg got him home, half conscious. A garbled report of the accident reached New York that evening. Booth was dead!

Booth was not dead. He had a broken arm and several broken ribs and innumerable bruises; he had some internal injuries which alarmed his physicians, but he was not dead. His recovery was slow, however, and it was weeks before the anxiety of his friends was entirely allayed. Newspapers sent interviewers to inquire about him and one actually saw Booth, a rare event in the life of a newspaper man in those days, unless he paid for his seat. Booth assured the reporter for the "Sun" that he was doing as well as could be expected. He expressed some astonishment that he was so badly injured. He had, he said, "been thrown out of wagons, over horses' heads, fallen twice through stage traps and walked out of a second floor window in an unfinished house"—truly an amazing career in minor mishaps, his—but never been badly injured before. It is possible that Booth exaggerated.

He had signed a contract to appear at Daly's early in October, the new Daly's; the old had burned in the autumn of 1873. He was forced to postpone his appearance, and when he returned to the stage on October 25, three weeks after his scheduled time, it was with his arm still in a sling. He was pale and worn. The audience was sorry for him, and greeted him with prolonged applause. There was something infinitely appealing about the man: he passed through catastrophe and bankruptcy and well-nigh fatal accident, and emerged by no means unscathed but with his head up. He had that quality of courage which is loved in the theater. Nothing could down him.

His latest misfortunes had prepared a special welcome, of course. The "Daily Graphic," a few days before he appeared, had published a warm eulogy, hailing him once more as "the greatest living American tragedian and the greatest Hamlet in the world" and recalling to its readers his "undeserved financial embarrassment," together with the other woes which had overtaken him. It even described his appearance anew, reminding any who might have forgotten that his face was "not only beautiful, but had precisely that style of beauty which is best adapted for stage effects."

And the "Evening Telegram" joined in the advance rejoicing, speaking of his happy recovery from his serious injuries and his projected appearance at Daly's as Hamlet. And it added: "At Booth's theater, reared by him to be a temple forever dedicated to the legitimate, Mr. G. L. Fox will jump through policemen, pop up from traps, play jokes on innocent citizens and go through all the intricate performances necessary to show 'The Adventures of Humpty-Dumpty in Every Clime.'"

So was the altar of the temple profaned, under Jarrett & Palmer. But it must have been rather amusing to see Mr. Fox "jump through policemen." A lost art, one fears.

Booth remained at Daly's for several weeks, getting his usual fifty per cent of the gross, and then went on tour under the management of John T. Ford, playing through the South with a company. The days of the visiting star and the resident stock company were passing. Booth appeared in Baltimore, whither Washington lovers of tragedy flocked to see him, and then started around the circuit, visiting Richmond, Charlotte, Columbia, Augusta, Charleston, Atlanta, Nashville, and many other communities before the company was disbanded on March 3. After that, Booth continued, without the company, to appear in Louisville, Cincinnati, and Chicago, where his father-in-law starred him in an engagement beginning April 6.

The season, while arduous, and especially so to a man still weak from serious injuries, was very profitable and the proceeds helped reduce his debt to McVicker. He finished in Chicago, traded the Cos Cob property for property in the Western city, and late in the summer traveled West to San Francisco. He was there, he wrote McEntee, just twenty years after he had left to try his luck in the East. He recalled his draft for five hundred dollars and remarked that he was not, now, much better off. He added:

True, I have done something—or rather I have tried to do something—for art, but when that hundred years have rolled by, I doubt if you'll find Edwin Booth on the art list—some centennialiated McEntee will refuse me admittance for being merely a profane stage player, while the "gorgeous temple of Dramatic Art" will have been long ago converted into a worse house of some sort.

It reads like a slap at McEntee, but if it were so intended, which is doubtful, it probably made no great impression on that industrious, conscientious, and not greatly inspired artist. He was a meek and patient man, Jervis McEntee.

In California, Booth came under the management of John McCullough, one of the lesser, but still remembered, tragedians of his day. McCullough was striving to wring from management the financial security acting had not given him. He was touchingly grateful that Booth would act for him, for he knew that the tragedian had had other offers. But Edwin had promised that when he appeared in the far West it would be as McCullough's star.

Booth opened in San Francisco early in September and was greeted as a favorite son come home. He was the city's own; unforgotten were the days he had played there, and gone hungry there; unforgotten by dozens of feature-writers for the newspapers, by many men who were, by twenty years, not so young as they had been. The theater was crowded nightly for eight weeks. The receipts averaged twelve thousand dollars a week, a very satisfactory average, even now, for the usual dramatic offering; phenomenal in those days of lower prices. "The engagement was the most remunerative that had ever been known on the dramatic, as distinguished from the operatic, stage of America." Booth's share ran close to six thousand dollars a week.

It occurred to Booth as he wandered the streets of the new San Francisco, that he was getting on. Everything was changed. Handsome buildings stood where shacks had been. He looked with particular interest for the site of one of those shacks. There had been a shack which stood magnificently in a considerable lot which a boy and an elder man had called "the ranch." He found the place. A tenement-house was built on it and it was in a back street. It was hard to remember how he and Dave Anderson had cooked and swept and lived carelessly there, before anything had happened to him.

He left San Francisco immediately on the termination of his engagement and came back, not by way of the Isthmus this time, to open in New York on November 20, under the management of McVicker. He appeared at the Lyceum Theater in Fourteenth Street. That is one of the comparatively few in which he played left standing in 1932. It is now the home of the Civic Repertory group.

Booth played at both the Lyceum and the Academy of Music until January, remaining under the management of McVicker, that probably having been stipulated in the agreement between the two, and being clearly to the advantage of both. Business was only fairly good after December 5, when the Brooklyn Theater burned during a performance, with the loss of three hundred lives, and New York was left chary of trusting itself to the playhouse.

In January he returned to the road, playing this time in the East.

According to one estimate,[1] Booth made, as his share, more than seventy-two thousand dollars from the beginning of the Lyceum engagement to the close of his season in May, 1877, this sum being exclusive of his profits on the coast. With them his seasonal profit was close to a hundred and twenty thousand dollars and from his appearance at Daly's in 1875 to his completion of the 1876-77 tour he made, Asia tells us, enough to discharge his debt and stand once more clear with the world.

[1] Made by Sally MacDougall in the "Century Magazine," December, 1928, and purporting to be based on McVicker's records.

Booth rested that summer at the home of E. C. Benedict at Greenwich and in the autumn returned to touring. His engagements took him to Philadelphia and Baltimore and then through the middle West. He seemed now, truly, on a straight road. Only work and the accumulation of "ducats" occupied him; for many months there was no Booth misfortune for the newspapers to report. He played through that season, rested that summer, leased and appeared in his own theater the next autumn, toured again under the management of McVicker late in 1877 and in 1878, all without incident. This is perhaps the longest period of unbroken quiet in his life. Nothing happened until April of 1878, when he opened at his father-in-law's theater in Chicago.

He was playing there on April 23, as Richard. The audience was engrossed; Booth was deep in his part. Suddenly the silence was broken by the report of a pistol. A canvas "flat" behind Booth shuddered as a bullet passed through it. There was another shot. Booth heard it whine past his head.

He had looked up toward the balcony as the first shot was fired. He saw the flash of the second. He advanced to the front of the stage and pointed. But his heroism was unnecessary. Already men had seized the marksman and prevented his firing the third shot, for which he had taken aim. He was hustled away while Booth, still outwardly calm, returned to his dressing-room. After reassuring his wife, the actor returned to the stage and continued his part.

The man under arrest identified himself as Mark Gray (his name seems to have been Mark Gray Lyon) and told a disconnected story. He was, he revealed, a dry-goods clerk in St. Louis when it suddenly came to him that he must shoot Edwin Booth. He further hinted darkly that he had good—oh, very good—reason for his act and talked of defending the honor of a female relative. He did not deny that the relative was his sister. All this was, in due course, printed in Chicago and elsewhere, but probably not very widely believed. Gray was too obviously unbalanced mentally.

Booth himself took the charges more seriously than any one, after his initial calm had worn through. He wrote Anderson, lamenting the "filthy scandals" which were being circulated and explaining that Gray thought himself "a great tragic genius, mad on the subject of acting." Gray intimated, along with his other intimations, that he was defending not only the female relative but William Shakspere, therewith shedding a new light on the term "destructive critic."

The affair brought out the largest head-lines in many newspapers, occupying four and five columns on the front pages of the Chicago journals, and it was generally taken seriously. Some, however, doubted and Booth condemned those who "throw doubt upon the terrible fact by calling it an advertising trick." He thought such suspicious persons "little souled" and their comments increased his nervousness until, as he wrote Stedman, "his temporary self control gave way to highly nervous excitement." But that, too, passed.

After examination, Gray, or Lyon, was removed from jail to an asylum at Elgin. Before he was taken there, however, he found opportunity to write Booth and to tell him that he must pay nine hundred dollars, or he would "dy."

Further incarceration gave him a calmer outlook, however, and late in the year he wrote again, thus:

Dear Sir—coming to look over this unpleasantness in a rational light I find you were right when you quoted from Hector O. Hallaron, "Mark, you got the wrong pig by the ear." Well, as the learned "heads" say we all are not infallible, hence it is human to err. And to forgive is divine.

Mr. Booth, I seen it announced in papers that you are taking a rest until the 1st of March. If you take in Chicago I hope you'll pay me a visit; then we will talk this matter over and understand one another in the future.

My cous. Jno. Rainey of Chicago paid me a visit three weeks ago he said he can liberate me through the law his brother-in-law is studying law under Noyrs one of the most prominent men in the legal fraternity. I hate law and think the following proverbs are well applied to law at the present time

"Fear not the law but the judge. Go before God with justice, before the judge with money."

I wish you a happy new year and many of them.

I remain sincerely and affectionately yours in friendship, harmony and peace.

MARK GRAY LYON,

care asylum.            Elgin, Ill.

He wrote several more letters, in similar vein, and Booth's first real fear of him diminished. Eventually he made no objection when the question of his assailant's parole came up, nor is there any record that Lyon showed further inclination to criticize with firearms.

Booth's somewhat odd humor, indeed, asserted itself in after years and he had one of the recovered bullets set in a gold cartridge cap, which was engraved: "From Mark Gray

.. . .*238*

to Edwin Booth. April 23, 1879." He wore this almost constantly thereafter. Perhaps it gratified his love of word-juggling, so evident in all his letters. It is grieving to report in this connection, that he once wrote Anderson at a time when the elder actor was considering some investment in a match factory, and mentioned the plan to start a "match-ri-money-all factory." Beyond this it is, one hopes, impossible to pun.

And after the near-tragedy in Chicago, Booth toured again, without adventure, and edited prompt-books of his plays, in association with William Winter. During the autumn and winter he played in New York and out of it, and in the early spring he appeared again at his own theater. But by then he was looking forward to a new professional adventure. The next autumn he wrote Anderson: "I shall try my British luck once more, though I have not much faith in the lottery over there."

# XV

## MR. BOOTH ARRANGES

SOMETIMES BOOTH WOULD WORK LONG AND HARD TO BRING something about and then afterward assure his friends that it had merely happened. "Chance," it will be remembered, had directed his steps to the stage. Partly, no doubt, this attitude was the economy of an indolent man, easily bored by details. After something had been accomplished he preferred to forget the steps which had led to the accomplishment; it was somehow brighter and more satisfying if he could think of it as emerging in full glory from a cloudless sky. It would have been a bother to tell interested friends that he had done this and then this and then that, until finally the other came about.

One may suspect, too, that there was another source, a source by Booth unsuspected, for this habit. We know how shy a man he was, and how self-conscious. In a man so burdened the fear of appearing ridiculous is always alive. And to such a one there seems always something ridiculous in a man who tries very hard and fails. The mountain labored and brought forth a mouse; and that was, undeniably, a trifle ridiculous of the mountain. But if the mountain were quite unconscious—why, then the mouse would be merely a mouse, no more absurd than most mice, and there would be no necessity of pretending that it was subtly an elephant.

Similarly, if Edwin Booth planned and schemed and wrote letters to prepare a reception for himself in London in 1880 and then that London appearance turned out to be another stupendous fizzle, Booth would look, he felt, very absurd. He wished things to come to him unsought; the world cannot better compliment a man than by giving him that for which he is too indifferent, too detached, to ask. And with no intention to deceive, Booth could pretend to himself, when something did come, that he had not begged for it, and he could give that impression to others, too. Still with no intention to deceive, and only for the good of his own soul. He must have, for himself, some explanation of failure, and lack of effort is always an excellent explanation, particularly if it be noted in advance.

· It is not surprising in the case of Booth, to discover that he worked eighteen months or more to bring about what he hoped would be an English triumph and then suggested · that it was merely something which had happened to him. He might write to a correspondent whose name is hopelessly lost in Booth's hasty chirography that he went to England "more for pleasure than for professional ends" but was induced to accept a flattering offer. He might know, as a mere matter of fact, that he had written letter after letter to intermediaries; that he had written to Henry Irving at the Lyceum; that he had consulted agents, and negotiated with one Walter Gooch. And still only a person insensitive to the dodges of a sensitive spirit which must keep itself warm in a cold world would think of Booth as falsifying.

Out of all these negotiations, which began early in 1879 or perhaps before, grew, after an· initial disappointment, a very real triumph. Out of them grew two visits to England and a tour of the Continent, the latter being all triumph; and it is largely because of these that we may think of Booth as a world figure in his art. However great his successes in his own country before 1880, and they were very great, Booth remained up to that time a provincial figure. He might be the foremost actor of the United States, but that did not prove that he was one of the foremost actors of the world; it did not make him one of that small company of international stars, a company which shines with the glitter of such names as Bernhardt and Duse, Salvini, and, in a measure, Henry Irving.

The weight of influence had not yet shifted across the Atlantic in things theatrical; it was not to shift, indeed, until new methods and new materials had played their part in changing the stage, in so far as it is a living stage, to a thing hardly to be recognized by Booth and his peers and not recognized by the few of their direct successors who still carry on a losing battle for old traditions.

Booth felt, as he had felt in 1860, but with far more reason, that he had done what he could for his fame and his art, within the boundaries of his own country. All that he thought was true in 1860, about himself, was true in 1880. He no longer, to be sure, believed that art was to be found only in the European capitals. He did feel that he could go no higher in the United ·States. He had played there all his rôles, a hundred times over. He had an artistic priority which there was none to challenge. He had given all he had to producing and could not hope to surpass himself in that endeavor. Now he needed new worlds to conquer; in 1860 he had only thought he needed them.

And in 1880, if ever, was the time to conquer those new worlds. Nothing held him in the United States. His debts were paid and his theater was gone. He was still at the height of his powers, but he knew that he could not indefinitely remain there. In a few more years he would be too old for Hamlet, could not hope to suggest, in form and feature, the lithe, unhappy youth who was his Dane. (It is even possible that he had then already waited a few years too long. But he did not think so.) Even his domestic life urged him to make the attempt at this time. Mrs. Booth's condition was again unsatisfactory; often she was hardly herself mentally; physically she was far from well. Treatment had availed nothing, but some physicians felt that she might be improved by a voyage, by a complete change of scene.

At that time, in London, Henry Irving was at the height of his fame at the Lyceum, which he now managed. His first triumph in "The Bells" had been followed by successes in Shaksperian rôles. He was devoted, almost as utterly as Booth, to "the legitimate"—as Bernard Shaw was later scathingly to note, while denying that "the legitimate" was in the least legitimate, when compared with Henrik Ibsen or even, for that matter, with Bernard Shaw. And Booth felt that Irving might feel much as he did, that it was time to conquer new worlds. He heard rumors that Irving might decide to visit America, in search of greater fame and a more generous outpouring of ducats.

It seemed a fortunate coincidence that the two foremost tragedians of the English-speaking stage should at one moment stand ready for new efforts. Booth had what seemed to him a happy idea; he had had it once before, while he still managed his own theater, and it had not worked out happily, but this was a better time for it. Why might not he and Irving exchange countries for a time? Why not make Irving's appearance in the United States and Booth's in England coincide? Why not, in short, have an "exchange of pulpits"?

Booth could think of no reason against this project, however phrased. He turned to Stedman, who had friends in England. Stedman thought the idea excellent and at Booth's suggestion wrote, early in the spring of 1879, to George Washburn Smalley, London correspondent for the "Tribune" and the author of several volumes of little sketches, part essay, part descriptive article. Smalley, whose pride was that he knew everybody in London worth knowing, knew Irving well.

Stedman hesitated to trespass on "the comity of our friendship," when he wrote to Smalley and edged otherwise a little awkwardly into the matter with which he was concerned, but he eventually reached the point:

Mr. Edwin Booth and myself long have been intimate and every day that I have known him has added to my respect for his talents, his character and accomplishments, and especially for his exquisite sense of all the modest and courteous proprieties which mark the true gentleman. His delicacy and reserve are notable; he is at the opposite extreme from the lesser lights of the stage who long to be always glaring in the eyes of the world.

For several years he has been urged to visit England professionally, and various managers, English and American, have made all sorts of offers to tempt him into London engagements. All these he has steadfastly declined, feeling that there would be an attempt made to make a furor over him, set him up as the "leading American tragedian" and evoke some sort of rivalry between himself and the great genius of your stage, within the latter's own domain.

He now learns that there is talk of Mr. Irving's visiting America next year. He tells me that he has nearly determined to write a personal and fraternal letter to Mr. Irving, having in view his (Booth's) own trip to England and endeavoring to make some arrangements so that it can be timed during Mr. Irving's absence; something, I think, like an "exchange of pulpits" between two preachers. He would long to act in the Lyceum Theater, if at all—a place honored by Irving's management and so complete in all those appurtenances for which Booth made his own theater unique in this country. Above all, he don't want to be "managed" or heralded by his in-law, Clarke, who now runs two theaters in London; would like to appear quietly and on his own merits, if at all. Of course Booth, like myself, is familiar with your letters, which have recorded and described Irving's impersonations from time to time. He has an idea, and so have I, that you may have the pleasure of meeting Irving often and on rather intimate terms. If so, it would be natural for Mr. I. to speak to you of Mr. Booth's letter. Should he do so, I think you know enough, without any statements, of Mr. Booth's gentle and unsullied character to assure Mr. Irving that whatever Mr. B. shall write, may be taken without reserve as the fresh and trustworthy expression of an honorable man. If you could do anything which would make Americans to see and hear your great and scholarly actor, whose salutation here has long been made for him, you would bestow upon our stage lovers a boon that would insure you their gratitude. And if Edwin Booth should appear in London, now, in the strength and beauty of his prime, I am sure that his season there would be satisfactory to your own feelings and honorable to the country of which you are a kind of "lay-plenipotentiary."

The matter was, evidently, one to be approached with great circumlocution and rather anxious observation of "the modest and courteous proprieties which mark the true gentleman." We find that approach repeated in Booth's letter to Irving, which was duly written on March 28, 1879, and forwarded after Stedman had approved. It read:

*68 Madison Avenue*

HENRY IRVING, ESQ.

DEAR SIR:

Contemplating a visit to Europe in the summer of 1880 and surmising that it may serve your convenience to come at that time where "you have been hotly called for," I venture to suggest for your consideration a plan which has but recently occurred to me, but which may not accord with your arrangements or views of business and may seem impracticable—if not absurd.

I am solicited, not by a few managers (and others with speculation in their eyes) to revisit London, while many disinterested friends, on both sides, have long urged me to go, but domestic and other causes have prevented me till now from entertaining such a project.

Detesting even the mere appearance of rivalry, I have remained deaf to many flattering offers, preferring to place before you—as a lover of the art we both are striving to advance—the proposition that I shall go to your theater during your professional visit to this country, to perform under your management for a stated number of weeks and on such conditions as shall be mutually advantageous.

I have now no theater to offer you in exchange for such a courtesy, but whatever service I may be able to render you among my countrymen I will cheerfully perform; my influence may not be very extensive, but you really need no more than your name already bears with it to secure the favor of all cultivated Americans.

This is a fertile field where you may be sure of a rich harvest of "ducats" to gild withal the laurels you will gather here, while I shall be contented with the endorsement of the British public (should I be so fortunate as to obtain it) and such emolument as will be consistent with your managerial expenses, which I know from severe experience must be great. With this knowledge I suspect that my desire to perform but three nights (or four at most) during the week will be objectionable even if the main feature of my proposition should receive your favorable consideration.

Like yourself, I have worked hard for many years and though my physical strength is equal to the nightly demands upon it, my nervous reservoir requires to be replenished by alternate days of rest.

This relief, with surroundings already prepared for the plays which comprise my repertory (I mean your present stock of scenery, costumes, etc.—no additional expense) and such actors as your judgement could select, would greatly enhance my comfort and consequently aid my acting. Of such advantages I very naturally desire to avail myself rather than to risk the danger of having a "scratch" company with its attendant cares.

A letter just received from my sister, Mrs. Clarke—in which she expresses her great interest in your Hamlet—advises me to make no engagement but to visit Europe as a tourist and to look about me, but I would feel more secure in going equipped and prepared for action, to one whose æsthetic sympathies are in harmony with my own than in "taking the chances" with any mere showman.

During the early days of my control of Booth's Theater, my business manager wrote to you relative to performing there, but your silence convinced me the letter never reached you. When you do come, I advise you to appear first in that house, for though, since I lost it, it has shared the desecration of many a "hallowed fame" it still retains, nor can it ever entirely lose, its Shakespearian prestige.

The son of a Boston manager, a Mr. Tompkins, may have already broached the subject of this letter to you; he has lately sailed for England partly, I presume, to negotiate with you for his father's theater. I regret having mentioned the matter to him, for it would be better to keep it from the public until near its consummation—if this should lead to such an agreeable conclusion—but at the time I spoke of it the idea was but barely taking form.

Sincerely wishing for you a happier result than my unfortunate efforts at management attained, and hoping to hear from you by early mail, I am,

Truly yours,
EDWIN BOOTH.

P.S. My friend, Mr. Stedman, the poet, with whom I have consulted, has written on this subject to Mr. Smalley, with whom, I presume, you are acquainted.

Irving was a very difficult man to bring to a final decision[1] but Booth did not know that. He waited, at first optimistically, then with growing surprise, but no answer came. Booth's next step was again toward Stedman, to whom he wrote on June 4:

My dear Stedman—

Should it chance—among the many good hopes I hope for you in England—that you should meet Mr. Irving, I shall deem it a favor if you will remind him of the letter I wrote him some two months since.

I have a note from Mr. Daly which tells me that Mr. Irving expressed the hope that I would visit England professionally and in a similar one to Mr. McVicker he speaks of the "Irving and Booth exchange" (the plan I suggested in the letter before mentioned) but—and for the present at least—I shall not stir in the matter until I hear from Mr. Irving. Besides, I would prefer a responsible and well-established English to an American manager to "handle" me in London.

I fear to add to the many friends' commissions with which you are doubtless already burthened, but I shall consider it an honor, my dear boy, to have you represent me in any preliminary confab that may arise between Mr. Irving and yourself relative to my acting in his theater. But do not, I beg you, let

---

[1] Shaw's efforts to get some final answer to his proposal that Irving produce "The Man of Destiny," revealed in "Ellen Terry and Bernard Shaw: A Correspondence" (G. P. Putnam's Sons, New York, 1931), amusingly disclose this characteristic of the actor-manager.

me or my affairs bother your brains if the least inconvenience
is likely to be incurred thereby.

"Farewell! My blessings season this in thee."

Adieu,

Faithfully yours,

EDWIN BOOTH.

Never was an appeal made to a better friend than
E. C. Stedman. He had hardly reached London, had not
yet found lodgings, when he was in communication with
Smalley, learning from him that Smalley had acted
"promptly and wisely"; that Irving had received Booth's
letter and "thought favorably of the idea"; that he might see
Irving. Ten days later he had seen Irving, talked long with
him, and received assurances which made it possible for
him to write Booth jubilantly, "Io triumphe! I have come,
have seen, have conquered." He continued:

You are all right here. It has taken over a week to bring
the acquaintanceship about with Irving, rightly, and make no
blunders—as he is in the pressure of the "season"—but at last
I have met with the fullest success. After considerable diplo-
macy on Smalley's part, and Irving's learning that I had your
full confidence, I arranged to meet him at his apartments yesterday. (They reminded me of yours—full of old furniture,
bric-à-brac, etc.) We passed an hour there together, Smalley
being of the party, and I was greatly pleased with the handsome manner in which Irving acted. In the first place, he desired
to assure me that he had not written you because Daly had
volunteered to express his wishes to you by word of mouth. He
had been urged by Daly to put his interests in America in his
hands, etc., but of this more anon. Next, he told me, that,
whether he should go to America or not, he would place his

theater and his company at your service in the autumn of 1880
—the time you suggested.

Again, you could either run the theater yourself, paying
him the rent he has to pay, or you can be "managed" by him,
as a partnership affair, and you and he share the profits of your
engagement. I told him I thought you would quite as lief act in
the latter way, under his auspices. Miss Terry will probably go
with him as his support—otherwise his superb company will
all remain to support you. His house is an expensive one,
including his own and Miss Terry's salaries, and costs £120
a night. In spite of this, he has made £9,000 the last six
months. He says he is sure of your success here; that you had
a great popularity when you played with him in the provinces,
that you were in the wrong theater in London, and of course
had everything here against you; that he admired you sincerely, etc., etc. He indubitably wants to come to America and
wants his theater to be sustained during his absence. Of course
I told him he must come—that we must have a "Booth and
Irving exchange," and that we would all do all we could for
him in America. I promised him that I would at once write
requesting you to advise him as to his course in America. It
seems that, besides Daly's overture (who wishes to star him,
etc.) he has offers from Wallack, who says Wallack's holds
£400 a night. Then there is the question of Booth's Theater
(Jarrett & Palmer). Had he better to go there or to Wallack or
to Daly's?

Please write him at once and give him your candid advice.
It will bring matters to a head. He says he does not care much
to play in a large theater. (I have heard him twice—Claude
Melnotte, Hamlet—and should not think he would. His voice
is queer—often inarticulate—a curious dialectic use of words.
His action is far superior to his reading. Frankly, I am greatly

251...;

disappointed in him as an actor, though he is most intellectual, scholarly, picturesque. But he certainly "carries the house" with him here and had crowded houses, besides. Miss Terry is pathetic, talented, charming, the best Ophelia I have seen. They both affect the pre-Raphaelite style—mediæval—"blessed damo-zel" and that sort of thing you see on tiles.)

You see Irving acts handsomely by you. You can have his theater yourself and run it as cheaply or as dearly as you choose; or you can act under his management and share proceeds. Take your choice. Write him at once covering the whole matter. Please also drop a line to G. W. Smalley, 8 Chester Place, Hyde Park Square, London, W., thanking him for his offices in the matter, as he will continue to be a most important friend when you visit London. Has great influence with the best critics, journals, clubs, etc., here. Besides, he writes letters to the Tribune. We have agreed to let nothing of this be known at present, until the right time. You can address Irving at the Lyceum Theater, Strand. He proposed to me to telegraph you —said he would bear the expense, but I told him it was scarcely necessary. I am to sup with him in a few days and will talk matters over. He told me that you could make money in the provinces after your town engagement. You see he is prospering and it makes him, Smalley says, generous and open in his views.

Thus did everything seem arranged. And then, without finally clinching the matter, Irving sailed away on a yacht, answering no letters, vanishing. Stedman, told of this, was amazed. He wrote from Paris, his last surprised gasp as a booking agent:

Before leaving London, I wrote Irving a letter telling him all I had written you, and saying that I supposed you would send him a letter of advice, as to his trip to America. This, as his theater had just closed, I sent to Smalley to forward to Irving. Mr. Smalley replied that Irving had gone off to the Mediterranean in the yacht of Baroness Burdett-Coutts (who is his backer) and that the letter should be sent after him.

I thoroughly understand, and as a gentleman fully sympathize with you in, your view of the matter. Probably I was an ass of unusually pure and ancient long-eared breed, in not accepting Irving's suggestion that he should "telegraph you." He said he "wouldn't mind four or five pounds" for that purpose. But his proffers were so open and fair, and it seemed so absurd to telegraph as to a matter of a year ahead, that I put the suggestion aside. Instead, I said, it would please you to receive something by mail from his own hand, which he said you should have. He also said he wished me to meet him at a midnight supper, for further talking, he being excessively driven by the close of his season. But the special invitation never came.

Stedman was worried lest it should appear that he had not been authorized to act for his friend, particularly if it came out that the firm of Schwab & Shatrock had been negotiating with Booth, through Winter. He was confused and annoyed about the whole matter and it is not now entirely clear whether negotiations were definitely broken off for some reason or merely allowed to lapse. The latter seems more probable. Irving preferred to let things lapse if he changed his mind, and it later became evident that he harbored no ill-will.

But Stedman was annoyed. He urged Booth to go on to London, anyway, and, somewhat later, expressed his italicized opinion that Irving was *not a gentleman.* Gentle

Stedman knew, one suspects, no harsher phrase of denunciation. Booth decided to accept the advice and Stedman's
encouraging assurance that he would succeed in London,
with Irving or without him. ("People accept Irving *faute
de mieux,*" Stedman wrote, "but all criticize his elocution
and seem to want a change.") So he turned to professional
agents, employing the firm of Simmonds & Brown. Morris
Simmonds, in London, began new negotiations in the winter of 1879-80. He interviewed Walter Gooch of the Princess
Theater, Mr. Hollingshead of the Gaiety, and the Messrs. A.
and G. Gatte of the Adelphi. On February 6 he wrote Booth:

> There is not the least doubt of your being able to arrange
> your own time and terms at either of the above theaters. Of the
> three referred to I would prefer the Princess—for the following
> named reason:—This theater will be closed for three months
> from June next to be entirely reconstructed and will be re-
> opened as a new theater in September next. Mr. Walter Gooche,
> the manager, would be pleased to open negotiations with you
> to inaugurate his new theater, commencing at your option
> either in September or October next.

The idea of opening a new theater appealed to Booth,
and Booth negotiated, this time directly. Clarke was brought
in, finally, despite his brother-in-law's wish not to involve
him, and represented the tragedian when the contract was
finally signed. This stage in the negotiations was not reached
until Booth had sailed from the United States and reached
England in the summer of 1880, which gives some color
to his subsequent assertion that he had no definite arrangements made when he sailed. The point, of course, is technical.

He knew very well that Gooch was going to make a "flattering offer," probably knew precisely what the offer would be. What it was is disclosed in the following excerpt from a letter written Clarke by Gooch on August 8:

As Mr. Edwin Booth has written me and referred me to you to definitely arrange for him to appear and act at the above theater under my management to play a starring engagement in a series of Shakespearian and other plays, I offer you the following terms:

Mr. Booth to take 50 per cent of the gross receipts per week after I deduct the sum of £450 (four hundred and fifty pounds) per week. These terms to apply up to £1,000 (one thousand pounds) gross receipts weekly. Mr. Booth to take sixty per cent of the receipts exceeding one thousand pounds weekly.

The piece or pieces selected during this engagement to be withdrawn as soon as practicable should the receipts in any one week fall below £650 (six hundred and fifty pounds). This engagement to continue for three months (3 months) commencing in October next. If extended by consent of both parties then the terms are to be the same for the renewal. Should this engagement not be extended as above, Mr. Booth agrees not to act in any other London Theater for twelve months from the expiration of this agreement. Six nights performance each week is agreed upon for Mr. Booth to play during said three months.

WALTER GOOCH.

It is understood that the name of Mr. Edwin Booth will be made the feature of this engagement.

These were the terms as eventually agreed upon. It is a little difficult to discover that they were "flattering" to a tragedian who had been starred for years, who had for years received fifty per cent of the gross, without deductions; who had wished to play three or not more than four nights a week. But they were accepted.

Booth, who had been touring while these lengthy negotiations were in progress, sailed from New York in June, after a breakfast in his honor had been eaten at Delmonico's on the fifteenth. It was given to speed him on his way, and toasts to his success were drunk. Barrett, Lester Wallack, Jefferson, Charles P. Daly, Parke Godwin, John R. Brady, and half a dozen more delivered addresses suitable to the occasion. Winter read a poem. He frequently read poems of his own composition on request. They were usually quite bad poems and this was no exception.

Before his friend left, Winter gave him some last-minute advice. "Open in 'Richelieu,'" he urged. That was safest, he argued; it was one of Booth's best parts, it had wide and obvious appeal. Later he could play his more subtle parts. No good purpose would be served by challenging Irving at the outset in one of the parts with which he was identified in the mind of the "B. P." But Mrs. Booth had other views. She was, as Winter remarks, "an impulsive, belligerent lady, who meant well but possessed no tact." She wanted Booth to open in "Hamlet." He did.

But first, with Edwina, they sailed at leisure across the Atlantic and at leisure explored Ireland, stopping at Dublin while Booth wrote to Anderson that he was disappointed in the place. "Saving the antiquities and the foul weather, we can bate 'em in Yankeedom. The lakes and hills and all the beautiful scenery they boast of are way behind us, so they are." Then they went on to London, where Booth met his new manager and was assured by him that everything would be beautifully in readiness for the opening. Gooch said he had a theater in which Booth would be proud to act; a company he would be proud to lead; scenery which would delight his soul.

Booth suggested opening in "Hamlet" and Gooch was enthusiastic. Booth explained that it was easier on his voice after a long period of rest than any other part. Gooch probably was delighted with the opportunity to advertise Booth against Irving.

But before that advertising began, Booth had begun to suspect that he had made another mistake.

# XVI

## HIS BRITISH LUCK—AND HENRY IRVING

WALTER GOOCH WAS VERY MUCH PLEASED WITH HIMSELF WHEN he thought what he had done with the old Princess Theater, which twenty years before had served Charles Fechter well enough but had subsequently fallen into decay. A London correspondent informed his American public:

During Mr. Gooch's management of the Princess Theater the old house was the home of melodrama, not classic melodrama, but strong, realistic—I had almost said "blood and thunder"—melodrama. It was practically an East End theater at the West. A Bowery theater in Madison Square is a parallel idea for New York. *Guinea Gold, Jane Shore, It Is Never Too Late to Mend, Drink, The Streets of London,* were its most successful plays. It was old, dusty, inconvenient. It smelled of sawdust, orange peel and gas. It was draughty, afflicted with rats and the stage was positively dangerous; but the cheap parts of the theater were crowded every night. Tom, Dick and 'Arry were there always.

Then Gooch decided to change everything. He would make the theater over, and he thought that to do that he need merely chase out the rats, sweep up the sawdust, make all shiny and new. He believed that, throughly renovated, the house would regain overnight its erstwhile esteem; that it would again be the home of tragedy it had been in 1860, when Booth played at the Haymarket and envied Fechter his fashionable playhouse. So for three months Gooch renovated.

Our correspondent continues:

Today the old house is no more. On the historic site has risen a clean, comfortable and handsome theater with a beautiful entrance hall, artistically decorated corridors, pleasant waiting-rooms, cheerful saloon and everything else in harmony therewith. The auditorium looks rather cold, perhaps the decorations are heavy, but the arrangements for the comfort of the audience are admirable.

Booth probably discovered before he had been long in London what Gooch's optimism blinded him to. It took more than new clothes to make a lady out of the old Princess. It was easier to drive Tom, Dick and 'Arry out than to entice Reginald and Colin and Cecil in. The former went away gladly, even eagerly, after one look at the new comforts and the perhaps heavy decorations; the latter stayed away just as gladly. Before he had been long in England, Booth suspected that he had once more picked a loser, with that uncanny luck of his. By the time he began to rehearse with the company of Gooch's choice he was sure of it.

There were then in England, one writer notes, "only a handful of artists who could speak blank verse." The handful was not at the Princess, working for Mr. Gooch. Booth was horrified as he observed his companions on the stage. "My support at the Princess often did more harm than good," he observed afterward. "Every one wanted to be the star of the play, whatever it was. Miss . . . was determined to act her tragedy of Ophelia, with my assistance as Hamlet." He had once more encountered, he realized with sinking heart, "a sort of 'cheap John' management, with a wretched company and poorly furnished stage, compared with Irving's superior settings."

The theater was not ready in October. It was barely ready on November 6, when Booth opened in "Hamlet." Gooch had not yet had time—he must be given that credit—to collect the stock of scenery necessary to mount Booth's plays properly. Perhaps he was hurried, also, in the matter of his cast. It is probable that, in sheer self-interest, he did the best he could in the time allowed. Evidently it was not a very high best. There was, however, a crowd for the opening night. Most of the Americans in London were on hand to greet their countryman.

The London "Times" reported on Monday, November 8, that London was "developing year by year greater centralizing force as a capital which draws to itself all that is most distinguished abroad upon the stage." It recalled those who had been drawn, in a gently chauvinistic glow. And now:

Mr. Booth makes his second visit to London and crowds are found to wait for admission from 2 till 6 o'clock on a Saturday afternoon till the queue stretches across the road at the pit and gallery entrances and other crowds watch the arrivals at the principal doors as if a levee were in progress.

It took the "Times" several paragraphs to reach Mr. Booth himself. It then reported him "obviously master of his resources and giving a thoroughly intelligible and consistent reading of a favorite part." Only now and then did the critic find his acting "labored and tricky." The "Times" was courteous to the visitor. It even praised the cast, mildly. All was, in a word, adequate. The "Times" was the most kind of the dailies; others were sharp with the tragedian and sharper with his cast. Booth had to wait for the weeklies, to hear the "crickets chirping pleasantly."

The "Saturday Review," one of the first to offer a considered report upon the American star, was both judicious and fair. Its review bears quoting:

Mr. Booth's first appearance has been in the part of Hamlet, and in undertaking this part he had two forces to contend against, that of his own celebrity in America which preceded his introduction (for so it may fairly be called, although he has appeared before in England) to the English stage and of the striking and lasting impression produced by the performance in the same part of the distinguished actor-manager, whose Hamlet was a surprise to those who only knew him before as a melodramatic and "character" actor of mark. It may be said at once that the result justifies Mr. Booth in choosing for his first part one in which he had what an American paper calls the "Irving canon" to contend against. . . .

Mr. Booth is markedly graceful, markedly perfect in elocution and both markedly and nicely courteous in his demeanor throughout the play. The fault which has been patent to most of his critics, that of want of passion, exists to some extent but has, at any rate, been exaggerated, possibly through misunderstanding of his purpose, possibly through the nervousness which generally affects even the most practiced actors on the first night in a new theater, and possibly in many cases through a combination of both causes. . . .

To sum up, Mr. Booth is, judged by his performance in Hamlet, a thoroughly well-graced actor. He has thought, poetic conception and complete skill in execution. His gestures and elocution are indeed admirable and his marked, but slight, American intonation gave a not unpleasing individuality to his performance. The effect of his acting is marred by the odd and old-fashioned trick of "taking the stage," and perhaps it cannot be expected that Mr. Booth will give up a habit which has presumably become a part of his method, although it might serve his immediate purpose to do so. Whatever Mr. Booth's faults may be, his performance of Hamlet is fine and interesting and leads us to look forward with agreeable anticipation to his promised performance of other and widely different parts.

Against this reasonable praise, may be set the charges of a few who found him a "ranter"; and against those charges, in turn, may be set the following, written by J. Palgrave Simpson in "Theater" for December:

Instead of being a slave of tradition, I found him constantly neglecting the old traditional points, of which his manner after the play scene, when his exultation would not give him time to wait until the crowd was wholly dispersed was, perhaps, the most notable example, for effects which commended themselves better to his matured intelligence. Another instance may be given in his delivery of the words, "I'll rant as well as thou" which were not howled and ranted as is commonly the case, but uttered with profound contempt for the ranting of Laertes. To my mind, and especially on the second occasion of witnessing his performance, Edwin Booth was eminently natural and to be looked on as an admirable exponent of the more approved new school.

. . .262

It has frequently been said that Booth, on his appearance in London, was contemptuously dismissed as an old-fashioned ranter, adhering to methods which had been discarded in England for fifty years. Mr. Simpson's reasoned criticism, even when reduced to a few words, as here, is interesting evidence in this connection.

But, whatever generous exceptions may have been made by the discerning, the press as a whole was not what Booth had hoped. Nor were the receipts. The first week brought in only £630, which was below the minimum agreed upon. The gain was not extravagant in the second week, when '£685 came through the box-office. Then Hamlet was withdrawn and "Richelieu" replaced it. Then history repeated itself, the public responded, and the receipts climbed through '£700 in the third week to £845 in the fourth. Almost precisely similar had been Booth's experience when he first visited London in 1860. Then, too, the public preferred Bulwer-Lytton to Shakspere, and 'showed its preference concretely.

And "Richelieu"—lest this be thought of as a mere popular success—found favor also in the press. Booth wrote Anderson:

It startled even the puffers, although some of them fail to see in me more than a mediocrity. But the public is with me; so is the profession, while from many high and noble sources I daily receive the most encouraging marks of approval. The best parts of the house have been nightly filled with noted people, but the pit and the gallery are not so well patronized, this being the worst season for plays as I am giving them. Titled folks that stand very close to the throne have graced my dressing room with their presence.

The "cricket" of the "Times" gave "Richelieu" a "mixed" notice, taking the opportunity to hedge somewhat on his previous endorsement of Hamlet and by inference moving to the side of those reviewers who objected to "the mannered style, the studied graces, the sententious speech, all the instances of an art which, if the phrase may be permitted, wears its heart upon its sleeve." The learned critic discerned also that Booth was "as an actor what Lord Lytton was as a dramatist," having not numerous forces at his disposal but maneuvering them with the ability of a consummate general.

The public remained pleased and "Richelieu" stayed on until December 24, although the receipts hovered generally around or slightly under £600 a week. Then on December 27, Boxing Night, Booth tried "The Fool's Revenge" and at that piece of dramatic shoddy the "Times" was considerably upset. For one thing, it did not think the play suitable to the season. And for another, Booth indulged in "curious leaping and contortions of the body" which the "Times" was "disposed to think rather in excess of those likely to be affected by a man of his apparent age, even though a court fool." The "Times" critic was really grumpy that day; he could not but wonder "if, as the advertisements of the theater tell us, the company has been specially selected, for what particular purpose the selection has been made."

As the engagement continued it became evident that it was to be tantalizing—neither flat failure nor real success. Sometimes Booth was hopeful, or trying to be hopeful. Then he wrote that the business, while in the United States it would be considered bad, was generally regarded as "pretty fair" for London. He expressed the belief that he would have "pulled through" with "Hamlet" if he had kept it on, and regretted he had gone to the less classical categories of his repertory. He hardly thought "the critics have shown me a kindly spirit, but they are very provincial and little in their views of art matters and this prejudice is not confined to the theatrical art, either."

But when he wrote to Anderson, early in the new year, he was "quite satisfied, particularly as I find the impression I have made is deepening and daily growing stronger." He felt he had triumphed with the "brains of England" and, if he chose, could point to Charles Reade as an example. Reade read the reviews, snorted, and announced, "the London press is an ass." Tennyson, however, invited Booth to dinner to tell him that his Lear was "most interesting, most touching and powerful, but not a bit like Lear." Booth reported subsequently that he thought Tennyson very conceited. He liked Browning when he met him, however, "a charming man." These friends, and those he met at the Garrick Club, encouraged him and berated the dissenting critics.

It was a mixture of good and bad, with bad uppermost. Over it all lay the shadow of Mary Booth's increasing ill health, mental and physical. For days, now, she was excited to madness and her wandering mind fixed itself curiously on illusions of persecution. She came to hate Edwina and, to friends, accused her of ridiculous thefts and purposeless cruelties. The social life which she and Edwina had begun when they first arrived dwindled of necessity as the

Darling of Misfortune

winter advanced. It became something of a struggle to keep Mrs. Booth out of the theater; one night she had convulsions and became unconscious in her husband's dressing-room while he was playing. It needed only that.

At the turn of the year there was the question of renewal with Gooch, who wished it, but insisted on changed terms. Booth was not making money; he made less during the extended time which was finally agreed upon, since Gooch, although the original contract stipulated that it might be renewed without change, insisted on larger deductions before the even division of receipts began. Booth agreed, probably dreaming that success was just around the corner.

But during the first eight weeks of the engagement he made only about six hundred dollars a week, a tenth of what he had often made in the United States. It was a question, too, whether his prestige was gaining. But he felt he had gone too far to turn back; that he had to go on to victory. He tried "Othello," alternating in the rôles with Henry Forrester, and the attitude of the press, except for the enlightened weeklies, remained lukewarm.

It was well into January before the clouds which hung so dully over Booth showed any signs of breaking. He could see, until then, no better engagement than he had with Gooch, and lamented as much in a letter to Bispham. Only— "perhaps some lucky sprite may upset something for me and open one of the doors now closed against me." The next sentence was significant and led Bispham to prick his ears. "Irving called yesterday and spent (to me) a most agreeable hour in social chat."

Booth and Irving had made friends during the autumn.

*Edwin Booth*

The earlier misunderstanding was more or less forgotten. Perhaps Booth was learning that Irving had a reputation for vagueness in business relationships. He treated others as casually as he had treated the American tragedian. Booth probably never felt any real affection for Irving, for Booth was incapable of entirely forgetting a slight; but they got along.

And as their acquaintance reached easier terms, one of them made a suggestion to the other. It is generally believed that Booth was the first, suggesting that he take over the Lyceum for morning performances. Irving agreed; then he had a better idea. He suggested that they should play together, in "Othello," alternating the rôles. Booth was elated. It was a definite play, on its way to fulfilment, when Booth closed at the Princess on March 26 and wrote to Stedman:

At last my *great* London engagement is ended. Thank God a thousand times, again and again repeated! I have never had such an uphill drag of it in all my professional experience, to say nothing of the many annoyances connected with the mean and tricky management of ―― and ――.[1] I've had dyspepsia in its worst form nearly half the time, the result of intense anxiety on my wife's account. For two weeks now she has been confined to her bed, just hovering twixt life and death. You can imagine my interest in acting under such circumstances. On the whole, the critics have used me well.

So Irving and I are at last to hitch together, but only for

[1] This letter, unlike the other Stedman-Booth letters quoted, appears in the Grossman collection. The dashes are doubtless Mrs. Grossman's, the names omitted presumably being those of Gooch and Henry Jackson, the latter having been a little obscurely involved in the management.

a short pull of four weeks in *Othello*. Every seat worth secur-
ing is booked for the brief term of our combination and
London is very much excited over it. Of course, I live in dread
anxiety lest my wife's death, which seems certain, may occur
either at the beginning or during the engagement. Edwina is
bravely assuming the duties so new to her, but I have fears
for her health also.

Concerning Mrs. Booth's illness, her husband was somewhat clearer in a letter to Bispham, written at about the same
time. "Poor Mary has been insane for two weeks," he wrote,
"and the doctors give no hope for life beyond a few weeks.
Her pulse rallies now and then; today, particularly, it is
quite strong, but her brain has not for a moment given a sign
of improvement."

With this worry fuming in his mind, Booth began
rehearsals for "Othello." Matters were hardly improved
when Mary's parents came to London from Chicago and
were horrified to discover their daughter's condition. They
apparently blamed Booth; they were none too enthusiastic
about him at best.

Horace McVicker, son of the manager, wrote Booth,
whom he greatly admired:

I wonder how you and your in-laws get on together? I
think I can see the thermometer fall into the depths of despair
and fail to register the last half of the freeziness. I suppose
mother is bothered at drawing the line between being the
mother-in-law of England's imported "lion" and the mother of
the abused wife of said lion. Hard lines for an inexperienced
old lady.

The inexperienced old lady was not Horace's mother; McVicker was married before he met Mary's mother.

Horace, whose letters at all times reflect a bright and cynical gaiety, would have written less briskly on this occasion, probably, had he known how sadly changed was his once sturdy stepsister. She was delicate enough now, poor thing, to satisfy any critic's longing for lilies and languors. And, most sad of all, she had periods of lucidity, during which she realized how rapidly she was failing. "Oh, Asia, my life is going from me!" she cried once to Booth's sister. That was the hardest; it was easier to bear her expression of the "virulent hatred of Edwina" which Asia thought the uppermost thing in her mind. When Asia was with Mary, Mary could talk of nothing else. No one believed she would live through the spring, yet she lived on.

Little notes flew between the two actors as they worked together in the Lyceum. Many of those from Irving, Booth saved; and they remain now odd and almost indecipherable mementos of a once historical association. They dealt with incidentals, for the most part. Only one, as indicating the progress of the arrangements, will serve to suggest their tenor. Irving wrote:

On Monday I propose to issue this preliminary announcement—particularly now as the subscriptions for our performances very soon commence. I should like, if possible, to play Iago first for it is new to me and the more rehearsals I can get the more comfortable I shall naturally be—besides, I should be most uncomfortable with the part hanging over my head—but all this you understand quite well. I say no more.

I believe, too, for the success of our engagement (which

promises to be a brilliant one) this is by far the best course, starting off the performances with great curiosity. I hope we may continue through June.

During next week, I will ask you to come down here to see the models of the scenes—that you make any alterations, should you wish to.

A few weeks later Irving wrote to say that about twelve hundred pounds had been booked at doubled prices—balcony seats, ten shillings; stalls from ten and six to a guinea. Subscriptions poured in and before the opening performance four thousand pounds had been taken at the box-office.

Rehearsals went forward, with Miss Terry playing Desdemona and finding the American gentle very nearly to the point of apathy and making few suggestions and those almost apologetically. She was not much impressed until, one day, Booth looked at her. "I have never, in any face, in any country, seen such wonderful eyes," she writes in her memoirs. In them, also, she sums up Booth's season at the Princess as a wretched one at a theater which when he went there "was on the down grade and under a thoroughly commercial management." During rehearsals, and afterward, each star played his own rôle and Miss Terry, with whom Irving seldom interfered, played hers. Irving chivied the rest.

The opening performance, on May 2, was very grand. Booth's admired nobility was present; the cream of the American colony went to pay tribute to the American representative. The house was gaily crowded and there were cheers. Once more, however, the cheers were not echoed in the newspapers. On this occasion the "Times" liked neither

Othello nor Iago. Irving's Iago was too "playful," although "spirited and original." Only the Irving soliloquies really pleased the critic. Booth's Othello was "indifferent as a performance as a whole, to call it by no harsher name." Yet it had its good points:

> One can hardly conceive any performance of Mr. Booth's in which there would be no good points; there would always be his rare training and knowledge of the theater; his admirable method of speaking, despite an occasional jar of accent; always, too, a thorough completeness and perfection of design, what objection soever we might be disposed to find with the design.

It had "individual utterances of great beauty and effect." But in the great scenes, "those tremendous scenes of passion, he was not good."

After a week the stars changed places and the "Times" had this to say of Booth:

> Mr. Booth's Iago is as different from Mr. Irving's as two presentments of the same character well can be. About the former there is none of the picturesqueness, the piquancy, if we may use the word, of the latter. It is, in truth, a conventional rendering, but it is a convention polished to a very high pitch. Where it is, in our opinion, distinctly inferior is in the soliloquies; but, then, Irving's soliloquies were what one seldom, if ever, gets from the stage. Mr. Booth's, on the contrary, were of the old familiar type, set pieces declaimed and acted, but certainly declaimed and acted with remarkable skill. This Iago is the more common, the more generally recognized, of the two. No one but Mr. Irving could have given us the ancient he did; whereas, though very few, perhaps, would give it as

well and as completely, most actors would give us more or less the ancient of Mr. Booth. . . .

On the whole, as a work of art, a piece of technical skill, we should be inclined to place the American's Iago above the Englishman's; the parts are better fitted, the colors are more skillfully blended; it is less startling, less brilliant, perhaps; to minds imbued with the Athenian yearning for novelty, and there are so many such to be met inside the theater, it may seem tamer, less spirited; but as a whole it is, we think, more artistic.

So critics split hairs, while the public crowded the Lyceum. It was much talked about, everywhere. It produced, in the general opinion as summed up by Dr. Odell, "two masterly Iagos and two unsatisfactory Othellos." It also produced increased fame for both men; discussion of it on the Continent, and particularly in Shakspere-loving Germany, paved the way for Booth's later unalloyed triumph there.

"Only my domestic misery prevents it from being the happiest theatrical experience I have ever had," Booth wrote to Winter. He lamented its brevity, but could not extend the engagement, because of Mrs. Booth's condition and the decision to take her home. It would have run on for several weeks at least, both actors believed. "I have made a solid mark here," Booth wrote to Anderson, "but, as fate will have it, I must leave in the midst of my success."

The engagement was ended on June 15 and a few days later the Booths and the McVickers sailed for New York. McVicker and his wife guarded Mary carefully and kept her as much as possible from her husband, who was the recipient of itemized bills for her expenses, from McVicker. He paid one of $705.80 covering amounts expended by her father. It was carefully itemized and duly receipted on payment.

The party went at first to the Windsor Hotel; but after a short time there the McVickers removed their daughter to another hotel near by and Edwin and Mary were definitely separated.

# XVII

## DEATH AND WRANGLING

MRS. BOOTH LINGERED DURING THE SUMMER, WHILE HER HUSBAND visited his mother in Long Branch and found her health not so precarious as he had feared. From there he went on to Greenwich, Connecticut, to stay a few weeks with Benedict, and then to Mount Vernon, New York, where he visited Magonigle. They lay in hammocks and smoked their pipes. But Booth longed to be at work. Prolonged idleness, he felt, would "only intensify the sadness that is hovering over my domestic life." On October 3 he opened again in New York City, finding his fame increased by his success with Irving.

The tensity of relations between Booth and the McVickers meanwhile increased. His communications with the theater-manager who had helped him so mightily after the collapse of the theater project was reduced to the curtest of notes. Two weeks after Booth opened he was writing from the Brunswick Hotel to McVicker that—

the removal of Mrs. Booth from the Windsor Hotel prevents my further payment of her expenses as hitherto. I write to say that while I remain in New York I shall be ready to pay all bills necessary for her comfort and support, and that in my absence the same will be paid on presentation to

Mr. E. C. Benedict, No. 29 Broad Street, New York; also to ask that I may be kept advised as to her health during my absence on professional engagements.

He adds that his interviews "having been so painful and unsatisfactory," he is "forced to adopt this mode of communication."

A few days later even this was too much, and Booth answered some intervening presentation from McVicker with the curtest of formality, thus: "The character and tone of your note addressed to me under date of October 18 is such that the only reply—if any—to which it is entitled is an acknowledgment of its receipt."

Under this hard crust of conventionality ran a current of recrimination and abuse. The McVickers honestly believed, apparently, that Edwin had treated their daughter badly. They doubtless did not sufficiently discount the insane imaginings which prompted Mary's denunciations of her husband. Mary had grown bitter at Edwin, would not allow him to approach her. What she had suffered from knowing her love for him greater than his for her, what she had known of jealousy of Edwina and, through Edwina, of Edwina's mother, whose memory did not fade from Edwin's mind, came out in that bitterness. And somehow, so far as the McVickers were concerned, money entered into the picture and was another reason for wrangling.

The wrangle leaked into the newspapers, as such wrangles often do. The greater freedom the press then allowed itself to publish abusive personalities permitted the public to learn much which was by no stretch of the imagination any of the public's business. "Scandalous tongues," as Edwina wrote later, "attacked the privacy of the home." The attacks began before Mary's death, on November 13, and continued after it.

Bitterness was not, apparently, laid aside even at the funeral. Edwin was curtly advised of Mary's death; a telegram read, "Mrs. Booth died at five o'clock," and was signed by a Clinton Wagner; and at the services he was isolated by the McVickers so far as was possible. He sat at the head of the coffin, holding his daughter by the hand, and "seemed much affected." The Rev. Robert Collyer read the service and delivered a eulogy in which, it appears from other accounts, he allowed himself several remarks aimed at the tragedian. The Rev. Ferdinand C. Ewer—the Ewer who had been one of Booth's first critics in California—was present and was shocked. To Booth he wrote a few days later that he could not trust himself to comment on the remarks at the funeral, and added:

It would have been a trying occasion for any clergyman, but how a man could wade in, regardless of taste, sound judgement and, I am bound to say, the first principles of Christianity, as Collyer did!—well, well, well! You, of course, are silent. But I, as your friend, pronounce the whole harangue a bare-faced insult to you, to Edwina—no, I will not say to me. There was a certain oily, patronizing manner which was exceedingly offensive. Well, let it go.

It must be let go. The harangue has not crossed the years, which is perhaps as well.

Mary's body was taken to Chicago for burial, Edwin attending it and being accompanied by Laurence Hutton and William Winter. There was at one time some thought of taking West, also, the remains of the child, which lay buried in Boston beside these of Mary Devlin. This was not done, however. Booth returned East after the funeral and soon resumed playing, this time in Philadelphia.

The attacks meanwhile continued and were finally answered, without Booth's sanction or knowledge, by Junius Henri Browne, a New York journalist, in an article in the Boston "Herald." (Booth knew so little of it that he was forced to appeal to friends to learn the name of his defender, which was not published in the "Herald.") Part of the article, which was severe on the McVickers, was suppressed by the "Herald," and there remained only a defense of Booth, printed under head-lines which read: "Domestic Discord, Facts Concerning Edwin Booth's Second Marriage, Sad Case of Incompatibility, A Complete Refutation of Base Slanders."

The writer began by describing the offending slanders, in which Edwin had been "outrageously traduced and arraigned as a drunkard, a profligate, a mercenary wretch, as a cruel, brutal husband, as a monster of baseness and vice." Poor, gentle Edwin! All this!

Browne rather cleverly contrasted the opposing temperaments of Mary and Edwin. To her, the journalist suggested, "he seemed indifferent to everything, wholly indolent, and all her energy, which was boundless, was employed to rouse him out of what she regarded as his laziness and lethargy." He "wanted, in brief, to be left to himself. She deemed it her wifely duty to keep him mentally active, in her sense of mental activity, and in her ceaseless effort to this end, she tired and tormented him, more or less, every hour of the day." But he was seldom, if ever, irritable to her, "despite this continual nagging."

The journalist, who must have obtained his information from some close friend of the actor, continued:

Booth never spoke of the incongruity between them; he was always patient, tender, chivalrous and in nearly all cases allowed her to have her way, as strong, self-disciplined husbands, not afraid of being thought hen-pecked, always do. Mrs. Booth, congenitally unbalanced, was more than ever so after the birth of her child (it lived but a few hours) thirteen months after their marriage. From that day she was subject to periodic derangements, which increased in frequency and violence as time went on. During their continuance, she was entirely irresponsible, frequently doing the very reverse of what she would have done if she had been sane. She had fits of raving and her piercing screams could be heard sometimes throughout the neighborhood. When she had come out of these periods she had no consciousness or recollection of them and nobody was cruel enough to remind her of their occurrence. After going to Europe with her husband, summer before last, her physical health, never firm, and her mental health, also, grew much worse. A good deal of the time she was a lunatic, and a lunatic who could hardly be controlled.

After they returned, Mary—

had been here only a few months when she began to disclose a marked aversion to her husband, of whom she had, in her impassioned, irrational manner, been hitherto dotingly fond. She had exhibited before a causeless antipathy to divers members of her family, all of whom were aware of her distempered mind, and not one of them had been able by any degree of

EDWIN BOOTH AND HIS SECOND WIFE

kindness or devotion to overcome or materially modify her aversion. She refused to receive the visits of her husband and, as his presence in her chamber threw her into convulsions of rage, he at last, after trying in every way to placate her, kept carefully out of her sight. But he still took every care of her, leaving nothing undone that could add to her comfort.

In explanation of the attitude of the McVickers—there may have been some disagreement concerning financial questions, because in the event of Mrs. Booth's death, the whole, or part, of what he had given her—and he had been very liberal—would have gone according to the particular law of the State, to her mother, Mrs. McVicker. This lady has, if the testimony of the actor's friends be of any value, hated Booth long and bitterly and has, by her energetic manifestation of it, earned from him some degree of reciprocity.

This presents, of course, only one side of a sorry contention, which unquestionably was one of the few misfortunes in Booth's life which did not serve, in the long run, to add to his popularity. But the picture painted by the defender accords with other evidence in the case; with the veiled hints of Booth's friends, with the attitude openly expressed in the letters from Horace McVicker, with a curious little anecdote, recalled by "Margaret" (Townsend) in her "Theatrical Sketches," in which Mary is sketched as a domineering wife, despatching to their beds at stated hours her obedient husband and cowed stepdaughter.

Very likely Booth was sometimes irritating; very likely there was a certain limpness about him, in repose, which was nicely calculated to drive so dynamic a person as Mary to the utmost fury. But that he was in any essential way ungenerous, and particularly that he was ungenerous in money matters, is flatly unbelievable. There is too much evidence of a generosity which approached lavishness.

He never, writes Hutton—
made any public expression of his personal feelings. He gave lavishly with both hands, concealing from his left hand the gifts of his right and, if possible, keeping even the right hand ignorant of its own well-doing. I have heard him say that a certain worn out comedian had a fixed income for life, and that a certain broken-down tragedian's mortgage had been paid, without the expression of the slightest hint that he himself had taken up the mortgage or had bought the annuity.[1]

That willingness to give was known to all his friends. Many of them profited by it. Sometimes his generosity was discovered; hundreds of times it was not. He seems almost never to have refused a bona-fide request; his chest at The Players, left since he died much as he left it in dying, contains dozens of notes—from institutions, from individuals—thanking him for his kindness. The kindness always meant money. His relatives had cause to bless the same characteristic in him; friends he had made as a boy had reason to be thankful for it when they, and he, were old.

There was the case of a "certain friend, a poor player who struts, etc., but one I love with all the tenderness a son might bear for a father—one of the oldest and dearest of duffers the good God ever made." And although William Bispham, to whom a letter about this friend was sent, observed Booth's injunction to preserve the anonymity of the recipient, it is perhaps now late enough to say it was almost certainly Anderson.

[1] Laurence Hutton: "Edwin Booth." Harper & Brothers, New York.

When Booth wrote, in 1881, to his friend Bispham, that other friend approached "now the time when the oil burneth low and the wick waxeth brief. He wants to settle in New York, his dear wife and he." And they had a small income, enough to run, perhaps, to a flat of four or five rooms. Would Bispham look about for such a home, and find out, too, what the cost of furnishing it would be, and the wages of a cook? "I want them near me, these antique babies," Booth added. A few days later, evidently in answer to a letter from Bispham, Edwin explained more fully, letting drop that it was he who would pay for the flat and provide the income, so that the antique babies might be relieved of all cares for the future. Bispham served him and respected his injunction to tell no one—respected it until Booth had died.

And Lawrence Barrett was accustomed to tell, to Booth's embarrassment, a story to the same point. Once, he said, he was walking in Philadelphia and the wreck of what had been a well-known actor staggered to him. He wanted money. Barrett, who had little sympathy with the drunken, and many demands upon his purse, refused. The beggar hesitated a moment. "Well, will you cash a check?" he asked. Barrett, naturally curious, asked to see it. The broken actor showed him. It was a check for fifty dollars, and signed by Edwin Booth.

A dozen pages might be filled with similar anecdotes, and that without touching on the charities which Booth was able to keep hidden from his friends. Booth made, during his life, many thousands of dollars and never did his eye grow dim to the ducat. But there is no evidence that he ever regarded his wealth as more than a means to comfort for himself and those he loved, and those who asked.

# XVIII

## TRIUMPH IN GERMANY

GRADUALLY THE GOSSIP, IN THE PRESS AND OUT, DIED AWAY, AND Booth played without adventure during the winter which followed Mary's death. Now, more than ever, he had no other concern than his acting and he looked for a new world to conquer. This time it would be Germany, Shakspere's other home. He had already been invited there; very likely would have gone on from London, after a provincial tour in' England, if Mary's illness had not forced the return to America. The invitation still was open.

‾ He would have gone abroad early in the spring but for an illness which for a time threatened Edwina's life. It was summer before she had sufficiently recovered to sail with him. They went straight to London and Booth opened there at the Adelphi Theater for a brief summer engagement prior to his tour of the provinces. Once again, with his genius for mismanagement, he found himself in the wrong theater. Once again newspaper correspondents assured their American readers that the playhouse of his choice was not one "in which an actor of Mr. Booth's distinction ought to be playing." Again they were forced to explain that he was in a house which "had been given over to melodrama and low forms of purely sensational nature."

But it did not matter to Booth so much on this occasion and, perhaps because it did not, it did not matter so much to the public, either. His fame still held from the Lyceum engagement and there were enough lovers of classic melodrama who had missed him on his previous visits, or who wished to see him again, to insure a fair success. So he could write Anderson, with unwonted crispness, "Reception great, business English, papers kind, weather too good for the theaters, audiences fashionable and enthusiastic every night." Also, Edwina was getting on splendidly.

Booth played into August, rested a month, and on September 11 began a provincial tour which took him to Leeds, Manchester, Hull, and elsewhere in England and across the channel to Dublin. His success was varied. Leeds had the grandest theater he had ever seen, except the Paris opera-house. It was "superb—and empty all the time." In Manchester, business was bad. The city was a "good one night stand." But Dublin was splendid for two weeks and he left with the business still on the increase. He was at it all the autumn, collecting minor bay leaves and some ducats. Then he spent the holidays in London and, after Christmas, crossed to the Continent, heading for Germany and the "German indorsement." He went first to Berlin.

And there it seemed that he was again to have trouble in getting the right theater—or in getting any theater, for that matter. He had expected to appear in the Victoria, but the manager of that theater had a success running and declined to withdraw it. Booth would have to wait. He waited, fuming. He was about to sign a contract binding him to wait indefinitely, if that were the pleasure of the manager, when his German agent rushed to him with a happy smile. The "lady star" who was to have opened at the Residenz Theater was ill. The manager wanted Booth. The tragedian moved, for once, expeditiously and wisely.

He visited the Residenz and was delighted. It was "a smaller, but more fashionable, house than the Victoria, which is a large and cheerless place." So he wrote Bispham. He appeared, acting in English, which was the only language he knew. The members of his supporting cast spoke in German. Such synthetic performances cause shudders to run down 1932 spines, but fifty years ago they did not surprise. The Germans loved it, whether or not they understood it, as the English and Americans had loved Salvini, whom they quite certainly did not understand.

But it was a task for Booth. "I have mentally to recite in English what the Germans are saying to make the speeches fit," he explained. He had, also, need to study a prompt-book—a little, worn book, still extant. In it Hamlet's speeches (he was acting Hamlet again, and this time, at last, he was right) are pasted on blank sheets opposite the German text. It is confusing even to consider and it is doubtful whether from it Booth ever learned the German cues. Probably he spoke whenever the German stopped, hoping against hope that he was in the right place. Evidently he was in the right place, usually, since there was no open objection.

Nothing could have been, indeed, farther from objection. Booth was greeted by the German press with an outpouring of adjectives fit to warm the heart of any actor. He was great, a genius; he was the foremost Hamlet of the world; it was possible that he was the greatest Hamlet of all time. He was *Meister!* In his art there was "infinite charm, so simple, so noble, so free from all attempts at mere effect." Oscar Welten, writing in the "Tägliche Berliner Rundschau," had never seen a Hamlet to compare with his, and Herr Welten had seen many Hamlets, as he proved by recitation.

The public followed the lead of the press, and met to *hoch!* His fellow-actors emotionally wept their enthusiasm and joined with representatives of the press in purchasing him a silver wreath. Doubtless royalty would have joined in to make the triumph complete, but the court was unfortunately in mourning for the death of the emperor's brother. But that was a tiny fly in an abundance of ointment.

He left Berlin, after a longer stay than he had at first contemplated, for Hamburg, and there the exciting cheers were repeated and, if possible, augmented. "The people and (I am told) the press seem wild over me," he wrote. The stage director, who had looked on Booth doubtfully at first, kissed his hand. *"Meister! Meister!"* said the stage-manager, and wept. "The actors and actresses weep and kiss galore," Booth wrote. "The audience last night formed a passage from the lobby to my carriage." He had thought himself surfeited with applause. "But this personal enthusiasm from actors old and young is a new experience and still stimulated me strangely. I feel more like acting than I have felt for years and I wish I could keep it up here in Germany for six months at least."

He went on, laden with more silver trophies, to Hanover and Leipsic, where his triumphs were repeated, and then to Vienna, where the critics were at first a trifle dubious but later open in their admiration. "My windup in Vienna was a triumph," he assured his friends, who were hearing of it through the newspapers in any case. He was urged to play on after his first engagement was ended and was urged, also, to play in Italy and France. He declined these offers, however, and on April 7 closed in Vienna "what I regard as the most important engagement of my life." He headed back toward the United States, then, stopping only for a few days in Paris and not playing. In June he and Edwina reached New York and went immediately to a house he had recently acquired near Newport. He called it Boothden.

It was a house in which, for several summers to come, he was to spend happy and lazy hours. It was not large, but large enough, and comfortable. Some four miles from Newport, it was set in grounds which slanted down to the Seekonk River and from the porch Booth could see his boats bobbing at anchor. He had several boats, including a small yacht in which he sometimes floated down the river to the sea. But he did not often adventure.

For the most part he lay in a hammock swung on the porch. It was contrived so that the occupant might draw up canvas sides, and even a canvas roof, to protect himself from hostile breezes. It was Booth's favorite retreat and there, with the sun lying warm on the porch floor, he would doze for hours. There would be pipes at hand; at the bottom of the slope the sun would glitter on the water. Sometimes he would read, often merely dream. No longer was there a sturdy little woman from the West to stir him to purposeless activity. Edwina was gentle with him and allowed him idle hours. Now and then, if he chanced to be boating after dark, she would hang a lantern for him in a little light-house near the river; on the first floor chickens were kept.

The house in Newport provided Booth a refuge, as he entered his fifties and felt the first almost pleasant caress of that weariness which during the next ten years was to settle over him. To it he could hurry after his far-flung tours; in it he could forget trains and bad hotels, barn-like theaters and incompetent actors—all the demands of his professional life. He could loaf while his dyspepsia vanished and his nerves relaxed.

He was not always alone there. He had many friends, and now there was more time for them. Benedict could visit him, and Magonigle; Jefferson could stay a week or two and so could Bispham. Now and then he kept open house for a day or so, but usually he was more content if only two or three friends were with him. He could welcome Stedman and Charles E. Carryl and Jervis McEntee and they could stretch in chairs or hammocks and talk idly, and idly watch smoke drift away, blue in the air. Now and then, possibly, Booth quietly made a pun and Stedman or Magonigle gently smiled over this idiosyncrasy of a man well liked.

Booth felt that the strenuous days were over. He had lived a full life; he had his full measure of fame; his purse was heavy again. Still he had one or two notions of things he might do; he was thinking vaguely of doing something for his fellow-actors. And he was glad to give what help he could —he, a poor player—to a "professor" who had come to him for aid. His old friend Horace H. Furness, indefatigable editor of Shakspere, asked his opinion now and again; and his opinions, expressed, became foot-notes in two volumes of

Furness's Variorum edition of Shakspere's plays. Those notes, which throw light on Booth's methods of playing, will be turned to on a later page.

It did not seem that there would be any occasion for new and violent efforts. He would continue to play for a few years yet, surely. His powers were still far from decline. But his career had reached its climax in the German triumph and he suspected that acting would hereafter partake of anticlimax. He rather dreaded going on. The life of an actor was one of "wearisome drudgery and requires years of toil and disappointment to achieve a position worth having," Booth cautioned a physician who had written to say that he thought of abandoning medicine for the stage. "The art is the makeshift of every speculator," Booth added, thinking of managers he had met.

But in the autumn of 1883, after a summer's rest at Newport, he went back to the drudgery, opening on November 3 in Boston, and two weeks later he wrote Bispham to say, with enthusiasm, that the engagement was splendid and that he had had lunch with a company which included his old friend Aldrich, Matthew Arnold, Charles Dudley Warner, Mark Twain, Oliver Wendell Holmes, and W. D. Howells. (And after lunch, probably, Aldrich provided his friend the tragedian with a dose of jamaica ginger; for the poet always kept a supply of that specific on hand against his Edwin's visits.)

Booth played steadily that winter and the next, apparently not meeting Irving on the occasion of his first visit to the United States—ignoring the matter altogether, so far as any record shows. Irving had been considered by the critics and found not so good as Booth, which evened that count and decided nothing. Irving was popular, making a great appeal as a curiosity, an appeal which, as is evident in his letter to Booth, he knew well how to capitalize. But he did not gain favor at the expense of his American rival, whose place in the hearts of his countrymen, a place secured by art and clinched by sympathy, was not one easily to be superseded.

Yet William Winter dates from the first appearance of the English actor the beginning of Booth's decline. Then, thinks the "Tribune's" one-time critic, the star of America's great tragedian had "passed its meridian and was beginning to descend." Indisputably that was, in a sense, true. At the close of his triumphant German tour Booth stood at the highest point of his fame, as he had somewhat earlier stood at the highest point of his art—those points being rarely superimposed in the life of any man and never, one suspects, in the career of any actor. And it is true that in 1883, although Edwin was only fifty, some reviewers had already begun to "go for his antiquity," the phrase being the player's own.

But on a summer afternoon the hottest hour comes long after the sun has begun to slide down the westward slope. Perhaps at four or five o'clock of such an evening the sun is not at its greatest glory, but it is certainly very difficult to ignore. And although Booth was already a good way post meridian in 1883, he was yet to have a persisting, even cumulative, effect upon his audiences for some years to come. And he did not, in 1883 or 1884 or 1885, lessen his efforts, whatever he thought of the drudgery of his life. He went on doggedly, riding bad trains, stopping at bad hotels.

It was as late as the spring of 1885 that he discovered and informed his daughter of "the worst hotel this side of the Rocky Mountains," adding that after the night he understood why there were no carpets in the place. "They had crawled away," he reported, with indomitable spirit. He had enjoyed these delights in the State of Massachusetts, at the city of Haverhill, very close to his loved Boston.

He went on to Boston later and bought another house, this time at 29 Chestnut Street. He and his daughter occupied it for only a short time, as it was extremely gloomy; but there, on May 16, 1885, Edwina was married to Ignatius R. Grossman, a stock-broker from Hungary, who had taught languages in a New England college before turning to a more remunerative activity. He was the brother of a young actor who had been in the United States some years before and had played with Booth at Philadelphia. This brother did not remain long, fleeing precipitately back to Europe after his struggles with English had led him, on one evening, to announce the appearance of a relieving regiment with a shout which brought down the house. "Here comes the forty-one-ers," he yelled. He returned to Europe, where he was popular on the German stage. It was indirectly through him that Ignatius and Edwina met.

Booth's mother died the next autumn, but her death had been long expected and the blow was lessened. She died happy, at any rate, in Edwin, although her later years had been darkened by the crime and fate of her youngest son.

After a short period of mourning, Edwin returned to the road and played on tour until spring, when he returned to Boston to act with Tommaso Salvini. From Boston the two went on to New York to appear at the Academy of Music. Their most successful merging of talents occurred in "Othello," with Booth as Iago and Salvini, somewhat quieted by the protests of his Desdemona, as Othello. The company this time was English-speaking. They also played "Hamlet," with Salvini appearing briefly as the Ghost.

There were twelve performances, altogether; and Salvini in his autobiography describes them as splendid beyond words: "I cannot find epithets to characterize those performances. The word extraordinary is not enough, nor is splendid. I will call them unique." They were, then, unique. They brought in $43,500. "In Italy such receipts would be something phenomenal; in America they were very satisfactory."

But in one respect, although Salvini was gentleman enough not to stress it unduly, the performances were anything but satisfactory. They gave rise to a scandal which might have hurt Booth sorely in the public esteem if he had not reached a popularity so enormous and a place so unchallenged that even a glimpse of clay feet did little but endear. On the evening of April 28, while playing Iago, Booth collapsed. He fell flat on the stage. There was no doubt about it and few had any doubt of the cause. The "Evening Post" was the most frank. With that engaging savagery so characteristic of the newspapers of the last century, the "Post" did not mince words. It reported:

The stage of the Academy of Music last evening presented a painful and humiliating scene—the actor who took the part of Iago appearing in a state of intoxication. In the most exciting part of the play, Iago fell among the footlights and was pulled out by Othello. An audible groan went through the house. Strange to say, a considerable number of the audience seemed to relish this kind of dramatic entertainment, for they applauded Iago vociferously and called him out twice in spite of the hisses of some and the silent departure of others. The hired claque of a French theater never did anything more untimely. It is to be hoped that such exhibitions as that of last night are not to be encouraged by the forbearance of the public. It should be added that the greatness of Salvini was never exhibited to better advantage than in the trying scene of last evening.

These were harsh words, and Booth writhed under them. He explained that he was not drunk, but ill. For two days, he said, his old enemy, dyspepsia, had made it impossible for him to eat. He had sought solace in his pipe and had smoked heavily. He had felt ill when he went on the stage; at the moment referred to he had been suddenly taken with vertigo and had fainted. He pointed out that, again on his feet and revived, he had been able to continue until the end of the play and suggested, reasonably enough, one would think, that no such quick or complete recovery would be possible to a man in a state of intoxication. His friends rallied to him, repeating their frequent assertions that since the death of his first wife Booth had not drunk enough of spirits to intoxicate one man at a sitting.

Knowing of Booth's long struggle against the indigestion which often made his life burdensome, it is easier for us, looking back, to accept his explanation. The "Post" had on its side tradition and Booth's early history. If an actor, even in the eighties, collapsed on the stage, it was naturally assumed he was drunk, although the tolerance which had once accompanied this assumption was missing. There had

been a day when the plunk of actors hitting the stage unconscious was almost part of the entertainments given in the
Bowery, and not only in the Bowery. But these were politer
days.

The scandal, however, blew over quickly. Perhaps it
confirmed the belief of those who saw the tragedian near the
end of his career; certainly, from then on, newspaper comments upon his supposed decline were more frequent. It was
after his collapse that spring, for example, that the "Chronicle" was moved to publish an article which read singularly
like a review of the life of a great actor already in retirement.
The writer reviewed Booth's past triumphs in detail. He
described the failure of the theater. "Since then," he went on,
"Booth has apparently had little ambition." He had visited
England, played with Irving, triumphed on the Continent.

He dreams and mopes and his mind preys on itself. His
health is delicate. When not playing he will sit all day and half
the night, smoking, reading. . . . He has helped most of the
members of his family constantly; he never recovered from the
loss of his first wife. . . . It is thought he will not play another
season, so weary, ill and despondent is he. His spiritual ailments
are inertia and brooding.

And he read late at night.

The writer continued in this strain for some paragraphs,
pausing to estimate Booth's fortune at two hundred thousand
dollars, and ending, not very consistently, with the statement that he was still genial and delightful as a companion,
although his friends had to seek him out.

So the "Chronicle" wept for Booth, as did others. But
they might have saved their tears.

# XIX

## EDWIN BOOTH AND
## LAWRENCE BARRETT

THERE WAS A PLEASANT COLONY IN THOSE YEARS AT COHASSET, on the Cape Cod peninsula. Joseph Jefferson and Lawrence Barrett had homes there, as did L. Clark Davis, editor of the Philadelphia "Ledger" and father of a promising youth named Richard Harding Davis. Richard Watson Gilder, editor of the "Century Magazine," spent much time there; sometimes Grover Cleveland visited Jefferson and fished the lakes near by. Now and then Booth visited Jefferson or Barrett. Both had long been his friends—Barrett since the days of Edwin's first appearance in New York.

In the intervening years, Barrett had attained fame as a tragedian only less than Booth's own. For two decades he had been starring in his own right, frequently managing his own companies. Booth had more or less given him his start with the invitation which, in 1863, brought Barrett from Philadelphia to support his friend at the Winter Garden and to win enthusiastic applause as Cassius—to find himself, indeed, after a long engagement of "Julius Cæsar" the player best remembered and most highly praised. And afterward Barrett had gone to England to try his luck, and had found it not much better than Booth's had been in 1860.

Their paths had been separate for some years, but had often crossed and now and then they had played together. Booth admired in Barrett a clarity of mind, a confidence in dealing with the details of the world, which he knew himself to lack; Barrett had for Booth the admiration which the talented man of logical mind, the rationalist who secures his effects by reasonable and clearly understood means, inevitably feels for those who are touched with unpredictable genius. Barrett was not precisely a plodder, but he did not think himself inspired. But in Booth, sometimes, a fire was lighted.

One of Booth's visits to Cohasset was in the summer of 1886, and then he went fishing with Barrett and the rest—or sat in the boat smoking while the others fished. It must have been some evening after such a day in the sun, when Barrett and Booth sat half drowsy and smoked their pipes, that Barrett, who was not really half so drowsy as he seemed, made a suggestion. And Booth must have sucked his pipe and listened reflectively, not half so sunk in dreams as he had been a moment before.

Then Barrett suggested that they tour together, while their strength and skill were undiminished, and give the country some seasons of Shakspere the country would not soon forget. He, Barrett, would get together a company which would be strong enough for its stars, and so for a time those who complained daily that Booth's supporting companies were unendurable would be silenced. Barrett would, moreover, take from Booth's shoulders all details of management. He would arrange the booking, plan the tours, provide, during the first season, a company manager. Booth would have only to star and accept his share of the proceeds.

For the season of 1886-87, Barrett was already promised, but if Booth were willing, the new arrangement would begin that season, regardless. Barrett would provide everything he had engaged to provide, except himself. Booth would tour alone with the company, which they would select together. During the season of 1887-88 and thereafter Barrett would join forces with him, the best actors would be retained from the two companies, and Barrett would play in his friend's support—would play Horatio, and Othello, assuming Booth preferred Iago, and the Chevalier de Mauprat to Booth's Richelieu, and Cassius.

Booth, who knew his supporting casts had been bad and had regretted it, if not to the point of action; who was skeptical of the honesty and good faith, to say nothing of the intelligence, of the average commercial manager; who found himself grown far too indolent to think of managing himself—Booth consented. They would make a good team, both thought.

It was under Barrett's management, and with a company selected and rehearsed by Barrett, then, that Booth began his next season, opening in Buffalo on September 13. The company was better; and, in the long months which followed, the company and Booth himself seem to have entered into trouping with a new and lighter spirit. So, at least, one would assume from the charming, sentimental pages of a recent book by Katherine Goodale, who was then Kitty Molony and a member of the company, and who has written agreeably enough about what was to her a long party.[1]

That tour of 1886–87 was so characteristic in its scope of the tours which followed it, and so characteristic, for that matter, of the yearly task undertaken forty-odd years ago by the traveling star, that it may be interesting to follow it in some detail. It began on September 13 and did not end until April 30, if it ended then. From Buffalo the company worked its way westward, playing one- and two-night stands in tiny towns and larger towns and now and then in cities, through Ohio and Michigan and Illinois; and then went on still farther to St. Paul, for three performances. From St. Paul it traveled to Chicago and a two weeks' stop. Then it turned east again, visiting St. Louis, Cleveland, and towns with the opera-house on one side of the square, and pausing nowhere for more than a day or two until it reached New York on November 1.

New York and Brooklyn then occupied Booth and his company for almost a month before they went back to the life of train and hotel, touring first into New England, with a longish stay at Boston and shorter ones at such cities as Providence and Hartford and Bridgeport. Finished there, they struck off again across upper New York State and before Christmas had cut southward once more, to pause but not to play in New York. With the New Year they were away again for Philadelphia and Baltimore and Pittsburgh and Cincinnati; and, as February came, they were working

[1] Katherine Goodale: "Behind the Scenes with Edwin Booth." Houghton Mifflin, Boston, 1931.

slowly—all one-night stands then—through Texas. Late that month they reached California and played that State from one end to the other. And then were they done?

Do not think they had finished then. Then they were ready to work their way back through the mountains, stopping everywhere a theater beckoned; playing in Denver for their longest stop; visiting Salt Lake City; finally reaching Kansas City, to bring their tour to a formal end on April 30. And then were they done? Mrs. Goodale says not. Then "at once began a supplementary season of six weeks. So we wended our way East, stopping overnight in New York that Mr. Booth might contribute an act of Hamlet for the matinée benefit for Mr. Couldock at Wallack's Theater." They cut the repertory to two plays, "Hamlet" and "Richelieu," during those six weeks.

It was exhausting but successful, tediously successful. In San Francisco, Booth broke the tedium by visiting two Chinese theaters and finding both boring; in Texas he was amazed at the "embryo cities of wealth and beauty" and at the audiences, "very cultured and in full dress." Everywhere they went the audience pleaded for Hamlet, "in spite of my antique appearance as the youthful prince." (But Mrs. Goodale writes that she finally, in San Francisco, persuaded Booth to wear a black wig over his graying hair, and had a hard time doing it.) From Denver Booth took the company for a tour through the Garden of the Gods. He wrote to Bispham:

By giving the boys and the girls a treat now and then I have succeeded in making them all miserable in contemplating the end of what to them has been a perfect season and, indeed (if it were not for acting every night), I should like to continue the tour indefinitely. It has been very jolly.

So perhaps it was a picnic, after all, as it seemed to young Kitty Molony. It was a jolly tour, and one thing of importance may have grown out of it. During it, according to Mrs. Goodale—who writes with the full realization that her account differs from the generally accepted ones—Booth first made mention of his plan to form an actors' club. They were, she says, crossing the Rockies on their way East and Booth invited all the men to meet him in his private car. The charming Kitty (she and two other girls had, she says, been called "the chickens" by the tragedian throughout and given special privileges), the charming Kitty got in and stayed in. So she heard Booth outline, roughly, plans for an actors' club which should be unlike any other actors' club, and saw Magonigle and the rest listen with interest and nod assent.

According to Mrs. Goodale, Booth explained:

We do not mingle enough with minds that influence the world. We should measure ourselves through personal contact with outsiders. I do not want my club to be a gathering place for freaks who come to look upon another sort of freak. I want real men who will be able to realize what real men actors are. I want my club to be a place where actors are away from the glamour of the theater.

The often repeated story of the idea of the club places its incipiency the following summer. But the ideal, whenever it was first expressed in words, is the ideal above indicated. For now Booth's new ambition was building itself in his mind. Now he was ready, although he did not so intend, to build that monument to his fame which his theater had failed to be; the monument which still exists and flourishes and once each year is the scene of a toast to his memory. The club Booth was thinking of and talking of was to be The Players.

According to the accounts of Winter, Hutton, and Brander Matthews, among others, the club which now occupies its original building in Gramercy Park, New York City, was conceived at sea in the summer of 1887, at the end of the tour described above and before the first Booth-Barrett season. In July of that year Benedict put his yacht *Oneida* at the disposal of Booth and sailed with him from Greenwich, Connecticut, Bispham being of the party. As they sailed along the New England coast they picked up Barrett, Aldrich, and Hutton. They sat in deck chairs, smoked, and planned a club. No formal organization was decided upon, although plans were roughly reduced to writing. Then, or shortly after, Aldrich suggested the club be called "The Players."

Nothing more was done that summer and Booth and Barrett carried the plans with them as they took to the road again, this time together, in the autumn. They began at Buffalo on September 12. They played until May 14 and their itinerary, which it would be monotonous to follow, included most of the towns and cities Booth had visited the year before; nor was the order of the visiting different, except in detail: first westward to Chicago; then eastward to New York; then through the South to California, and back across the Rockies to Omaha and St. Joseph, Missouri, and Topeka; and then across the Mississippi Valley and into

New York State, to end at Williamsburg. And always they were prodigiously successful.

It is difficult, now, with the "road" dead, with the children of the theatergoers of the 1880's and their grandchildren weaned from the theater by the automobile and the talking pictures and devoting themselves to bridge and dancing and road-houses and healthy love-making out of doors—it is difficult to visualize the enthusiasm with which Booth and Barrett were everywhere greeted. It is hard now to realize that any star of the stage could create a furor by his mere passing; that the country people would flock to the rail lines merely that they might see flit past the train which carried Edwin Booth and Lawrence Barrett. It is almost impossible to understand that then, when they stopped in some city like Des Moines, theater-lovers came in from all the rural communities about and crowded the hotels and paid willingly, if not with enthusiasm, the high prices asked—five dollars for the orchestra seats, generally, and other prices proportionate. And the money rolled in; Booth's financial success of the year before, although he had once averaged seven thousand dollars a week, clear, for seven weeks, was eclipsed. It was a most spectacular triumph.

Naturally, it did not proceed without some hostile criticism. There were many objections that the company was no better than the admittedly bad companies which had supported Booth in other years; there were many charges that, in the engagements in less important cities, Booth walked through his part with no external evidences of being in the least interested.

Certainly, in such a circus tour, neither stars nor company could keep up the highest standards. Edwin Milton Royle was a member of the cast and he has suggested, a little acidly, that an applicant for membership in the company when it was being formed had found "the essential thing with the management was that he should provide a handsome wardrobe for a large repertoire." [2] Royle reports that on a salary of thirty dollars a week he himself was called upon to provide costumes costing between seven and eight hundred dollars. And he adds:

> The Booth-Barrett tour in the South degenerated into a money grabbing device. Much of the time we played twice a day like a traveling vaudeville show, and we were exploited like a circus and played to advanced prices to which the speculators added an additional iniquity. To travel and give two performances a day is quite beyond the powers of any combination.

One might imagine so, indeed. Yet the public seems to have had few complaints, for it supported the Shaksperian evangelists not only that year but the next as well. The tour was a great theatrical event to the public, whatever it may have failed to be to Mr. Royle. And even now, perhaps, those who still are loyal to the theater might be glad to be assured as much as was given then for five dollars a seat.

Nym Crinkle, the ever lively critic, had his own ideas of the combination, and expressed them in an article entitled "Mr. Booth and Mr. Barrett," which appeared in "Once a Week." Of the two actors, in association, he wrote thus:

[2] Edwin Milton Royle: "Edwin Booth as I Knew Him." "Harper's Magazine," May, 1916.

## Edwin Booth

My friend Mr. Ticknor of Boston has pithily characterized the association of Edwin Booth and Lawrence Barrett as a partnership of the erratic ease of genius with the formalism of industrious talent. I suppose this is true. Almost every observer of the pair has wished for the power to shake them up together and redistribute their qualities. What an illustrious, dominant, compelling man Ned Booth could be if he had some of Barrett's indomitable will and enthusiasm. What a superb actor Mr. Barrett would be if he only had a little of Booth's declamatory balance, music and repose. What a splendid work Booth could do for the American stage if he had Barrett's ambition and energy. But he hasn't. He is apparently an indolent and somewhat soured genius. He doesn't believe that he was ever called upon to create a part, out and out. The best he can do is to show his inheritance and repeat the traditions. . . .

Mr. Booth has the divine faculty, as the French call it. I don't think he knows how he does anything. I don't think he would do it with the same facility if he did. I don't believe that an anatomical knowledge of all his tendons and muscles and nerves would make Mr. Sullivan hit any harder. But I'll tell you what it would do. It would enable Mr. Sullivan to do something else than hit.

There is not any sensationalism about the Booth and Barrett series. They appeal to the conservative community and I suppose you know that the conservative is always the largest and solidest part of the community. It isn't heard of so often as the Drydock Gang. It doesn't do anything to command newspaper notoriety and headlines but it swings a quietly majestic force all the same. It can go to see Booth and Barrett safely, and take its daughters. It has the plea of classic literature and the authority of dramatic art. It will not be offended, or shocked or abashed. If Mr. Booth is not in his best condition it will still be interested; if he is, it will be delighted. It will come away in either case with the conviction that Mr. Booth can act when he wants to and that Mr. Barrett always wants to.

This is fair enough, notwithstanding certain errors and certain oversights; notwithstanding Mr. Crinkle's failure to suggest what he would have liked John L. Sullivan to do besides hit. It represented the opinion of a cultivated minority, without animus; it described, accurately enough, the classes of society appealed to in 1887 and 1888 by Mr. Booth and Mr. Barrett.

In all the larger cities they visited, this conservative element was particularly appealed to by astute managers, and this in an age in which satin programs were generally considered the height of elegance. There were, for example, satin programs in Kansas City late in October of that season and an appeal was made to the choicer spirits of the community.

But the conservative element was for once shocked to the marrow, with its conservative daughters. It was the fault of one Warder, ambitious builder of Warder's Grand Opera House, a commodious theater later known to residents of the city as the Auditorium. That autumn it was to be completed, and all summer Warder planned how it was to be opened, with satin programs, by Booth and Barrett. Nothing else could give to it quite the tone sought by its owner.

During the autumn, as the construction work was delayed and again delayed, Mr. Warder's plan came to hang on the outcome of one of those dramas of convergence always so popular with the writers of melodrama. The spirit of the drama lay in the clutches of dilatory bricklayers, while from afar could be heard the galloping of the Booth-Barrett company, coming to the rescue. It was nip and tuck, but for once the villain triumphed. The Shaksperian rescuers galloped into town on October 24. Then the satin programs were printed, the newspapers carried enthusiastic announcements. But the theater had no roof.

Warder had sworn that his house should be opened as planned, come what might. When its first curtain rose, Edwin Booth and Lawrence Barrett should, must, stand revealed. A newspaper correspondent of the time writes with understandable glee:

But when they arrived on Monday, October 24, 1887, the theater had never been closed—four walls were standing but there was no roof. Warder had sold hundreds of seats and had satin programs printed, but there were no chairs in the house. The interior was full of scaffolding. There was no effort made to open on Monday, all that day and night and all the next day men worked furiously, doing little. On Tuesday, a very cold night, they were still working. The scaffolding in the building began to come down at 8:30 and at 9 o'clock undertakers' chairs were hurried in. Meanwhile, the streets all about were filled with carriages and eager theatergoers who had been assured that all would be in readiness. The play was Julius Cæsar, the costumes for which were anything but appropriate to the chilly stage, swept by the breezes from above. It was fortunately a clear night and the stars shone down, plainly visible from the stage and to most of those in the orchestra, if they lifted their heads. The audience crowded in, looked around and most of them crowded out again.

The matinée the next day was, according to Booth's own amused comment, played to "about sixteen cold boys and girls." ("Julius Cæsar" was played for the matinée, according to custom, the opening performance having been "Othello"; the correspondent had erred.) That evening, after stoves had been set up and a tarpaulin stretched over the top, fully two hundred persons shivered through "Hamlet."

This memorable performance gave Booth the material for several letters to his friends. One of his letters to Bispham at this time, however, had a more serious subject. He announced that he had decided to continue another season with Barrett and added that Barrett was urging him to join in the purchase and management of a theater. He was of two minds about it. "I do not think I shall take any financial risks in another such venture," he wrote, being a burned child. "It seems, however, that I ought to make an effort before I quit to establish some abiding place for my profession where the legitimate may find a home."

The old bee was buzzing; the old dream stirring. Bispham took one horrified look at the letter and wrote instantly, anxiously, urging him to consider no such proposal. Perhaps Booth was only playing with the idea; perhaps Bispham's letter added needed weight to the balances and swung them against the plan. At any rate, when he wrote next, it was to assure his friend that he had "no intention to risk my health or wealth in management again." Bispham heaved a sigh of relief. That was in February. By then the new bee was buzzing so loudly as to drown out the old. By then The Players was, in all but its home, an actuality.

On January 7, 1888—the last night of the Booth-Barrett engagement in New York—the club was incorporated by

Booth, Barrett, Bispham, Samuel Clemens, Augustin and Joseph Daly, John Drew, Joseph Jefferson, John A. Lane, James Lewis, Brander Matthews, Stephen H. Olin, A. M. Palmer, and General William Tecumseh Sherman. Officers were elected after the tour had been resumed. Booth was chosen president; Augustin Daly, vice-president; Hutton, secretary; Bispham, treasurer; and the directors, in addition to the officers, were Palmer, Henry Edwards, Jefferson, and Joseph Daly. Booth thought, and told Bispham, that a man more competent in everyday affairs should have been chosen president, although he admitted he had expected the honor. "I am so easily bored and confused even by business immediately connected with my profession," he wrote, explaining his attitude.

During the rest of the winter Bispham, whose fears were not easily allayed, wrote and wrote, arguing against a new theater, until Booth heartily wished he had never brought the matter up. Finally, from San Francisco, he wrote that he was "after something else" and besought Bispham's aid. "I can tell you now," he said, "that from the first I've had a wish to make a donation of a suitable house (on certain conditions, of course) and with such a start there is no reason why the Players can't spread their sails."

This seems to have been Booth's first definite announcement that it was his plan to endow, as well as organize, The Players. He asked Bispham to look around for a suitable building and to tell no one what was in the air. Booth suggested that the house should be at least forty, better fifty, feet in width—a building rather like that of the Century Club in Fifteenth Street, of which he had thought. But he

Darling of Misfortune

had decided that that club-house might better be utilized, later, for an "Actors' Fund House," a charitable endowment. He was contemplating that, also.

He thought the cost of the house for The Players might run to seventy-five or eighty thousand dollars and that of the other around fifty thousand; tentatively he estimated his outlay for the two at not over a hundred and fifty thousand. But that proved optimistic as Bispham investigated, and Booth reported a few weeks later that he was willing to spend the entire sum on The Players, letting the other project go over until some future time. The other, incidentally, remained a dream unfulfilled until the end of Booth's life.

Bispham, with the limit thus raised, continued his search and found a four-story dwelling at 16 Gramercy Park which seemed to him to answer every purpose. He wrote Booth, describing his find; and, on April 17, Booth telegraphed him from St. Joseph, Missouri, approving the choice and authorizing him to close with the owners. Bispham did so and Booth, when he returned to New York at the end of the tour and saw the house, was pleased. Stanford White was called in to take charge of alterations and the work was started almost at once. Booth began to arrange his books and pictures for removal to the club-house, but on May 21 he found time to appear at the Metropolitan Opera House in an "all-star" benefit performance of "Hamlet" for Lester Wallack. Poor Wallack was aging and ill and penniless.

It was a prodigious benefit, in its fashion historic. Booth, of course, was the Hamlet. Barrett played the Ghost and Frank Mayo the King. John Gilbert was the Polonius, and

. . .*308*

the first and second grave-diggers were respectively Joseph Jefferson and W. J. Florence. If the dreary punning of those two hallowed bores was ever comical it must have been so on that occasion. Helena Modjeska was the Ophelia; Gertrude Kellogg the Queen, and Rose Coghlan enacted the rôle of the Player Queen. The others in the cast, down to the last Rosenkrantz and Guildenstern, were proportionately notable and the net outcome was, naturally enough, an arrestingly bad performance of "Hamlet." No play, not even "Hamlet," could overcome the glitter of so many bright and detached stars. But the audience was large and paid well, so that poor Wallack lived at his ease until he died, early the next September.

Booth that summer could snatch only a few weeks out of New York to visit his daughter and her husband, and his small grandson, at Narragansett Pier. There was much to do about The Players, where the rehabilitation of the old house for its new tenants went on. Long before the club-house was ready, Booth and Barrett took to the road again, leaving it to the clever, over-ornamenting hands of Stanford White. The aspect of the building began to change. The staid inhabitants of the staid houses around one of New York's two or three private parks looked on with distant disapproval. A club-house! A club-house for actors! Was it to this Gramercy Park had come?

But that first, natural fear was speedily allayed as the neighbors learned the names of those who were members of the club. These were not really actors, in the common sense. These were gentlemen of the stage, and mixed with them were many gentlemen not of the stage. It was not, evidently, going to be at all common. Booth sensed the changing view and nodded to himself. That was precisely what he wished. His actors were not to be freaks, to be stared at by other freaks. This was to be no bohemia for loose livers, but a meeting-place of gentlemen.

"The Players is already popular with the very best sort of folk," Booth wrote his daughter that November. Always eager for the "very best sort of folk" was Booth; always a little surprised, deep in himself, to discover that he was one of them. Never did he dream, one imagines, that there was in him some fugitive spark which was worth all their respectability. Never for one moment did there occur to him that fleeting, impish suspicion that the "professors" after whom he would have liked to model himself were very ordinary men. He crowned them in his mind and was modestly gratified that they were pleased with him and with his club. They smiled approvingly, and what could a poor player ask more?

# XX

## THE PLAYERS AND AFTER

THE CLUB-HOUSE IN GRAMERCY PARK WAS FORMALLY OPENED AS midnight marked the passage of the year 1888 and the city's bells saluted the new year. The members of the club gathered around the fireplace, in which a great log lay and Junius Brutus Booth in portrait looked down on the scene, past his broken nose, from the commanding wall. The son of Junius, gray and tired, but now buoyed up by excitement—slender still and lithe—stood in the center of the company. Briefly, before the bells sounded, he spoke, conveying the house to the Players. Briefly Augustin Daly, as vice-president, answered. The deed passed between them. There was a moment's pause and the bells sounded.

"Now," said Edwin, his voice low, "let us fire the yule log, sent from Boston by my daughter, with the request that it be burnt as her offering of love, peace and good will to the Players. While it burns, let us drink from this loving cup, bequeathed by William Warren to our no less valued Jefferson and by him presented to us—from this cup and this souvenir of long ago, my father's flagon, let us now, beneath his portrait and on the anniversary of this occupation, drink to the Players, perpetual prosperity." He drank and passed the cup. The Players drank. The fire licked around the log.

He had learned his little speech, had Booth; written it and conned it carefully. Yet as he neared the end of its careful periods his voice broke and for a moment he halted. Everything went well but that, he told his daughter in a letter the next day. Still, he felt, it had passed off well. "I cannot describe the universal joy which pervaded all hearts present, the sympathy expressed, the entire success of everything," he wrote Edwina, who must have thought with tenderness of the graying man whose voice had broken when he was with his friends. "White, the architect, went into ecstasies at the success of everything, and exclaimed, 'Even the log burned without smoking!' which we had feared it would not do in the new chimney." And all the exclusive neighborhood was pleased, not at all offended.

He was excited still and happy when he wrote Edwina. The party had lasted most of the night. It had been a lively, friendly night, giving warmth and reality to the formal hope expressed in the papers of incorporation that it would promote "social intercourse," that frigid name for so warm a thing. It was to promote social intercourse "between the representative members of the dramatic profession and of the kindred professions of literature, painting, sculpture and music, and the patrons of the arts." It was to result in "the creation of a library relating especially to the history of the American stage and the preservation of pictures, bills of the play, photographs and curiosities."

In words not so formal Booth wrote to McEntee. The club was "for the ultimate benefit of actors." It would, Booth hoped—

be a beacon to incite emulation in the "poor player"—to lift himself up to a higher social grade than the Bohemian level that so many worthy members of my profession grovel in from sheer lack of incentive to go up higher. In time it will have a better effect on the morale of the actor than can possibly be produced by all the benevolent "funds" and "homes" that have been or may be provided for him.

If Booth seems snobbish, many things must be remembered—his own irregular birth and isolated childhood, his limited education. These things he had conquered, and he was proud of it. And he had conquered, too, the prejudice which still existed, socially, against actors; a prejudice which was fading but not gone in 1889. Booth had overcome much and, when he had done so, he wished to aid other actors to follow in what seemed to him the proper paths.

He had chosen for his friends, his closest friends, only a few leading players. For the most part his intimates came from outside his profession: they were poets like Stedman and Stoddard; financial leaders like Benedict and John B. Murray; writers such as Brander Matthews and Aldrich; some critics who, like William Winter, were accepted also as men of literature. He believed that from these associations he had gained much, had widened his understanding, broadened his life. Doubtless he was right. The life he led seemed to him, in such aspects, ideal; he looked forward to a day when it might be a life characteristic of the player.

Booth's ideal, with which it would be difficult to quarrel, although the clannish spirit is by no means limited to actors, found expression in the membership of the club. It still finds expression there. Those directly connected with the stage predominated at the beginning, and probably still predominate; a majority of the board of directors must be made up of actors or managers. But its membership is heterogeneous. Even in 1891, Brander Matthews had heard one wit assert that one could divide The Players into four sections: the players, proper, including actors, managers, and playwrights; the artists; people who lived near Gramercy Park; and millionaires. But that was what Booth wanted, roughly.

It remains as he planned, although it has in recent years taken on a more public function than is discharged by the average club. Its leading members now look upon the club as a custodian of theatrical memories as well as a pleasant meeting-place. Booth's library, largely of Shakspere, and his pictures formed the nucleus of a collection which is constantly growing. In the library of The Players the history of the stage to-day is being conserved in thousands of newspaper clippings, in long rows of a magazine called "Cast" which catalogues, week by week, the plays in New York. Hundreds of theatrical relics—costumes, properties, and the like—which passed in other years through the hands of great actors are preserved and the collection of such mementos is constantly augmented. To an outsider entering for the first time it has very much the look of a museum.

This new function does not, however, seem to have interfered with the old. It is still a meeting-place for the players and their friends; still reading-room and library and restaurant and billiard-room are crowded. It is much as it was when Booth left it for the last time.

Booth lived there, when in New York, from the day of its opening until that of his death. He reserved the third

*Courtesy of the Albert Davis Collection*

THE PLAYERS, WITH SARGENT'S PAINTING OF EDWIN BOOTH

floor for the use of himself and Barrett; he himself occupied a pleasant room looking out over the square. From it to-day one may see the statue of Booth in the center of the square; glancing around it, one may see the portrait of Mary Devlin which Booth carried with him, after her death, wherever he went, and the portraits of his father and mother and of Wilkes. Mary looks out from her picture serenely, facing the world as if she trusted it.

Barrett moved into an equally comfortable room at the other end of the hall, overlooking the garden in the rear. The two settled down, within calling distance of each other, for the few days they remained in New York before taking to the road again. Then they packed once more and quit the pleasant club. Booth was tired but happy. They traveled westward to Pittsburgh and then retraced their steps to appear in New England. In March they visited upper New York State and dropped down to the city on the thirtieth to attend a supper given at Delmonico's by Augustin Daly and Albert M. Palmer to signalize the establishment of The Players. There were more speeches and more toasts and Booth was happier than ever, and more tired.

Without rest Booth and Barrett took to the road again. They traveled up to Rochester and prepared to appear there, in "Othello," on the night of April 3.

They left their hotel together and drove to the theater. Booth had been tired all day; now he felt . . . odd. He said nothing about it and the two actors left the carriage together at the stage door. The door-man nodded to Booth with the deference and friendliness of an old acquaintance. Booth tried to respond; with sudden amazement he discovered he could not speak. Bewilderment and fear were on his face and surprise on that of the door-man as he went on into the theater. Booth tried to speak to Barrett, but could not. Barrett realized that something had happened. Something in the mechanism which had stood so well against so much drudgery had snapped.

Barrett, when it became apparent that Booth's voice was gone, went before the curtain. The audience listened in shocked silence while he said that "the world has probably heard for the last time the voice of the greatest actor who speaks the English language." The audience filed out. Booth was taken back to his hotel and a physician summoned. The newspapers echoed Barrett's dismal prophecy and went farther.

Booth was dying, they said.

And once more, while they thus direfully reported, Booth improved. After a few hours of rest he found himself able to speak again; after a day or two he was himself. It had been nothing, then, after all. Booth laughed at it. But underneath he had his doubts. He began to think of himself, for the first time, as an old man. He was only a little over fifty-five, but he was an old man. He was going downhill now. The strain of all the planning, all the excitement, of the past year had tipped him down the slope.

The tour was interrupted only briefly, Booth feeling that, since he was promised, he must go on. His daughter pleaded with him to curtail his season, as did many friends. Her letter evidently implied that the fault was Barrett's, for when Booth answered he was mildly indignant. "I do not consider it very complimentary to have my over-anxious friends blame others for leading me by the nose," he wrote.

He did, however, consent to the elimination of a few of the many one-night stands scheduled as the Booth-Barrett company worked westward through Ohio and Michigan, through Iowa and Nebraska and turned southwest to play in Denver and Salt Lake City and then traveled on, once more, to California. San Francisco, on this occasion, provided a tame earthquake for its visitors. But Booth did not like the city now. "I wouldn't live here if the city were presented to me free of taxes," he wrote Edwina, longing for his peaceful room at The Players.

It was now the turn of Barrett to fail physically under the strain. Before the season ended—which it did not until Portland was reached on June 24—Barrett had to leave the cast, to seek treatment for peculiar swellings on his face. Then it was Booth's turn to shake his head sadly and fear his friend would never play again. The melancholy of day's end swept over him as he journeyed back to New York and the club.

He spent much time there, that summer. Old friends came in and talked with him. They remembered other days, when they had all been young. Booth remembered days when he was not tired, as now he was always tired. He remembered when he had trudged fifty miles through the snow in the far West and thought little of it; he remembered when he had been the "fiery star" and the sheriff had pursued; he remembered when as a boy he had gone to Australia, and when he had come East, finally, full of rant and promise, for good or ill. He remembered when he had listened, through a keyhole, to his father's mighty voice; he remembered when he had stretched before the fire and read his lines to the gentle promptings of Mary Devlin. He remembered strange little things he had long forgotten; he remembered when he and Mary had sailed home with a tiny baby not so large as his grandchildren now were.

He had grandchildren, now. "Tell the babies to keep their heads out of the soup," he wrote Edwina, and signed himself "your loving papa." Sometimes he visited the Grossmans at the Pier and played on the floor with the children. But he found he was often sleepy and he would doze off, sometimes, when he could not pretend he needed sleep. But he could rouse himself.

He roused himself in the autumn to take to the road once again. Barrett was not with him this time, although he was still the manager. Instead Booth played with Helena Modjeska when they opened, in Pittsburgh, on September 30, 1889. It was strange to be without Barrett, but Barrett was better. He was rehearsing a new play in Chicago. That gave Booth confidence. It was reassuring that Barrett should be better.

Booth and Modjeska, both of whom were past their prime, played their way eastward in the autumn, stopping at Cleveland and opening in New York on October 14. They played at the Broadway Theater, at Forty-first Street and Broadway. That is now Times Square, the theatrical district of 1932. Booth had first played in Park Row, below Five Points, at the National Theater. He had seen the theaters move uptown almost all the distance the theaters have gone since there were theaters on Manhattan

Island. He had seen them at Union Square, and at Madison Square, and in lower Fifth Avenue.

Booth and Modjeska played at the Broadway until December 7 and then went along the beaten paths through New England and upper New York State to Chicago and St. Louis and played on through the winter and spring, to end on May 10 at Buffalo. Very little had been clipped from the usual tour—not enough, probably. Booth came back very tired. And that reassurance which Barrett's apparent return to health had brought had ended suddenly. Before Christmas, Barrett had been forced to abandon work on his new play and go to Washington for treatment. "I do not think he will ever act again, even if he lives," Booth wrote sadly. Barrett went from Washington to Germany, for treatment at a spa. In the spring he seemed to have improved, but Booth was doubtful.

Booth rested and dreamed again. He may have looked over his books of clippings—seen how doubt had given way to enthusiasm with the critics, how they had magnificently praised him, how now doubt was creeping in once more. Crinkle, the gadfly, was at it again. "Nowhere," he wrote cruelly, "but at a public funeral or a public performance of Shakespeare do we parade the relics of departed worth." That stirred Booth in his lethargy. "Relics . . . relics . . . departed worth." But there were still some to praise. His daughter reminded him of this. "Yes," he answered, "it is indeed most gratifying to feel that age has not rendered my work stale and tiresome, as is usual with actors (especially tragedians) at my time."

But he could not forget that phrase—"relics of departed

worth." There had been a time when he was young; a time
when it was Edwin Forrest who was a relic, when Forrest
was "backing slowly out of sight with the dignity and the
distress of a paralyzed titan."

It was time, and past time, for Booth to quit the stage.
He had nothing more to gain . . . but ducats. And of ducats
he had no lack. Yet he went back to the road in the autumn
of 1890, joining Barrett—who had played alone for several
weeks, apparently quite recovered—on November 3. They
played in Philadelphia and Boston and Providence until
December 15, when Booth returned to New York to rest
and Barrett went on alone during the winter. They came
together again on March 2, 1891, at the Broadway, and played
together for something over two weeks. The critics were
not kind; or they were too kind. During that month the
declining tragedian wrote his daughter:

> I have long since ceased to read theatrical news. From this
> point in my career, little else but abuse or pitying, faint praise
> will be my portion of the dramatic critics' notice. 'Tis the fate
> of all artists after they have reached their zenith, and I have
> long expected my turn. I'm not in the least disturbed by these
> so-called critics. The public tells a different story.

But Booth was reassuring his daughter. He fought
against the realization, but could not down it, of his growing
feebleness. Often now, he admitted, he had not "my usual
clear mental grasp of the character" and he acted "with
uncertainty of gait and thinness of voice—at least to my own
ear." Other ears were as sharp, unfortunately. And other

eyes noted even more acutely Booth's lack of grasp of the characters he portrayed.

Then, on the evening of March 18, they played "Richelieu," with Barrett in the rôle of De Mauprat, a young man's rôle. Before the performance began, Barrett was ill. Booth found him in his dressing-room, leaning against the wall. He had not removed his hat or overcoat, and he was softly crying to himself. Booth urged him not to go on, but Barrett insisted, and played until the end of the third act. Then when, in his rôle, he leaned over the bed on which the cardinal reclined, he whispered, "I can't go on." The curtain was rung down. Two days later Barrett died at Cohasset, of pneumonia.

Booth went on alone. He canceled his engagement for the next season, however. He remained for a short time at the Broadway and then went to the Academy of Music in Brooklyn. His engagement closed there with a matinée on April 4. Word had spread that he would not appear the next season. The house was crowded. Hundreds listened intently to "Hamlet." They applauded long and insistently. Finally Booth came to the front. He thanked them.

"I am not saying good-by for good," he told them, in a voice which had not been robbed of its beauty. "I intend to rest next year for the benefit of my health and I expect to appear before you in the near future. Again I thank you— and I hope it will not be for the last time. Au revoir, not adieu."

The members of the company and the theater's staff formed a double line for him as he left the theater. As the

stage door was opened for him he stepped back, involun-
tarily. Outside, a crowd had gathered, cheering. The police
opened a way for him to his carriage; the police held off
those who would have unhitched the horses and drawn the
carriage through the streets. Booth drove away for the last
time from a theater in which he had finished playing for
the day.

# XXI

## THE SANDS RUN OUT

BOOTH DID NOT KNOW WHAT ALL HIS FRIENDS KNEW. "'I AM steadily gaining strength," he wrote Horace Furness in Philadelphia a few days after he had acted Hamlet for the last time in Brooklyn. "Having canceled my next season's engagements, I shall devote my entire time to playing off the stage, after so long a frolic on it. Don't be alarmed in the least concerning me."

He had frolicked on the stage for upward of forty-one years. Now, even while he planned an easy future, his health was failing rapidly. He was not gaining; he was not to gain again. The physicians who cared for him, who set him to taking exercises on a rowing machine, who gave him electrical treatments, knew this. They fought against his increasing inertia; against a stupor which was always pushed back only by their patient's will. But he could not fully rouse himself for long.

His appearance was shocking to those who had known him earlier. The stroke had been the signal for the beginning of decay. Otis Skinner had played with him in 1880 and with a firmly written recommendation in his pocket had left a man of youngish middle life. "It is a pleasure to me to recommend those who evince such decided ability and interest in their professions as you have manifested during the past six weeks, and you have my cordial wishes for your success," Booth had written. Now, after a part of that success, Skinner had returned. He played with Booth and Modjeska and was shocked when he looked at the tragedian.

"Ten years had dug devitalizing claws into his strength, his spirit and his ambition," Skinner writes.[1] "It was the shell of the great actor, old and tired and unhappy."

And since that time he had failed still more. Now his friends looked at him and winced, trying unhappily to disbelieve the evidence of their eyes; trying to think with Booth, and against what was plain enough, that he was gaining. He was almost daily more feeble that summer as he stayed with the Grossmans at Narragansett Pier, although he managed sometimes to play as of old with his grand-children. In the autumn he returned to The Players, his home. Now his friends visited him in his sitting-room, which opened off an alcove bedchamber. Many days, now, saw him moving no farther than the dozen steps or so from bed to easy-chair.

Winter sat near by often and talked with him; and the two elderly men, whose days had passed, talked together of what their days had been. They talked, too, of the change that was already in the air. They talked of Ibsen and of all that this strange new force in their theater meant to it, and to them. From that they turned again, eagerly, to the old days.

[1] Otis Skinner: "Footlights and Spotlights." Bobbs-Merrill, Indianapolis, 1924.

Booth tried to describe himself, knowing how the world thought of him. "I was always of boyish spirit," he said once, and then he must have looked with amazement at the tired legs of an old man stretched out before his eyes and wondered, in irrational amazement, that he had ceased to be a boy. "But there was always an air of melancholy about me which made me seem more serious than I really was," he added. Winter nodded.

Other old friends sat with him, too. Magonigle and Hutton and Bispham were frequent visitors. Jefferson came sometimes. Booth's presence shadowed the club, but not unpleasantly. There was a little, friendly hush for him. He was saluted gravely and with respect as, on very sunny days, he and one of the others rode down on the elevator and went out under the wrought-iron decorations to walk slowly or to sit for a while in the fenced park across the way.

On the last day of 1891 he joined the other Players at the ceremonial before the fireplace, drinking once more to the health and prosperity of all players, everywhere. And he stood in the center of the group as they drank his health, it being Founder's Night. Perhaps he whispered to Jefferson afterward, "They drink my health tonight, Joe. When they meet again it will be to my memory." If he did, as is reported, then he knew, although whether for only a revealing moment no one can guess, that he was not long to frolic off the stage.

He grew very slowly weaker through the winter and spring, and that summer at Narragansett did not play with the children, although he could sit and watch them, when he was not dozing, in a chair set out on the lawn. It became apparent as the summer drew to a close that it would not be well to leave him alone, so the Grossmans took him to the Laurel House at Lakewood, New Jersey.

There Booth sat, for the most part, in a chair on the porch, from which he rose with difficulty as his daughter approached. Now and then he went with Edwina for a short drive; sometimes he met friends, although most visitors were intercepted by Grossman. He answered, in brief notes over which he would sometimes doze, the letters of friends and assured them, with no conviction now, that he was slowly gaining. He was seldom left alone; now and then he had attacks of vertigo and once, in his room, had fallen heavily.

But though all were kind, he ached to be back at The Players. There late in the autumn, when there were no more sunny days at Lakewood, they took him. He lived there dreamily that winter, between sleeping and waking. "I am exceedingly lazy," he wrote his daughter. "I do nothing but snooze all day and see very few to talk to except the doctors. I have three now who apply electricity and all sorts of disagreeable but not painful remedies every day. I spend most of my time in my gloomy room." But the room is not really gloomy.

His condition seemed unchanged in the winter and spring; even, if there was any change, it seemed for the better. He did not see Mlle. Duse when she visited New York that year, but wrote to Edwina that they said she was the "greatest yet." But in March he was strong enough to start reading the diary of Marie Bashkirtseff who, he noted, "beginning at twelve years of age, moralizes and philosophizes like Hamlet." And during the next month he was strong enough to visit the theater and to watch a performance from a box—his last glimpse of the stage. But, between sleeping and waking, it took him a day to write to his daughter the not long letter in which he told her about Marie Bashkirtseff.

When he went to bed on Tuesday night, April 18, he was apparently as he had been for months. But the next morning he did not ring at the customary time and, after a period of waiting, Magonigle went to his door and knocked. There was no answer and Magonigle entered. Booth lay on the bed, breathing heavily, unconscious. His right side, examination by hastily summoned doctors proved, was paralyzed. News of his sudden collapse reached the newspapers and reporters gathered outside the club-house to lean against the iron fence of the park. They waited.

From the first, there was no hope of real recovery. Booth rallied enough to make it seem that he might go on living, although paralyzed, for an indefinite time; he sank back into the coma from which it seemed he would not rouse. And then he again rallied. The Grossmans thought of taking him with them to Narragansett, hoping that the air there might aid him to partial recovery, and the physicians agreed. But on June 3, when they were ready to go, he sank again into unconsciousness. The next day, while the waiting group of newspaper men opposite increased, a bulletin was posted in the club:

In regard to Mr. Booth's condition it may be stated that he has gradually grown weaker during the past twenty-four hours and there is now very little hope left of even a partial recovery.

On the night of June 6 he began to slip away. "Mr. Booth is slowly sinking and it is doubtful if he survives the night," read the bulletin about which the other Players clustered in the lower hall. Edwina and her husband, Bispham, Magonigle, and Carryl gathered in the room as midnight approached, with the doctor and nurses. Outside a magnificent thunder-storm raged through the city, lighting the room fitfully. Then, after one prodigious crash, the lights went out. "Don't let father die in the dark!" Edwina screamed hysterically. Lightning played in the room. Then the storm died away. Booth died with it, breathing his last at a few minutes after one o'clock on the morning of June 7. He died peacefully. It was like "the passing of a shadow."

As he died a handkerchief fluttered from the window in signal. Newspaper men broke for their offices. The next morning long columns told of Booth's death, and of his life. From one end of the country to the other his passing was mourned in the head-lines; his career was summarized in crowded paragraphs.

On the morning of June 9 the body was carried from the club-house in Gramercy Park. It must have been on its way when, in Washington, the old Ford Theater collapsed. After the assassination it had not again been used as a theater, but was utilized first as a museum and, afterward, as an overflow office for the pension-record division of the War Department. It had been condemned some weeks before and, as the "Sun" caustically noted, the important records had been removed. However, "with a refinement of discrimination between what could be replaced and what could not so easily be supplied, the clerks were trusted in the unsafe building." Twenty-two of them were killed and fifty seriously injured when the building crashed down—and the total of those who died in the old playhouse, victims of governmental inefficiency, was raised to twenty-three.

The body of Booth, who had been a victim, too, was taken to the Little Church Around the Corner, followed by the Players. Services were held over it, Bishop Henry C. Potter officiating, and that afternoon it was taken to Boston, where it was buried in the plot in Mount Auburn which held the bodies of Mary Devlin and the little boy born so fatally to Mary McVicker.

Not long afterward, Booth's will was filed and was found to dispose of an estate of about $605,000. Magonigle, Benedict, and Bispham were made executors. There were numerous bequests to relatives, four to charity—three of them to agencies for the relief of impoverished actors—and the balance went to Edwina for life, with the provision that it be afterward divided among her children. Mrs. Edwina Grossman lived, as these pages were written, in the Gramercy Park neighborhood, not far from The Players.

The extent of Booth's fortune was surprising to many. It represented his surplus earnings since about 1875, when he had started over again, financially, after the debacle of his theater project. He had earned for fifteen years after that, had lived well, had met scores of calls on his generosity, had purchased and deeded to the Players the club-house in Gramercy Park. His clear earnings must have been well over a million, and most of the fortune came from his acting in the plays of Shakspere and in the play of Bulwer-Lytton.

During that period his weekly gain, while he was actually playing (he rested during the summer almost always in those years) ranged from the $500 or $600 he received from Gooch in London to the occasional $10,000 and better which was sometimes his weekly share of the earnings of the Booth-Barrett tours. In one season that partnership is reported to have earned him close to $300,000; his clear income from it, between 1886 and 1891, is reliably estimated to have been $579,000.

It may be of interest to the theatrical economist to recall that most of his money he made not in New York but on the "road"—in Leavenworth, Kansas, and Des Moines, Iowa; in Fort Worth, Texas; and Haverhill, Massachusetts.

Memorial services were held for Booth in the autumn after his death, on November 13. On that day he would have been sixty years old. The services, under the auspices of The Players, drew many thousands to Madison Square Garden to hear Jefferson and Salvini and Henry Irving speak in praise of Edwin Booth. Jefferson spoke of his boyhood; Irving recalled how Booth had floated "across the horizon, bright, brilliant, full of vigor and the fire of genius" when he first went to England in 1860; Salvini spoke, in sounding Italian phrases—which were read, in translation, by Henry Miller—of a great actor and a great man.

And after that it was The Players which sponsored a memorial window in the Little Church Around the Corner, which was unveiled by Jefferson on June 24, 1898; so it was The Players which sponsored, and paid for, the statue in Gramercy Park which shows Booth in the rôle of Hamlet.

It may be seen from the window of the room in which he died; it dominates the park. It was unveiled, by one of the actor's grandchildren, twenty years after his death.

It was not until 1926 that the memory of the tragedian was further honored, as New York honors the great of the land, with a bust in the hall of fame of New York University. Three years before, a picture of Booth had been placed in the Shakespeare Gallery at Stratford, by the Rotary Club of America. The portrait was donated by E. F. Albee, head of a vaudeville circuit.

But his monument is The Players, and if he revisits any place it must be his room, which remains untouched as he left it in dying, with the book of Winter's poetry he was reading on the last night of consciousness held open where he laid it down.

# XXII

## EPILOGUE

"IT IS HARDLY TIME FOR THE COLD APPRAISEMENT OF CRITICISM which shall fix with accuracy the shortcomings of the actor's conception and interpretation. Such appraisement is inevitable, but it cannot be contemporary."

So wrote Nym Crinkle of Edwin Booth, after the tragedian's death; so, if not always as honestly, did other critics of the day seek to pass on to the future a task which they must have known the future could hardly attempt, let alone accomplish. Mr. Crinkle, who was astute, must certainly have realized he was suggesting that only the meteorologists of to-morrow can measure the depths of to-day's snowfall. He must have known that the art of an actor vanishes like the snow; that even snowfalls, in a day of statistical records, are not so impermanent as an actor's art.

Nothing dies quite so completely as an actor when he dies. He takes everything with him. He is dead with the peculiar finality of something which never really existed. Crinkle must have known that, and have written with tongue in cheek, having so a quiet joke at solemn contemporaries who were always taking the long view and assiduously courting scholarship.

# Edwin Booth

When an actor dies he dies all over. His memory, as his contemporaries follow him, becomes a name—a name and two dates. What do we know now of Edmund Kean? What can we say of him that we have not learned by rote? We cannot mark his passage by outside things. Napoleons leave wreckage. Something of what the Bismarcks build remains to mock their descendants. A writer lives in what he writes; a painter in the slowly fading colors of his masterpieces. They, too, are artists. And they can be valued and revalued until the world ends, for they do not really die. But an actor works in the perishable gestures of the body; the instantly dead inflections of the voice. He leaves, as one editor said of Booth—as if it were his special failing—"nothing but the memory of his own shining achievements." Booth left as much as any actor; more than most. And, by the time those who watched him play are dead, he will be a name only.

Something remains to tell us of the man—a letter, the record of a remembered action. Of the actor we have only the hastily scrawled impressions of his contemporaries; impressions which contradict one another, which fall short, at best, of the evocation of clear images. Perhaps a phrase lives. We remember that to see Edmund Kean was like "reading Shakespeare by flashes of lightning." And the outward appearance of the man, who was also the actor, persists in photographs and paintings. With these before us we may read the painstaking words in which yesterday's critics sought to picture him. We may read detailed analyses of his fleeting expressions, and try to imagine them as they must once have crossed the face registered for us by Sargent or by the sensitive chemicals of some camera.

Darling of Misfortune

Do not think that this failure to capture in words the essence of an actor's art is peculiar to the day of those who wrote of Booth. Not their fallibility, but an essential limitation is involved. When he writes of acting, the critic of the theater is as unhappily situated as is the critic of music when he reluctantly leaves off describing the musician and turns to his real task. A listing of gestures is not, to the reader, much more helpful than might be a note-by-note description of the rise and fall of sound. These things are the husks.

Your critic, then, retreats to the subjective and conveys to his readers that Miss Soandso was "tantalizing" or "vibrant" or "delicious" in her rôle; or that Alfred Lunt captured the true spirit of sex comedy when he played with Lynn Fontanne in "Reunion in Vienna." And that is doubtless helpful, if the reader knows what the critic thinks the true spirit of sex comedy is, or what the critic finds delicious.

So far from being peculiarly prone to failure in this regard, the critics of yesterday had one device, lacked by their descendants, which gave them some chance of success. William Winter, for example, could always beat his way back to comparison. When he wrote of Booth, he wrote of one artist in a series. He did not have to describe an incomparable object, as one might describe a single wave to a person who had no conception that waves come in series. A wave, one supposes, is merely a bump in water, considered by itself. But it is larger or smaller, rounder or sharper, foamier or smoother, than the waves before and behind.

In the old days tragedians were like that. They came one behind the other, usually close enough together so that several might be seen at once: yesterday's and to-day's and to-morrow's. Then the critic might evaluate Edwin Booth in the terms of Junius Booth, or Charles Kean in the terms of Edmund Kean, to take two examples in which the relationship was not only of art but of blood. There was a continuity. That continuity existed for many years unbroken, and then with Booth it broke.

It was not that none was born to follow him. One can imagine, without too much difficulty, that John Barrymore might have taken Booth's place; might have picked up the scepter when Booth, last of the tragedian-monarchs, laid it down. Or, if not Barrymore, another, if the conditions favorable to what Winter called "the elocutionary no less than the mimetic art" had not changed. These conditions made a successor to Booth in the dynasty of the tragedians impossible. He was the last. So there must once have been a last fully equipped saber-toothed tiger, and after him no more such tigers, conditions favorable to the production of that gaudy beast having ended.

The tragedian is now extinct as the tiger. Human tastes being more mutable than natural phenomena, it is possible that the tragedian may return, while the recurrence of the tiger is as unlikely as it is undesirable.

The tragedians thrived in surroundings of theatrical luxuriance, as the tiger thrived in surroundings of natural luxuriance. The tragedian relied on a kind of dramatic giganticism; upon the playwright's acceptance of a scale of values and events which resembled everyday life only as a fireworks portrait of Herbert Hoover resembles a harried gentleman in the White House; only as the clarion promises of the "Star-spangled Banner" reflect conditions in a land ideally of the brave, in a home symbolically of the free.

The drama of yesterday, of the tragedian's yesterday, was ideal drama. That is perhaps its most significant difference from the drama of to-day, which essays to be the drama of the real. As heroic poetry is idealized human speech, so the poetic drama was idealized human action. Its medium was blank verse, and not only because Shakspere had written so and the natural thing was to imitate Shakspere.

And realism, such realism as there was, took its place well below the salt. Dion Boucicault was, in his day, a "realist" and Dion Boucicault was below the salt. It is difficult now to think of him so, but he brought melodrama into the terms of actual contemporary life. His were not the murders of far away and long ago, but of the sidewalks of New York or London or Liverpool; his was not the voice of some heroic Brutus, but of some brave young bank clerk. He was, in that sense, among the forerunners of what was, by Ibsen's time, to be called "realism," the term coming to have a peculiar absolute meaning, instead of a simple relative one.

And that new realism, of which it is convenient to think Ibsen a typical practitioner, came to the top. It was democracy crowding out monarchy; the ideal was crowded from the throne. The battle was brief and decisive. Protestants might go on wailing for years, as Winter did, but they could do no more than catalogue themselves as unreconciled. The change came a little before Booth left the stage and died. He saw it coming and lamented it, but, perhaps because his life was nearly over, he maintained a tolerance impossible to the crusading critic who was his friend. But perhaps he had a better reason to be friendly with the conquerors.

He could not fully have joined them, perhaps. His art could not have lived, in the more obvious of its aspects, on the close-cropped action and dialogue which succeeded the old luxuriance. New conditions called for new actors; actors who could thrive on clipped speech, who could express passion in understatement. The distance between Edwin Forrest and Hope Williams is precisely the distance between the old dramatic conditions and the new. At first glance the distance between Edwin Booth and Miss Williams may seem the same. If it were, there would be little hope of our now achieving any real understanding of Booth as an actor. If he were the last of the tragedians, and only the last of the tragedians, we should be as baffled to place him as to measure the depth of the snow which fell on New York in the blizzard of 1888.

But the elements were mixed in Booth. In some respects he also was among the moderns. There was a vein of new running through the rock of the old. This his first critics perceived dimly. They did not diagnose it as we may diagnose it now. Only when a transition is complete is it possible to see the steps through which it came. Looking back now to discover Booth's early efforts toward a natural style, as revealed in Mary Devlin's letter to him, we may perceive that in so far as he was a significant figure in what may be called the living theater, he was so as a figure of transition. He was an artist going somewhere. He did not know where, probably, but he went.

We have seen how his first digression from the established standards puzzled his early critics. Some of course missed that digression altogether, attributing to inexperience rather than to intention such divergence as they dimly saw. Others, more astute, perceived clearly that the new tragedian was missing the established "points," but considered these misses as errors in understanding.

It was not until some ten years after his first appearance in New York that any clear idea was achieved by the critics of what Edwin Booth was doing, and by that time, so rapid were changing tastes already beginning to manifest themselves, what he was doing was no longer surprising. Some time before his middle period, he seems to have fixed his style, and thereafter, as Crinkle has remarked, he brought "the same eggs to market," content with the knowledge that they were good eggs. By the time he died, the artist who had been once, rather timidly, a pioneer was close to being outmoded as a reactionary. But that, one takes it, is the almost inevitable fate of "transitional" figures.

Among his early critics, an anonymous writer for the "Nation" of 1866 probably had the clearest understanding of Booth as an artist. His summary, printed about ten years after Booth had made his début in the metropolis under Burton's direction, merits space here:

We regard it as Mr. Booth's misfortune that he is divided between two widely differing schools of acting—the romantic and the natural. The traditions of his youth, his early observation and training, compelled him to the romantic or heroic school. His organization, taste, aptitude, perhaps his later study also, inclined him to the side of nature. But he seems never to have made a deliberate choice between the two; his favorite plays are romantic; in his treatment he aims at naturalism. Hence the incongruity. Shakespeare's tragedies cannot be acted naturally, for they are entirely out of *our* nature, and to play them after the old unnatural style of the last century would be simply intolerable. How, then, can they be played at all? Even *Richelieu* cannot be acted naturally, for such episodes in French society cannot be reproduced as real to our audiences. They will always remain something to be caricatured by strained action, artificial gesture and stilted declamation. Mr. Booth does all that man can do, but no man can bring *Hamlet* or *Richelieu* into modern life. We think that if he would abandon the endeavor and devote his remarkable talents to the studies in the school of nature he would achieve triumphs worthy of the greatest artists of the age.

The "Nation" was, of course, a bad prophet. Mr. Booth attained triumphs without those "studies in the school of nature" of which his critic writes with such confidence, although one is now, looking back to the production lists of that day, rather put to it to determine what they may have been. Boucicault, probably, or "Life Among the Mormons." Shakspere was better, as it proved. And one can imagine with how blank an expression the "Nation's" critic, if he could have looked forward, would have noted the "modern-dress" "Hamlet" offered in New York sixty-odd years later.

But this was by far the keenest analysis of Booth's peculiar position. Possibly it overstressed the difficulty, the insolubility of the problem. But it must be admitted that Booth never entirely solved it. He went as far as he might, and stopped. His style was always two styles. Most of those who watched him saw one or the other; few saw both. When he went to England in 1880 he was not, as sometimes reported, dismissed as a "ranter." But many did accuse him of rant. And others, it will be recalled, found him the personification of naturalism. He did not "rant as well as thou" with Laertes; he did, certainly, touch off set-pieces, on occasion, in the old manner.

It was as a naturalist, one suspects, that he was at his best. The rôle of Hamlet was played by him in a relatively minor key. He was a famous Iago, but never a satisfactory Othello. In his best rôles, wrote Augustus Pitou in 1914, his art "was the best of the actor's art that is now prevalent. His school was the natural school of to-day, for it was he who introduced it; he was neither declamatory nor strident."[1] And Otis Skinner testifies to the same effect when he writes of Booth that "extravagance never marred his work."[2] Mr. Skinner, as one whose work also is not marred by extravagance, speaks in the tongue of to-day, and by to-day's standards. "Edwin Booth's genius, when he was at his best, would as surely thrill a Broadway audience to-day as it did in the past," Pitou added. "He would not be 'hooted from the stage' nor would he be considered an 'archaic curiosity.' "

As we consider Mr. Pitou's assertion, which goes to the heart of this matter, we may turn for a moment to Booth's own theories of his own art. He did not, on the whole, write much about it. One of his few considerable essays on acting discusses in some detail the art of his father and includes his own interpretation of Hamlet—"to my dull thinking, Hamlet typifies uneven or unbalanced genius . . . Hamlet's mind, on the very edge of frenzy, seeks its relief in

---

[1] Augustus Pitou: "Masters of the Show." New York, 1914.
[2] Otis Skinner: "Footlights and Spotlights."

ribaldry" [3]—but is not helpful as far as his esthetic views in general are concerned. Chance remarks, such as his comment to Skinner that he thought his own art "somewhat quieter" than that of his father, are more illuminating. So, in a letter to James E. Russell in 1871, he commented that he could not—

paint with big brushes—the fine touches come in spite of me, and it's all folly to say: "Don't elaborate, don't refine it"—I can't help it. I'm too damned genteel and exquisite, I s'pose, and some buster with a big voice and broadaxe gesticulations will oust me one of these fine days.

Booth had, it will be noticed, not the faintest idea of artistic trends.

But his most significant comments on his own methods, and our best evidence concerning the nature of those methods, are to be found in his foot-notes to "Othello" and "The Merchant of Venice" edited by Horace H. Furness in his variorum edition. Furness and Booth were, as we have noted, close friends; while these two volumes were in preparation (1886 and 1888 respectively are the dates of publication) the editor wrote the actor, asking him to throw light upon his interpretations of the rôles. Booth responded with lengthy letters and detailed references; stage directions, really. These Furness embedded in the mountain of notes piled over the poet. A scholar's Shakspere is one line of poetry to twenty of comment, and Booth's contributions

[3] On Edmund Kean and Junius Brutus Booth, in "Actors and Actresses of Great Britain and the United States," edited by Brander Matthews and Laurence Hutton.

sound a clear note in the dry whispering of scholastic wit and erudition which fill the pages of the variorum "Shakespeare."

These notes are written as if intended for injunctions to actors. And those injunctions, a dozen times repeated, are one injunction. "Play down!" commands Booth, as earnestly as any modern director of the quietest modern tragedy. "Play down!"

In the notes one finds, specifically, such advice as this ("Othello," Act I, Scene 1):

> Iago, at back, watches this curiously; let him not be obtrusive; he must keep in the background and assume the expression and feel the curiousness, even if only one person in the whole audience sees or understands it. The censure, as Hamlet calls it, of that one is worth all the rest.

No more accurate description of the method adopted in the twentieth century by the Russian players of the Moscow Art Company and of the Chauve Souris, a method highly and justly praised, could be written in 1932. And this quietness, this subtlety, is even more urged in connection with Iago's speech on reputation (Act II, Scene 2), of which Booth writes:

> Do not smile or sneer or glower—try to impress even the audience with your sincerity. 'Tis better, however, always to ignore the audience; if you can forget you are a "shew" you will be natural. The more sincere your manner, the more devilish your deceit. I think the "light comedian" should play the villain's part, not the "heavy man." I mean the Shakespeare villain. Iago should appear to be what all but the audience believe he is. Even when alone there is little need to remove the mask entirely. Shakespeare spares you that trouble.

Imagine an actor of the old school trusting thus to his playwright, even to Shakspere! Imagine such a one discerning that Iago is a part for the "light comedian," not for the heavy tragic hand; a part to be whispered, a part of malevolence, not of bluster! (It is significant that almost all the many notes to "Othello" are concerned with the acting of the rôle of Iago, not of the title rôle. Booth knew well enough he was not fitted to play Othello. It took, he perceived, a certain bluff, soldierly quality which was not his.)

The notes on "The Merchant" are even more specific. "This in a lower tone," he counsels, again and again. "Subdued tones, between your teeth, as it were." . . . "Not too loud. Not too loud. Softly, here." No ranter wrote those injunctions. Nor did any "natural genius," guiltless of study, conceive so shrewd a conception of Shylock's character as this:

If we side with him in his self-defense, 'tis because we have charity, which he had not; if we pity him under the burthen of his merited punishment, 'tis because we are human, which he is not. . . . Do not forget when you read the poet's plays that he was a player and, mark you, a theatrical manager with a keen eye to stage effects; witness the "gag" of Shylock's sharpening his knife—a most dangerous "bit of business" and apt to cause a laugh. Be careful of that "point." Would the heroic Hebrew have stooped to such a paltry action? No, never!

These, and the many more which might be quoted, are specific items of a general theory of acting. The easy assumption of Crinkle and others that Booth had no theories, but acted only in response to instinct, falls to earth when confronted with these notes. Reading them, noting their clarity, we find it almost possible to believe with Pitou, himself an actor, that Booth's "school was the natural school of today, for it was he who introduced it."

That he did not invariably attend that school as religiously as he might have; that, always in many of his rôles and at times in all of them, he violated the rules he himself laid down, and played as the vast majority of his audience loved to see him play, is incidental. That he was often tired, too tired to do more than walk through his rôles, is incidental, too. Nor is it hard to understahd how in his later years, when ambition was dying, he allowed bad companies to make of the plays a dreary waste, rendered noteworthy only by the mountain of his own skill. His intentions still are clear.

He was not in theory, nor was he often in practice, so wholly of another day that he would be incomprehensible to this. That is surely clear enough from the evidence; and that, one suspects, is the matter of greatest interest now to those who wish to find what points of contact are possible between Edwin Booth and the theater which has followed him. If we wish now to know anything of Edwin Booth as an artist it is this: How, if he returned to-day, would he seem to us? What manner of actor was this?

It is reported that on January 25, 1931, Edwin Booth returned to this earth. Only as a voice, unfortunately, and as a voice only to a little group of the anointed—to, specifically, a "small private group of psychical researchers meeting on Sunday evenings at the house of a physician in New York." A report of this appearance was duly made to The Players by Frederick Bligh Bond, editor of "Psychic

*Edwin Booth*

Research" and one of the "researchers." Mr. Bond reports that the ghost of Booth urged the institution of a club for indigent actors and the support of a youth even then attending dramatic school; the particular youth being accurately enough identified. These things The Players were to do. The Players have taken no steps.

But suppose that, instead of this limited return, Edwin Booth were to reappear to all of us. Suppose he were to-morrow night to walk the stage of the theater which bears his name—not the old theater, but a new theater; not the playhouse in Twenty-third Street, but that in Forty-fifth. Should we thrill to him as did those of his day? Would his Richelieu take the town by storm; his Hamlet rouse us anew to the glories of elder days? It can never be tested; the answers can never be known. But it is my opinion that the old magic would live again.

# INDEX

# Index

# Index

# Index

# Index

Printed in the United Kingdom
by Lightning Source UK Ltd.
136469UK00001B/64/A